PUTIN

ALSO BY RICHARD LOURIE

NONFICTION

Sakharov: A Biography

Hunting the Devil

Russia Speaks: An Oral History from the Revolution to the Present

Predicting Russia's Future

Letters to the Future: An Approach to Sinyavsky–Tertz

FICTION

A Hatred for Tulips

The Autobiography of Joseph Stalin

Zero Gravity

First Loyalty

Sagittarius in Warsaw

SELECTED TRANSLATIONS

Memoirs by Andrei Sakharov

The Life and Extraordinary Adventures of Private Ivan Chonkin by
    Vladimir Voinovich

Visions from San Francisco Bay by Czeslaw Milosz

My Century by Aleksander Wat

RICHARD LOURIE

PUTIN

HIS DOWNFALL AND RUSSIA'S COMING CRASH

THOMAS DUNNE BOOKS / ST. MARTIN'S PRESS ≈ NEW YORK

To Katya,
May we discuss all this someday

THOMAS DUNNE BOOKS.
An imprint of St. Martin's Press.

PUTIN. Copyright © 2017 by Richard Lourie. All rights reserved. Printed in the United States of America. For information, address St. Martin's Press, 175 Fifth Avenue, New York, N.Y. 10010.

www.thomasdunnebooks.com
www.stmartins.com

The Library of Congress Cataloging-in-Publication Data is available upon request.

ISBN 978-0-312-53808-8 (hardcover)
ISBN 978-1-250-13596-4 (ebook)

Our books may be purchased in bulk for promotional, educational, or business use. Please contact your local bookseller or the Macmillan Corporate and Premium Sales Department at 1-800-221-7945, extension 5442, or by email at MacmillanSpecialMarkets@macmillan.com.

First Edition: July 2017

10 9 8 7 6 5 4 3 2 1

CONTENTS

ACKNOWLEDGMENTS

I want to thank George Soros for a valuable idea.

There are quite a few Russians I would like to thank for their insights and hospitality, but see no good reason to do so here when the current situation in their country does not reward association with books of this sort.

There was another American who was indispensible to this book, its editor, Marcia Markland. In all my years working as a writer, I have always taken pride in making the deadline whether it involved a restaurant review or a long tome. But this book thwarted me at every turn. Day after day my mind was as blank as the paper I stared at. The few pages I did manage to produce did not, when held between thumb and forefinger, provide the satisfying heft that indicates the coming of a book. Months passed, years.

In all that time Marcia and I would meet fairly frequently for lunch. The pleasures of conversation never faltered, though there was, of course, one subject that could prove awkward if broached. But Marcia never once mentioned the overdue manuscript. And when I could no longer stand it and said something on the subject, she would invariably reply—"Just make it good." She was, if such an expression can be used, "a perfect gentleman."

PREFACE: PUTIN TRUMPS AMERICA

Until quite recently Russia was an exotic country, distant, huge, both more brutal and cultured—Stalin at the Bolshoi—but then suddenly it was right here with us in the intimacy of the voting booth.

By the time the House Intelligence Committee convened in open session on March 21, 2017, the nature of that intrusion was fairly clear; the Russian state used hackers to break into the computers of the DNC and of Democratic Chairman John Podesta and then revealed their contents via WikiLeaks in an effort to tilt the election in Donald Trump's favor. The fact that there was no such parallel hack and leak of Republican computers is itself compelling circumstantial evidence of intent. And that in turn indicates that the Russian intelligence services were in no particular hurry to conceal either their favored candidate or their involvement. Had they wanted to remain invisible, they would have. But sometimes they prefer to send a message as in Soviet times when, after a surreptitious search of an apartment, a KGB agent would leave a cigarette butt floating in the toilet, as if to say: We were here.

It will never be known with quantitative certainty how significant the Russian meddling in the 2016 elections was. In time the Russians themselves might come to rue their choice, finding Hilary Clinton, for all her animus toward Moscow, a more seasoned and competent professional, more reliable and predictable than Trump.

But the most important question of all is one that probably can and certainly must be answered. As Adam Schiff, the ranking Democrat on the House Intelligence Committee phrased it: ". . . if the Trump campaign or anyone associated with it aided or abetted the Russians, it would not only be a serious crime, it would also represent one of the most shocking betrayals of democracy in history."

Those are the terms, the stakes.

What's less clear is how much solid evidence there is of collusion. But there would appear to be enough for the question of collusion to be an integral part of the investigation the FBI is conducting. As FBI director James Comey said at those hearings: "I have been authorized by the Department of Justice to confirm that the FBI, as part of our counterintelligence mission, is investigating the Russian government's efforts to interfere in the 2016 presidential election and that includes investigating the nature of any links between individuals associated with the Trump campaign and the Russian government and whether there was any coordination between the campaign and Russia's efforts. As with any counterintelligence investigation, this will also include an assessment of whether any crimes were committed."

The problem here is that counterintelligence operations are typically long and drawn-out, taking months, even years—the FBI has already been looking into Russian meddling since July 2016. That means for the foreseeable future, the White House will be under a "gray cloud" of suspicion to use the expression of Devin Nunes,

Chairman of the House Intelligence Committee. Mike Morrell, the former acting director of the CIA who made no secret of his support for Hilary Clinton or his disdain for Donald Trump, used a different metaphor: "There is smoke, but there is no fire at all." In any case, whether it's gray clouds or smoke, it is clear that we're in for a long spell of obscurity that can only make the current climate of jittery uncertainty all the more so.

Another point where clarity is of the essence is in assessing Putin's psychology and forestalling his actions, for there is general agreement that the Russians will strike again.

In his opening remarks, Chairman Nunes said: "A year ago I publicly stated that our inability to predict Putin's regime and intentions has been the biggest intelligence failure since 9/11 and that remains my view today."

There are many reasons why America is constantly outwitted by Putin. American categories of thought about Russia are too neat and clean. To the American mind government, crime, business, and the secret police are four quite different things. In Russia they easily shade into one another and it could be argued that at various times, Putin has had his hand in all of the above. Another reason is that the U.S., for all it shortcomings, remains a country of laws while Russia is a more Darwinian society where the law of the jungle, or, as the Russians call it, the law of the wolf, tends to prevail.

For Putin the game of power has only three rules—attain, maintain, retain—and all the rest is nonsense and pretense. Putin views American lack of historical memory not only as the naiveté of a young culture, but a convenient means for eluding responsibility. American can partake in the assassination of leaders—Allende, Hussein, and Gaddafi—and thereby change regimes, but when Russia does anything of the sort it is a crime against humanity.

To Putin the Orange Revolution that broke out in Ukraine in 2004 was no spontaneous uprising of the people but an integral part of the West's campaign to outflank and weaken Russia. In Putin's KGB-conditioned worldview, there are very few spontaneous events and the few there are immediately coopted and exploited by those quickest afoot. Someone is always behind everything, every organization is a front.

The expansion of NATO between 1999 and 2004, now flanking Russia from the Baltic to the Black Sea, and the uprising in Ukraine in 2004 were not discrete events but part of a pattern his training and experience had taught Putin to recognize. In interfering in the U.S. domestic political process, Putin was just doing unto others what others had already done unto him, and, if anything, feeling a little guilty about being so remiss in retaliating.

Does Putin have any particular power over Trump and how long have the Russian intelligence service been taking an active interest in Trump? The second part of the question is easier to answer than the first. Trump began making noises about running for president as early as 1988 having switched from the Democratic to the Republican Party the year before. That alone, along with his wealth, celebrity, and later attempts to do business in Russia, would have been more than enough to open a file on him.

Putin made his career by gathering sexually compromising video on Russia's attorney general, who had launched a potentially ruinous investigation into the economic wrongdoings of President Boris Yeltsin and his family. Saving Yeltsin won Putin the president's ultimate trust in the deal in which Yeltsin gave Putin power in exchange for immunity. So, Putin needs no convincing that compromising material can be important, even decisive. Does he have any such material on Trump, who has been so fulsome in his praise of Putin and so woefully slow to accept the intelligence community's assessment that the Russians had conducted politically motivated hacking during the 2016 campaign?

The largely unsubstantiated dossier compiled by former MI6

agent Christopher Steele claims that Trump hired prostitutes to urinate on the bed in the presidential suite in the Moscow Ritz Carlton where Barack and Michelle Obama slept, thereby to defile it. "The hotel was known to be under FSB control with microphones and concealed cameras in all the main rooms to record anything they wanted to."

If any such material exists, its principal value is in the threat to use it. And oddly enough, developments in modern technology would make it easier to deny. Anyone, a la Zelig, can be photoshopped in, or out, of any image, proving ample grounds for denial. The only way to guess if Putin has any such compromising material on Trump is to watch Trump's behavior for any unusual constraints on his usually unconstrained behavior.

But the real point here is that the hold Putin has over Trump need not be based on any such lurid material. If there was indeed collusion between the Trump campaign and Russian intelligence, Putin would have ample evidence of that in his possession and could release it at any moment to WikiLeaks, making FBI director Comey's drawn-out investigation over in the blink of an eye, the click of a key.

"You know the closest I came to Russia, I bought a house a number of years ago in Palm Beach . . . for $40 million and I sold it to a Russian for $100 million," was Donald Trump's way of combining his two favorite activities—denial and braggadocio.

The buyer was Dmitry Rybolovyev, known as the "fertilizer king," with a net worth that hovers around the $10 billion mark. After buying the house in summer 2008, Rybolovyev never spent a night in the place, which had a severe mold problem. The house is now slated to become the most expensive tear-down in real estate history.

This might simply be a case a case of hucksters and suckers. Or maybe someone too rich to be the least bit price conscious. Rybolovyev garnered headlines by purchasing an $88 million dollar

Manhattan apartment for his daughter, a student. He is also currently suing his art advisor, claiming that he fraudulently overcharged him and sold him Rothkos and Gauguins for something like twice their actual market value.

But there is another explanation that fits nicely with other of the events that have led to the investigations by the FBI and House Intelligence Committee. The Russian leadership could have indicated to Rybolovyev that doing the American real estate magnate a $50 million favor was a good investment all around. For Rybolovyev there was really no downside—he would also have done the Kremlin a service and acquired yet another piece of fancy property which, if he could find the proverbial "greater fool," he could sell at a profit. That now seems to be the case with the house torn down and the 6.3 acres divided into three parcels, one of which is already sold.

Trump said that was the closest he got to Russia, but in the meantime Russia kept getting closer to him in the person of Felix Sater.

Born in the USSR in 1966, Felix Sater came to the US when he was eight, his family fleeing persecution as Jews. He adapted quickly to American life, both to its brighter and darker sides. He dropped out of Pace University to become a broker at Bear Stearns, a hungry young immigrant on the make. In 1991 at an altercation at a bar in a Manhattan Mexican restaurant, Sater smashed a Margarita glass on the counter and stabbed its jagged stem into his opponent's face, causing injuries that required 110 stitches to close. He served more than a year in prison for the crime. In 1998, Sater pleaded guilty to one count of racketeering in a $40 million stock fraud carried out with four Mafia families of New York. But Sater would not spend a day in jail for his crime because, as Loretta Lynch would state in her hearings to become U.S. Attorney General, Sater had "provided valuable and sensitive information" to the government, his work "crucial to national security and the conviction of twenty individuals, including those responsible for committing massive financial fraud and members of La Cosa Nostra."

Sater apparently had important connections in the missile black market, negotiating to buy back Stingers before Osama bin Laden could get his hands on them and begin shooting American passenger planes out of the sky. For all the obvious reasons, little is known about this side of Sater's contribution, but its significance can be judged by the scale of the government's forgiveness.

By 2001 Sater joined Bayrock, a development company with offices in Trump Towers. By 2005 Bayrock got a one-year deal to develop a Trump luxury high-rise in Moscow, a deal which like most other of Trump's Russian ventures, oddly came to naught. Between 2006–2010, Bayrock and Sater are integrally involved in Trump SoHo, a hotel/condominium in lower Manhattan. This is the time period referred to by Donald Jr. when he said in 2008: "Russians make up a pretty disproportionate cross-section of a lot of our assets, say in Dubai, and certainly with our project in SoHo."

If Sater, who it must be remembered came to the U.S. at the tender age of eight, was able to return to Russia and the former Soviet republics and work to buy up missiles on the black market, it would not have been too difficult for him to help raise significant funds for Trump projects, especially since at that time Russia's prosperity was at an all-time high, with oil reaching nearly $150 a barrel in July 2008.

Trump would later disavow any real connection with Sater, saying, under oath, that if he "were sitting in the room tight now I really wouldn't know what he looked like." But other Russians were taking a closer look at Trump as the first decade of the twenty-first century came to a close, at least according to the Christopher Steele dossier whose sources allege as of June 2016 that "the Russian authorities had been cultivating and supporting . . . TRUMP for at least 5 years . . . the TRUMP operation was both supported and directed by Russian President Vladimir PUTIN. Its aim was to sow discord and disunity both within the US itself, but more especially within the Transatlantic alliance, which was viewed as inimical to Russia's interests."

Russia also drew nearer to Trump in the person of Paul Manafort, his campaign manager from April to August 2016, who lost that position "after his name surfaced . . . in a secret ledger listing millions of dollars in payments from a pro-Russian party in Ukraine." Those payments reportedly ran to $12.7 million. "I don't think he represented Russia . . . I think he represented the Ukraine or Ukrainian government or somebody, but everybody knew that," was Trump's defense.

Some questions arise here. Isn't it odd that of all the possible candidates to run Trump's campaign, it was someone so lavishly rewarded for serving the pro-Russian party that ended up with the job? And what were the services Manafort provided that warranted such extravagant compensation? One possibility was reported in a *Daily Beast* article of 11/7/16: "Trump and Russia: All the Mogul's Men," by James Miller:

> In 2006, a series of protests forced the cancellation of a scheduled NATO exercise, dubbed Sea Breeze, which was planned to take place on the Crimean Peninsula. A leaked legal memo shows how [pro-Putin Ukrainian politician] Yanukovich organized that protest, part of a strategy to raise ethnic fears that NATO was somehow making a move that could endanger the Russian-speaking population of the peninsula. Yanukovich organized the political response to the protests . . . The memo cites a senior Ukrainian prosecutor whose investigation determined that the organizer of those protests was none other than Paul Manafort.

Manafort protested such charges saying: "I am trying to play a constructive role in developing a democracy. I am helping to build a political party."

And it is while Manafort was still running Trump's campaign that the Republican Party platform underwent a curious change—its plank about "providing lethal defensive weapons" to the Ukrainian armed forces now became "appropriate assistance," it being unclear how you kill an enemy with that.

Stopping a NATO exercise and changing a plank in the Republican platform to a more pro-Russian position would have been worth several millions, by any standard.

Selling a house to a Russian oligarch for a tidy $50 million profit, developing a SoHo property with a Russian-born businessman who may have beat a racketeering rap by buying back missiles on the Russian and Central Asian black market, and hiring a man to run your campaign who had profited mightily from supporting pro-Russian forces in Ukraine, might seem like a lot of things Russian for one presidential candidate but it was only the tip of the iceberg, one that might yet sink the Trump Titanic.

There is the also the issue of Trump's suspiciously fulsome praise of Putin, who in 2007 he said, "was doing a great job in rebuilding the image of Russia and also rebuilding Russia, period." Trump often compared Obama to Putin unfavorably, saying of Putin that, "at least he was a leader unlike what we have in this country."

Praise is all fine and dandy but by 2005 Manafort had figured out a way to monetize it. According to an AP report, "Manafort proposed in a confidential strategy plan as early as June 2005 that he would influence politics, business dealings and news coverage inside the United States, Europe, and the former Soviet republics to benefit the Putin government . . ." In the plan Manafort states: "We are now of the belief that this model can greatly benefit the Putin government if employed at the correct levels with the appropriate commitment to success." Manafort signed a $10 million contract, not with Putin, of course, but with aluminum magnate Oleg Derepaska, a likely candidate to do the Kremlin's bidding. While Manafort denies he was acting for putin's benefit in his relationship with Derepaska, the political side of the relationship reportedly lasted from 2005 to at least 2010, though elements of the purely business side continued through 2014 when they had a falling out that ended up in a Cayman Islands bankruptcy court.

Manafort, sadly, did not stay with the campaign long enough to taste sweet victory in November. But the Russian connection issue got even more snarled and tangled once Trump was elected.

Ten days after his election, Trump appointed three-star Lt. General and former Defense Intelligence Agency chief Michael Flynn to be his national security advisor. And that gave Felix Sater an idea. His face-stabbing, fraud-committing, missile-retrieving youth was behind him and in the best American fashion he had reinvented himself as a patriot and philanthropist, having twice been chosen as Man of the Year by the Orthodox Jewish religious group Chabad in Port Washington, New York. To that impressive new list of attributes, Sater would now add peacemaker. Working with Trump's personal lawyer Michael D. and Andrii Artemenko, a Ukrainian lawmaker who styles himself his country's own Donald Trump, they hammered out a peace plan that would settle the problems in Ukraine and Crimea once and for all. Sanctions would be lifted on Russia, which would withdraw all forces from Eastern Ukraine with Crimea now, instead of being a possession, would be rented to Russia for the next fifty to one-hundred years, a long kick of the can. The plan was "hand-delivered" to the desk of National Security Advisor Flynn. Aside from its inherent unworkability, there was another element that would doom it immediately—Flynn's career was busily imploding.

Michael Flynn had been paid handsomely by the Kremlin's media propaganda arm, RT, but it was lying about his secret conversations with Russian Ambassador Sergei Kislyak that brought him down.

John Schindler, former NSA analyst and counterintelligence officer, says: "Ambassador Kislyak surely knew his conversations with Flynn were being intercepted, and it's incomprehensible that a career military intelligence officer who once headed a major intelligence agency didn't realize the same. Whether Flynn is monumentally stupid or monumentally arrogant is the big question that hangs over this increasingly strange affair."

But perhaps clarity could be achieved and justice done by the right appointment for attorney general. Except that at his own hearings, Jeff Sessions failed to tell the Senate about his own meetings with the Russian ambassador at the Republican convention, but also at a more private meeting in his office. Exposed, Sessions had to recuse himself from any relationship to his own justice department's investigation into the possibility of collusion between the Russians and the Trump campaign for which he himself worked. The situation begins to hover at the fine line between the hilarious and the nauseating.

The Trump administration betrays a lack of intelligence about how intelligence works. That, along with the damage done by Trump's earlier contemptuously disparaging remarks about the intelligence community and the obvious connections with the Russians, have caused some members of the intelligence community to begin withholding information from the White House. Schindler says of his former NSA colleagues with whom he is apparently still in touch: "A senior National Security Agency official explained that the NSA was systematically holding back some of the 'good stuff' from the White House . . . Since NSA provides something like 80 percent of the actionable intelligence in our government, what's being kept from the White House may be very significant indeed . . . a senior Pentagon intelligence official . . . stated that 'since January 20, we've assumed that the Kremlin has ears inside the SITROOM' meaning the White House Situation Room, the 5,500 square-foot conference room in the West Wing where the president and his top staffers get intelligence briefings. 'There's not much the Russians don't know at this point,' the official added in wry frustration."

That's probably an overstatement. And it's important not to ascribe too much importance to Putin's various tactical successes. Putin looked tough and successful in Syria but the bill for that particular venture has yet to be paid in full, the downing of a Russian jet in the Sinai desert killing 224 in December 2015, and the assassination of the Russian ambassador in Ankara in December 2016 by a killer shouting he was avenging Aleppo are only the first of more such incidents to come. Russia's attacks on NATO and American democracy may inadvertently end up making both stronger. The results of the investigation into the Russia connection can also force the U.S. take the necessary steps to make the country less vulnerable to the various forms of cyber warfare that will increasingly dominate the international scene.

Trump and his supporters have a different view of that investigation, taking it more personally, more politically, the two almost inseparable in Trump's case. "The Russia investigation is being used by his political opponents to delegitimize his entire presidency and to delegitimize his agenda," said Sam Nunberg, identified as a "longtime Trump political advisor who remains close with West Wing aides."

Though it may be difficult for Trump and some of his supporters to fathom, national security is of greater importance than Trump's presidency and agenda. Yet there is also no denying that for Trump's political opponents the Russia investigation offers the tantalizing prospect of a Trump impeachment. Still, Trump and his rise to power prove that this is a time where even the most grotesquely improbable events can and do occur.

And there is, as historian Douglas Brinkley put it, "a smell of treason in the air."

But even in all this swirling murk a few things are definite and clear. There are simply too many points of connection between the Trump campaign and the Russians to be mere matters of chance. On the opening day of the House Intelligence Committee hearings, ranking member Adam Schiff stated the matter with eloquent logic in this abbreviated version of his remarks since there are simply too many instances to cite here:

> In December, Michael Flynn has a secret conversation with Ambassador Kislyak, about sanctions imposed by President Obama on Russia over attacking designed to help the Trump campaign. Michael Flynn lies about the secret conversation. The vice president unknowingly then assures the country that no—no such conversation ever happened. The president is informed that Flynn has lied and Pence has misled the country. The president does nothing.

> Two weeks later, the press reveals that Flynn has lied and the president is forced to fire Mr. Flynn. The president then praises the man who lied, Mr. Flynn, and castigates the press for exposing the lie.

> Now, is it possible that the removal of the Ukraine provision from the GOP platform was a coincidence? Is it a coincidence that Jeff Sessions failed to tell the Senate about his meetings with a Russian ambassador, not only at the convention, but a more private meeting in his office and at a time when the U.S. election was under attack by the Russians?

> Is it a coincidence that Michael Flynn would lie about a conversation he had with the same Russian Ambassador Kislyak, about the most pressing issue facing both countries at the time

they spoke, the U.S. imposition of sanctions over Russian hacking of our election designed to help Donald Trump?

Is it possible that all of these events and reports are completely unrelated and nothing more than an entirely unhappy coincidence? Yes, it is possible. But it is also possible, maybe more than possible, that they are not coincidental, not disconnected and not unrelated and that the Russians use the same techniques to corrupt U.S. persons that they employed in Europe and elsewhere. We simply don't know, not yet. And we owe it to the country to find out.

And there was one other point that that was raised by the Committee Chairman Devin Nunes with equal clarity and urgency, concerning the fact that "our inability to predict Putin's regime plans and intentions has been the biggest intelligence failure that we have seen since 9/11 . . ."

To resolve the issue of collusion is the task of congressional investigative committees and the FBI.

To illuminate Putin, his background, his mind-set, his style of rule, and to indicate where he has brilliantly succeeded and grievously failed, is the task of this book.

I cannot forecast to you the actions of Russia. It is a riddle, wrapped in a mystery, inside an enigma; but perhaps there is a key. That key is Russian national interest.

—WINSTON CHURCHILL

The politics of Russia flow not from her true interests, but from the individual inclinations of specific persons.

—AUSTRIAN CHANCELLOR VON KAUNITZ TO
MARIA THERESA, IN 1745

PART ONE

THE PRESENT AS PROLOGUE

*The war between the security services
is our separation of powers.*

—YULIA LATYNINA

1

ARMS AND THE MAN

On April 5, 2016, Russian president Vladimir Putin did a most extraordinary thing—with the stroke of a pen he created his own personal army, 400,000 strong. To be known as the National Guard (and also as Rosguard), it will be staffed largely by troops from the Interior Ministry, including the fearsome OMON a mix of SWAT and riot police. Possessing nine battle tanks, thirty-five artillery pieces, twenty-nine airplanes, and seventy helicopters, the National Guard will be about half the size of Russia's regular army and among the world's ten largest. The guard was created by presidential decree without a scintilla of public discussion or debate, but, as one Russian commentator waggishly put it: "As is often the case in Russia, the creation of the National Guard was long anticipated, and therefore, caught everyone by surprise."

Unlike any other part of the Russian administration from agriculture to space, the National Guard will not report to a minister but directly to Putin himself and so has already been dubbed Putin's Praetorian Guard. Putin, of course, remains commander in chief of Russia's armed forces, but as such he has to contend with an array of strong-minded generals and admirals, not to mention the highly popular minister of defense.

The National Guard is unique in reporting directly to Putin, and the man who will lead the National Guard and do that reporting, Viktor Zolotov, is considered unique in his loyalty to Putin. Whether based on demonstrated trust or complicity in crime or the acquisition of wealth, loyalty has always been of the essence for Putin. In a Darwinian society only loyalty stands as a bulwark against greed and violent ambition.

"When it comes to President Vladimir Putin's personal trust, Viktor Zolotov has no peers," wrote Mikhail Fishman in a *Moscow Times* article, "A Bigger Bludgeon." Zolotov has all the basic characteristics to pass Stage One of Putin's Loyalty Test. They are both from the same city, Leningrad, and from the working class, and they are of the same generation, less than two years apart in age. They even look somewhat alike, with very Russian blue-gray eyes that stare intently and allow no entry. Most important, they are both former KGB, and as Putin is wont to remark, there is no such thing as that.

Stage Two of Putin's Loyalty Test is prolonged, close contact, especially in sharp and sudden situations when there is no time to dissemble and true colors come out. His relationship with Zolotov goes back to the early 1990s, when Zolotov was assigned to head up the bodyguard for the mayor of St. Petersburg and his deputy, Vladimir Putin, recently returned from five years of KGB service abroad in Dresden. Zolotov became Putin's sparring partner in boxing and judo, attempting to punch or flip him when he was not ensuring his safety.

Between 2000 and 2013 Zolotov was chief of security for the president and the prime minister of Russia, both of which offices Putin would occupy in that time. Little is known about Zolotov, as befits a secret service chief, yet there are fascinating and ominous glimpses of him in *Comrade J,* the memoirs of Colonel Sergei Tretyakov, who ran foreign intelligence for Russia in the United States after the end of the Cold War.

Newly elected president Vladimir Putin was scheduled to attend the UN Millennium Summit in New York in the first week of September 2000. The deputy head of Putin's advance team Aleksandr Lunkin was an old friend of Colonel Tretyakov's, and pumped Tretyakov for information about Zolotov. Lunkin recounted a conversation between Zolotov and an associate trying to decide which of Putin's rivals and enemies should be assassinated to better secure the new president's hold on power. Methods were discussed—how to make the killings look like a Mafia hit or the work of a Chechen terrorist. But one killing would necessitate another, the targets ranging from political figures to members of the press corps who might investigate the crimes. After much serious consideration, Zolotov concluded: "There are too many. It's too many to kill—even for us."

When, Zolotov himself, accompanied by a general, arrived in New York for a final security review, Colonel Tretyakov took the three of them to the popular Tatiana Café in Brighton Beach in Brooklyn. There Zolotov bragged about the superiority of the Russian secret service—its use of multiple armored limousines in a motorcade so an assassin wouldn't know which one bore the president, the quality of the weapons used by his "Men in Black," so called because of their black suits and black sunglasses. Those weapons included Gyurza pistols whose magazines contained eighteen bullets that could penetrate bulletproof vests from more than fifty yards away and also portable "Wasp" rocket launchers. Each man in the presidential guard was also an expert in martial arts, added Zolotov, and could kill with a single blow.

To demonstrate his point, Zolotov, without a word of warning, struck Tretyakov in the temple, knocking him unconscious to the floor. He came around a few seconds later, the general yelling: "You could have killed him!"

That may have been the tipping point for Colonel Tretyakov, who defected a month later to the United States, for which he had been covertly working for three years and which paid him more than $2 million, the highest sum any defector had ever received.

Officially, among the National Guard's several functions, the most important would seem to be "countering terrorism and extremism," categories that can cover a multitude of sins, especially the latter. Yet the real purpose of Putin's personal guard is to prevent Putin's personal nightmare scenario from becoming a reality. That scenario has several interlocking elements: military pressure from Russia's chief enemies, which, as in the Cold War, are again NATO and the United States; an information war by those same enemies designed to create unrest among the populace, leading to a Russian equivalent of Ukraine's uprising; and maintenance of the sanctions and, in the Kremlin's view, the deliberate keeping of oil prices low to bring Russia to its knees, since economic suffering will only exacerbate the discontent of workers, some of whom have received no salaries for months. Economic pain and social turmoil will set the stage for a palace coup by ambitious officials and oligarchs disgruntled because Putin has gone from making them money to costing them money. In that worst-case scenario Putin is dragged through the streets like Qaddafi.

The creation of the National Guard, a sort of national secret service, is the sign of a person feeling vulnerable, not one brimming with confidence. So it was probably no coincidence that the American guided missile destroyer USS *Donald Cook* was buzzed dangerously close by two Russian Su-24 bombers in the Baltic Sea off the coast of Kaliningrad on April 12, 2016, a week after the decree creating the National Guard. That this is an area where Russia feels particularly vulnerable was demonstrated two days later when a U.S.

reconnaissance jet was buzzed by a Russian fighter. It came close to creating an incident. Secretary of State John Kerry called the behavior "reckless," "provocative," and "dangerous," adding that "under the rules of engagement that could have been a shoot-down." A Russian official responded: "We will continue to use force to prevent any attempts by foreigners to come close to our borders. If they blink, we will shoot them down without a second's hesitation."

The Baltic states—Estonia, Lithuania, and Latvia—as well as Poland were particularly alarmed by the Russian annexation of Crimea and incursion into eastern Ukraine. They all have long memories of Russian occupation and oppression under tsars and Communists. Some, like the city of Narva in Estonia, would seem ripe for the plucking. Narva is 94 percent Russian-speaking and 82 percent ethnic Russia. Fewer than half its residents are even citizens of Estonia. In Narva on February 24, 2015, during a parade that included U.S. troops and armored vehicles, the Estonian prime minister said: "Narva is a part of NATO no less than New York or Istanbul, and NATO defends every square meter of its territory."

The irony is that Poland and the Baltic states really have nothing to worry about—Putin is happy to rattle the populace and humiliate NATO from time to time, but he has no vital interests there for which he would be willing to risk a confrontation with NATO. On the contrary, it is Putin himself who feels most vulnerable in the Baltic region.

Russia has a fleet at every point of the compass. The Northern Fleet, near Murmansk in the Arctic, and the Pacific Fleet in Vladivostok have always been secure. The southern Black Sea Fleet was secured with the annexation of Crimea; until then its use was ultimately dependent on the pleasure of the government in Kiev. It is the Baltic Fleet, which operates out of the Russian exclave province of Kaliningrad, that is the most unprotected. What Russia fears most— being surrounded by NATO—has already happened in Kaliningrad, a piece of Russia about the size of Connecticut, totally disconnected from the "mainland" and encircled by Poland and Lithuania.

Oddly enough, though surrounded by NATO in Kaliningrad, the Russians don't seem the least cowed. In fact, they've used the area quite aggressively. Both President Putin and President Dmitri Medvedev have threatened to place missiles there, including some with nuclear warheads, in response to U.S. plans to install missile defense systems in Eastern Europe beginning with Romania, operational as of May 2016, to be followed by Poland in 2017. Russia launched live-fire war games in Kaliningrad right after the invasion of Crimea; the Poles and Lithuanians were so shaken that they invoked Article 4 of the NATO charter, which calls for consultation when "territorial integrity, political independence or security" is threatened.

But Kaliningrad is not so much Russia's extended fist as its Achilles' heel.

The Kremlin fears that the West can question the validity of Kaliningrad's belonging to Russia. The original agreements about the postwar boundaries of Germany, Eastern Europe, and the Soviet Union were set out in the Potsdam Agreement of 1945. Those agreements were provisional and only became final forty-five years later, on September 12, 1990, with the signing of the Treaty on the Final Settlement with respect to Germany. In the 1994 Budapest Memorandum the Russians agreed to respect Ukraine's sovereignty and territorial integrity when Kiev surrendered its nuclear weapons. If Crimea can be an exception to that agreement, why can't Kaliningrad be an exception to the Final Settlement? This is a pressure the West could bring to bear.

In fact, Russia believes that its sovereign control of Kaliningrad is already under assault by the West.

Kaliningrad itself has already become an active front in the information war, though it isn't clear how much Russia's "enemy" is actually firing. Yet the counteroffensive is being waged on the highest levels. The governor of the province has said: "It's no secret that Western intelligence agencies are carrying out operations for a Ukrainian-style revolution in Kaliningrad."

Those Western operations take many forms, many of them seemingly small and innocuous, like "creeping Germanization"—demanding that the historical name of the city, Königsberg, be sometimes used or that the region's five-hundred-year history as part of Prussia and its being the birthplace of the philosopher Immanuel Kant not be entirely downplayed. But Germany has not evinced the slightest desire to reclaim this territory, which no longer has any ethnic Germans. And so: "Senior Russian intellectuals and officials have gone on record saying they strongly believe that Washington has secretly approved of the transfer of Kaliningrad to Lithuania." Fear of outside agitators uniting forces with a "fifth column" inside Kaliningrad is rife.

Pressure on regions like Kaliningrad is one way of raising tensions within Russia; maintaining the sanctions and artificially keeping the price of oil low are another. Proof that Putin respects sanctions is that he chose to inflict economic, not military, pain on Turkey when it shot down a Russian jet that strayed into Turkish territory in November 2015.

But if Putin were merely worried about unpaid workers and an unhappy middle class taking to the streets, he could easily have left the OMON riot police and other troops as part of the Interior Ministry and not created an entirely new entity, the National Guard. The creation of a "superpower agency can be considered as the official recognition of the significance of a new threat—the threat of the internal enemy," to quote a recent article from one of Russia's still fairly free newspapers.

Who exactly is that internal enemy? The National Guard's mandate to counterterrorism and extremism has some relevance here because many Chechen rebels have already pledged their allegiance to the ISIS caliphate, and from the Kremlin's point of view, people like opposition leader Alexei Navalny are at best just this side of extreme. But even though those are real concerns for Putin, especially as jihadists with Russian passports begin returning home from Syria, it's not what was foremost in his mind when creating the National Guard.

That creation was meant as a signal both to specific individuals and to the power elite as a class. The minister of the interior was humbled and humiliated by losing so much of his forces to Putin's National Guard. The Federal Security Bureau (FSB), successor to the KGB, also lost much of its mandate to the National Guard, terrorism especially having been its purview. For Putin, security types are both natural allies and natural enemies; those not bound to him by loyalty could easily have the wiles and ambition to move against him. They could collect compromising material, what the Russians call *kompromat*, on those around Putin or on Putin himself for that matter. If Putin has significant wealth stashed abroad, the FSB would be the organization most likely to initiate the search for it. Putin's own rise to power was based on obtaining compromising material on the prosecutor general who was investigating President Boris Yeltsin's family's financial dealings in the late 1990s. And so there would be a certain poetic justice, or at least bookkeeping symmetry, if *kompromat* was involved in Putin's fall.

The creation of the National Guard was also a signal to Minister of Defense Sergei Shoigu, whose popularity with the army and the populace cause some to view him as a natural successor to Putin. Because of his military achievements in Crimea and Syria, Shoigu consistently places second only to Putin in polls of Russia's most trustworthy leader, not an enviable position. Shoigu is said to harbor no political ambitions and is often described with a line from the poet Mikhail Lermontov: "A servant to the tsar, a father to his men." Others contend that no one with an Asiatic last name could ever be president of Russia. Still, the head of the Foreign Intelligence Service is part Jewish, as are many of the oligarchs close to Putin, which would seem to indicate that on some level Russia is either becoming more progressive or has finally lost all of its traditional values, anti-Semitism included.

Putin's message is straightforward: My National Guard will quash any demonstrations or terrorism, and I will come down especially hard on anyone trying to exploit social disturbance for political purposes.

Putin's creation of the National Guard was not widely covered by the Western media, consumed with America's political circus and immigrants streaming into a stagnant, disunited Europe, though some coverage was given to the buzzing by Russian planes because it was sensationalistic and because there was good video. The lack of coverage was in a way appropriate if Putin's move was essentially directed against an "internal enemy." But sometimes local politics go global. It is not in the least encouraging to see the leader of a nuclear superpower feel insecure enough to surround himself with a 400,000-strong Praetorian Guard—especially when that is coupled with a mounting mistrust of the West. In fact, both Russia and the West (NATO and the United States) have now openly declared the other their number one threat, though, according to the diplomatic nuance required, the choice of nouns may vary—"opponent," "target," or, to use Defense Secretary's Ashton Carter's memorably dweeby phrase when describing Russia and China, "stressing competitors."

When stepping down from leading NATO's Allied Command Operations in May 2016, General Philip Breedlove strongly warned about the dangers of a Russia that "has not accepted the hand of partnership but chosen a path of belligerence." Saying that Russians "may not be 10 feet tall, but they're pretty close to 7 feet tall," Breedlove was referring to Russia's armed forces, which had surprised and impressed the world in Syria, though even that distant incursion has its connections with the new National Guard.

Putin had many motivations for supporting Assad in Syria—to regain a position of power in the Middle East, to show up the West as meek and feckless, to test and advertise Russia's new generation of weaponry. Those weapons have in fact won the approval of international experts, and sales have already picked up; as soon as some of Iran's funds were unfrozen, Tehran's defense minister flew to Moscow with an $8 billion shopping list.

Putin is decisively against authoritarian leaders being toppled and their societies abandoned to chaos. The Syrian incursion is also a message for domestic consumption, especially now that a National Guard has been created: See what amount of force I am willing to use against the enemies of a semi-important ally? Imagine how much force I would use to protect my own power, position, life.

In Putin's view, Russia has both external and internal enemies. The external seek to weaken Russia's society and economy through sanctions, low oil prices, information wars, and pressure on possible weak points like Kaliningrad. The internal enemies—political rivals, opposition leaders, unhappy oligarchs—share a common goal with the external ones: the removal of Putin. It is even possible they will collude. After all, in 1917 Lenin was sent by Russia's enemy Germany in a sealed train to Petrograd in the calculation that a revolutionary Lenin would not wish to continue Tsarist Russia's imperialist war. All of these are the sort of moves Putin himself might make if he were on the other side of the chessboard—why shouldn't he pay his opponent the compliment of considering him equally intelligent and devious?

Putin's fears may seem extravagant, but when viewed against the backdrop of Russia's history, many of them do not seem so extravagant at all.

PART TWO

BACKGROUND CHECK

. . . the time is right for fighting in the streets.

—THE ROLLING STONES

2

THE EDUCATION OF V. V. PUTIN

All decent people get their start in intelligence. I did too.

—HENRY KISSINGER TO PUTIN IN CONVERSATION,
EARLY NINETIES

Any portrait of Putin must necessarily be streaky, ambiguous, elusive. His KGB training made him duplicitous, poker-faced, and his years in power have airbrushed his past. Besides, Russian psychology and behavior always tend to baffle Westerners. America's experts know Russia, they just don't know Russians. This is what Defense Secretary Robert M. Gates was getting at when, bemoaning deteriorating U.S.-Russia relations, he said of himself and Condoleezza Rice: "For the first time both the United States secretary of state and secretary of defense have doctorates in Russian studies. A fat lot of good that's done us."

Putin's time in the KGB lends him a sinister charisma that also obscures his true face. The way he views the KGB and the way it is seen by outsiders is one of the true impediments to penetrating his psychology and predicting his behavior. For Putin, membership in the KGB is a source of pride and identity; he's gone so far as to say that there is no such thing as ex-KGB. For him and many in the KGB, the organization was not evil but heroic. It helped win the revolution, beat the Nazis, and steal U.S. atomic secrets, thus preserving a balance of power in the world. Many KGB veterans, though they will in passing acknowledge their organization's complicity in Stalin's crimes and the oppression that continued after his death, are also acutely aware of themselves as victims and martyrs. There was no more dangerous job in Stalin's USSR than head of the KGB, and when a KGB leader fell, immediate purges of his confederates would decimate the ranks. The principal intelligence school that Putin attended during his training had been established by Stalin's personal order in 1938 to replace the agents killed in Stalin's own purges.

In KGB eyes the blame for the crimes committed against innocent civilians and against "innocent" KGB personnel lay with the party. The KGB was only the party's sword and shield—it did what it was told.

So when someone like John McCain says he looks into Putin's eyes and sees "KGB" he means thug and oppressor, but when Vladimir Putin says the same word, it has associations of victor, victim, and, at worst, inadvertent villain. This is not the best basis for communication and also violates the cardinal principle: Know thy enemy.

Our image of Russia lacks nuance and perversity. A Westerner might be able to understand why Russians would remain faithful to the original image of the KGB man as bold and valiant. It would, however, be considerably more difficult to understand the nostalgia some former prisoners of the Gulag for their time there. In the Gulag everything was more vivid and real. There was no ambiguity— friendship was friendship, betrayal betrayal. Speaking of some music he had by chance overheard and whose beauty sustained him for days, one Zek (prisoner) said to me: "You hold things dearer in there. Hearing music in there in not like hearing music out here. I would not have missed it for the world."

But Putin eludes even Russians. A politician who worked closely with Putin in St. Petersburg in the 1990s says: "When he became President I threw open my photo album to see us together—I knew he'd be there next to me at one of so many events we were at together. But he wasn't in a single one. He'd slipped out of every frame. I sometimes wonder if he even has a reflection in the mirror."

Vladimir Vladimirovich Putin was born in Leningrad in 1952. The time and the place are both important. It was only seven years since the end of World War II in a Soviet Union still ruled by Joseph Stalin, with whom Putin's family had a strong personal connection—Putin's grandfather cooked for Stalin.

Leningrad and Moscow had very different fates during the war. Moscow withstood Hitler's blitzkrieg attack of 1941, though it was a close call. German bombs hit Red Square. On the road into Moscow from Sheremetyevo International Airport there is a monument of oversized tank traps, which mark the point of the closest German advance. The Nazis were in Queens.

Moscow displayed heroic resistance, Leningrad heroic endurance. The latter city was besieged by the Nazi army for some nine hundred days. A million people died from hunger, cold, and the unrelenting shelling of the city. At the apex, ten thousand were dying a day. In the winter, dynamite was needed to blast the frozen ground to make mass graves. Putin tells the story of how his mother almost became an inadvertent victim: "Once my mother fainted from hunger. People thought she had died, and they laid her out with the corpses. Luckily, Mama woke up in time and started moaning."

The most terrifying sight in the world in the Leningrad of those days was that of a well-fed man—it meant he was a cannibal and out hunting for more.

Those were the stories Putin heard at the kitchen table when the grown-ups drank tea. Even Chancellor Angela Merkel, who grew up in East Germany, has nothing in her biography that comes close.

The year of Putin's birth was the last year of Stalin's life and the time of his last purge. The anti-Semitic Doctors' Plot accused Jewish doctors in Kremlin hospitals of murdering high Soviet officials. It was always dangerous to be too close to the Kremlin or Stalin and his inner circle, though that didn't affect Putin's grandfather, who cooked for both Lenin and Stalin. He must have had a very high clearance if he was not actually an official member of the security apparatus. Putin's father survived hazardous duty performing sabotage behind Nazi lines, fighting in a demolitions battalion of the NKVD, precursor of the KGB. He was seriously wounded—they never got all the shrapnel out of him and he limped for the rest of his life. The only casualty in the immediate family was a baby who died of diphtheria during the Siege, another having died shortly after birth before the war. Putin was thus an only child, "the sun, moon and stars" to his mother, who had him baptized on the sly from her party-member husband. Putin still wears that baptismal cross. There may also be a special sense of significance or destiny instilled in only children whose predecessor siblings all died, opening the way for them, as was the case for Stalin.

In World War II the USSR lost something like twenty-six million people, and innumerable buildings were destroyed. Like many others, Putin grew up in a communal apartment where several families lived together, usually one family per room, and shared a kitchen. There was no hot water, no bathtub. The toilet, out on the landing, was filthy and freezing. A teacher who once visited his home found the bathroom "horrendous." The stairs were infested with "hordes of rats" that Putin chased with sticks for fun, though it wasn't so much fun when, cornered, they turned and attacked.

Not all the lessons he learned were harsh. Friendship with a Jewish family that lived in one of the communal apartment's rooms helped inoculate him against anti-Semitism. He would also have close relations with Jewish teachers and martial arts mates. One of his Jewish teachers, Vera Gurevich, was responsible for Putin's learning German. Spotting his "potential, energy, and character," she decided to devote time and attention to him even though he seemed hell-bent for a life of street fights and petty crime. Under her tutelage, he developed a taste for German that would in time play an important part in his KGB career. He continued studying it in high school, where his chemistry teacher also noticed his force and drive, but still remarked, "He was ordinary, there were so many like him."

Yet not only did that rough and ordinary boy become president of Russia, but when in Israel in 2005 he found time to visit that old teacher and tell her that he remembered her as "honest, fair and kind," and then he bought her an apartment in Tel Aviv.

But back in his youth it was street fighting that was his passion and best skill. The lesson that the streets of Leningrad taught was simple, and it stayed with Putin his whole life: The weak get beaten. Weakness is both disgrace and danger. "The greatest criminals in our history," Putin would say when president, "were those weaklings who threw power on the floor—Nicholas II and Gorbachev—who allowed the power to be picked up by the hysterics and the madmen."

The streets would shape not only Putin's worldview but his tactics as well. In discussing preemptive attacks on ISIS in Syria when justifying his support of the Assad regime, he said: "The streets of Leningrad taught me one thing—if a fight is unavoidable, throw the first punch."

The streets of Leningrad were Putin's playing fields of Eton. They also taught the value of loyalty. Loyalty is both a useful attribute and a sign of strength, for it is often tested. The cult of strength and loyalty is Putin's true religion.

What saved Putin from the street was a sport and a dream. The sport was Sambo, a Soviet blend of wrestling and judo that was for

Putin a discipline, a philosophy, a way of life. He would eventually attain a black belt and become city champion of Leningrad. This was before he was important and opponents knew better than to beat him.

But it was not a career in sport that became his dream. It was the KGB for him. He was under the spell of KGB exploits lauded in books and films but especially in the black-and-white miniseries *The Sword and the Shield*, which recounted the adventures of a Soviet agent whose German was so perfect and composure so cool that he could even infiltrate the SS. Putin saw it when he was sixteen. "Books and spy movies like *The Sword and the Shield* took hold of my imagination. What amazed me most of all was how one man's effort could achieve what whole armies could not. One spy could decide the fate of thousands of people."

It all goes back to adolescence and the movies, even the difference between dissidents and KGB agents, as the Polish poet Stanislaw Baranczak observed in "The Restoration of Order":

> *They went to see different movies. For them*
> *being a man meant wearing a shoulder holster,*
> *driving fast cars screeching around corners,*
> *and shooting like a pro from a half squat, using both hands.*
> *For us being grownup was more like Bogart's grimace*
> *a bitter irony that had to be swallowed*
> *because you don't spit out such things with people around.*

Though Putin no doubt fantasized about acts of derring-do, what drew him most was the power to decide the fate of thousands. In an attempt to make his dream a reality, he went to the "Big House," KGB headquarters in Leningrad, and inquired about the process of becoming a spy. He was rebuffed, but learned two important things. The KGB didn't accept people who "came on their own initiative."

If the KGB wanted you, they found you. It was the state that decides, not the individual. And the KGB was only interested in people who had served in the army or had some higher education. "But what kind is preferred?" asked Putin. The answer: "Law school." As he says: "From that moment on, I began to prepare for the law faculty of Leningrad University. And nobody could stop me."

Even the little he knew about the KGB's role in the purges could not slow him down. Not that such things were much discussed at home. His father was a "silent man" who said with Soviet wisdom that "only a fool would open up his soul to the world. You have to know who you are talking to." "I didn't think about the purges," said Putin. "My notion of the KGB came from romantic spy stories. I was a pure and utterly successful product of Soviet patriotic education." It wasn't only the purges he didn't think about. *The Sword and the Shield*, the miniseries that so entranced the young Putin, came out in 1968, the same year that Warsaw Pact tanks rolled into Czechoslovakia to crush the Prague Spring that had tried to create "socialism with a human face." No doubt in Putin's household the reaction was the same as in many others—ungrateful Czechs, we liberated them from the Nazis and now look what they do. As usual, the intelligentsia summed up their bitter disappointment in a quip: Question: What is the most neutral country in the world? Answer: Czechoslovakia—it does not even interfere in its own internal affairs.

After graduating from Leningrad State University's Law Department in 1975, Putin was recruited by the KGB. Either they had remembered him or he had been spotted by one of their scouts.

Putin's romantic image of the Chekist—bold, incorruptible, wearing a long black-leather coat and dispensing revolutionary justice from a Mauser, or later, infiltrating Nazi circles or stealing atomic secrets from the West—was all part of the past. These were the Brezhnevian seventies, the era of stagnation, when dissidents were hounded and ended up in work camps or psychiatric hospitals where, as one former inhabitant described it, "After a breakfast of mush came shock therapy. You're given a large dose of insulin, the sugar disappears from your blood and you go into shock. You're tied to your bed with strips of torn sheets, not ropes. When they're in shock, people go into convulsions. They scream and howl. Their eyes look like they are going to pop out of their head."

If he was even aware of such things at the time, they would have been easy for Putin to justify. In any case, he was too happy and excited to be a part of the secret elite that really ran the world. A friend of Putin's, Sergei Roldugin, who went on to become the lead cellist in the Mariinsky Theater Symphony Orchestra, recalls Putin as a young KGB operative: "Once, at Eastertime, Volodya called me to go see a religious procession. He was standing at the rope, maintaining order, and he asked me whether I wanted to go up to the altar and take a look. Of course I agreed. There was such boyishness in this gesture—'nobody can go there, but we can.'"

On the way home drunken students tried to bum a cigarette from Putin, who refused. One of them then shoved or punched Putin. As his friend remembers: "Suddenly somebody's socks flashed before my eyes and the kid flew off somewhere. Volodya turned to me calmly and said, 'Let's get out of here.' And we left. I loved how he tossed that guy! One move, and the guy's legs were up in the air."

Though their paths diverged—the KGB for Putin, classical music for Roldugin—they kept in touch, bound by youth, the streets, a shared sense of loyalty. In early 2016 the Panama Papers would reveal that Roldugin was at least nominally in charge of some $2 billion in offshore capital, pretty good for a cellist.

Putin is only intermittently visible in the ten years between entering the KGB and surfacing in Dresden, East Germany, in 1985. Odd had it been otherwise. He was now a soldier on the "invisible front." As his friend noticed, this offered the secret satisfactions of knowing what others did not know and being able to do what others could not. He was being initiated into a secret elite. Part of that initiation was a new relationship to oneself that relieved him of the need to be sincere. The difference between the inner and the outer man, which might be called hypocrisy in a common Soviet citizen, was, in the case of a KGB officer, an operational necessity. In KGB training there is also an element of self-mastery that would have been familiar to Putin from martial arts, except that now it was used to manipulate others. Upon entering any training facility an agent would be given a new last name, to break his conditioned response to his own name, to free up his relationship to his own identity, the easier to slip into aliases and disguises.

Another force would begin shaping any new recruit, imperceptibly but implacably. Paranoia was both the strong suit and an occupational hazard of the KGB. Their task was to be suspicious. History had clearly demonstrated that it was always better to err on the side of excess suspicion. The KGB would agree with the Sicilian proverb that says To trust is good, not to trust is better.

But the trouble with paranoia is that it cannot set limits on itself, and so grotesqueries are committed. For example, when the Soviets wanted to transfer submarines from their southern bases to those in the north, they would not send them out by the short and easy route through the Black Sea, then to the Mediterranean and out to the Atlantic, from where they would pass over Scandinavia to Murmansk in the Arctic Circle. That route would expose the submarines to the spying eyes of NATO. To avoid that unacceptable risk, the subs were placed on floating dry docks, covered with tarps, and hauled on a fifty-one-day journey through the country's internal river system as detailed in the book *Rising Tide: The Untold Story of the Russian Submarines That Fought the Cold War*: "Only the nineteenth century Mariinsky Canals presented a true problem. Too shallow and too old, they often required the crew to pull the dock along and at the locks old women and pack animals pitched in to force the old controls to do their job."

Old women! Pack animals!

But there was nothing new in any of that—a Frenchman who served in the tsar's armies in the late 1500s said of Russia: "This is the most distrustful and suspicious nation in the world."

After some on-the-job training in counterintelligence, Putin received his first schooling between February and July 1976 in KGB School 401 in the Okhta region of Leningrad, a school he calls in "no way distinguished," which is either an accurate characterization or a way of deflecting attention from the subject.

His training there was no doubt largely operational—tradecraft, surveillance and avoiding surveillance, the art of recruitment. One danger KGB agents faced was that the sources they were developing were in fact working for the other side, "dangles" as they were called. For that reason it was recommended that a KGB officer meet with a potential source at least seven times before beginning to work with him, the "first stage of operational development."

KGB School 401 may also have had something of the boot camp about it. In a description of another such school Major Yuri Shvets, author of *Washington Station: My Life as a KGB Spy in America*, observes: "We parachuted from planes, mastered a variety of weapons, learned to plant mines, negotiated a napalm-drenched obstacle course, captured 'prisoners' for interrogation, 'blew up' bridges, and 'destroyed' enemy supply lines."

Putin had entered the KGB just as it was undergoing a fundamental change in course in part influenced by, of all things, an American movie, if one is to believe the post-Soviet station chief for foreign intelligence in New York City, Sergei Tretyakov, who writes that the 1975 Robert Redford film *Three Days of the Condor* "convinced the KGB generals that the CIA was spending more money and putting more effort into analytic work than the KGB was," and on that basis a shift of emphasis occurred between the operational and the analytical.

Though the KGB was undergoing certain changes in the mid-seventies, the organization bore the clear impress of its leader, Yuri Andropov, who would not only be Putin's commander in chief but his hero and role model as well. Andropov was the only person before Putin to pass from being chief of the security services to head of state. When Andropov took the helm of the USSR in 1982, the choice was even welcomed by a portion of the dissident intelligentsia who, along with Andrei Sakharov, believed that the KGB was "the least corrupt institution in the country." Moreover, it was assumed that the KGB possessed the best information and therefore had to realize that the country was in critical need of reform.

Andropov had been traumatized by the Hungarian Uprising of 1956, which he, as Soviet ambassador, would treacherously and viciously suppress. But first, as historian Christopher Andrew put it, "he had watched in horror from the windows of his embassy as officers of the hated Hungarian security service were strung up from lampposts. Andropov remained haunted for the rest of his life by the speed with which an apparently all-powerful Communist one-party state had begun to topple."

But Andropov would not be given long to show what course he would set for the Soviet ship of state. In fact, his initial actions—raiding movie theaters for people shirking work, enforcing labor discipline—betrayed a petty, fussy cast of mind, not the broad horizons of a reformer. He had served a little more than a year when he suffered renal failure that first debilitated him, then took his life. It is the great paradox of Andropov's life that his kidney problems had caused him to travel to the south of Russia to take the waters. On his sojourns there he became friendly with the local party boss, who in time became his protégé and whom Andropov introduced to the highest political circles in Moscow. His name was Mikhail Gorbachev.

Putin joined Andropov's KGB in 1975 as the Apollo and Soyuz spacecraft linked up in space. It was the height of the euphoria of détente, a policy of rapprochement and the relaxing of tensions that Nixon and Brezhnev had launched in the early seventies. Like the "reset" under Putin, détente would end in suspicion, recrimination, and invasion—that of Afghanistan in late 1979.

Not that the KGB itself ever took détente all that seriously. In fact, during Putin's first year at work in the Leningrad KGB, it was involved in a complex, risky, and ultimately highly successful operation directed against the American consulate in Leningrad. "Beginning in 1976, the KGB successfully installed sophisticated electronic eavesdropping equipment and burst transmitters inside 16 IBM Selectric typewriters used by the staffs of the Moscow embassy and Leningrad consulate, which copied everything being typed on the machines, then periodically broadcast their take to KGB engineers manning listening posts just outside. . . . In the end, the NSA concluded that the Soviet eavesdropping operation had most likely compromised every document typed on these 16 electric typewriters over a period of eight years from 1976 to 1984."

Putin at this time was a low-level operative, fresh from law school with a quick six months' training behind him. But he was working in the field of counterintelligence. On both sides, it was assumed that certain embassy, consulate, and mission personnel were spies, but the question always remained, precisely which ones? To determine that was the task of counterintelligence. The material gleaned from the bugging of the electric typewriters would have been valuable in determining which of the Leningrad U.S. consulate's personnel were intelligence officers. At the least, Putin's task would have been facilitated by this information, and he would also have shared in the general rise in esprit de corps that a successful operation always brings to an organization.

The KGB was on a roll. On September 7, 1978, on a crowded

London street, Georgi Markov, a defector who broadcast for the BBC's Bulgarian radio service, often ridiculing the Bulgarian Communist regime, was assassinated with a poison (ricin) pellet fired from a miniaturized gun in the tip of an umbrella, a masterstroke of disguise in forever rainy London. Coincidentally, or not coincidentally, the date was also the birthday of the Bulgarian Communist dictator Todor Zhivkov, who must have been gladdened by this gift. Coincidentally, or not coincidentally, the assassination of the gadfly journalist Anna Politkovskaya would take place on Putin's birthday.

Putin was in his element. The USSR may have been run by an increasingly doddering and sclerotic Leonid Brezhnev, but the KGB was vigorous and flush with success. Penetration of the enemy's embassics and crafty assassination in the name of the cause—what could be better? Since he was in his element, he thrived and so came to the attention of the people in foreign intelligence, the classiest and most coveted branch of service, since it meant foreign postings, action on the front line, access to goods. He was called in by the foreign-intelligence people for a series of conversations. They liked what they saw and sent him to Moscow for a year's worth of advanced training at the Dzerzhinsky KGB Higher School. Named for Felix Dzerzhinsky, often called with jocular affection "Iron Felix," the founder of the first Soviet secret police, the school specialized in "skills enhancement" and had itself suffered greatly in the purges of 1937–38, when practically the entire teaching staff had been shot.

Nowadays, in one measure of progress, the KGB Higher School, a sprawl of yellow-brick buildings in southwest Moscow, is so famed for its computer experts that the lampposts outside the institute's grounds are festooned with posters offering high-paying jobs in IT.

Nineteen seventy-nine, the year Putin spent immersed in his studies and training at the KGB Higher School, was a time of tectonic shifts within the Islamic world, and between the Western and

Islamic worlds. The Iranian Revolution ousted the pro-Western shah and replaced him with a theocratic government. Radicals seized the holy places of Mecca, and the Saudis could not expel them without outside, i.e., French, help. In late December the USSR invaded Afghanistan in what would prove a protracted, failed, and fatal war, instrumental in the collapse of the system and, ultimately, in the rise of Vladimir Putin.

After returning to Leningrad from Moscow, his skills enhanced, Putin worked for three and a half years in the First Directorate, intelligence. Or did he? Some observers maintain that Putin also spent time in Directorate 5, which was charged with crushing dissent.

Andropov strove for "the destruction of dissent in all its forms" and, foreshadowing Putin, declared that "the struggle for human rights was a part of a wide-ranging imperialist plot to undermine the foundations of the Soviet state." He was, no doubt, sincere. Andropov had seen what had happened in Hungary. A small discussion group named after nineteenth-century poet Sandor Petofi begins considering reformist ideas and the next thing you know security officers are hanging from lampposts.

Two figures dominated the opposition landscape: the writer Aleksandr Solzhenitsyn and Andrei Sakharov, creator of the Soviet H-bomb and leader of the human rights movement. In 1971 an attempt had been made on Solzhenitsyn's life in a Moscow store, where he was smeared with a gel most likely containing ricin from the KGB's poison factory. He became violently ill, but Solzhenitsyn, who had survived World War II, the Gulag, and cancer, wasn't easy to kill. In early 1974 the KGB simply put him on a plane and exiled him to the West.

Sakharov, however, was a trickier business for the party and the KGB, which never acted in important matters without directives from the party. Of course, the KGB had ways of getting the party to do what it wanted, like feeding the leadership false or misleading information, as Andropov is believed to have done during the Prague Spring, which he wanted crushed at once. Sakharov had made the Soviet Union a nuclear power and had three times been awarded the Hero of Socialist Labor, one of the country's highest civilian awards. In 1968, the year of the Prague Spring, *The New York Times* had published the complete text of Sakahrov's long essay "Reflections," which grappled with cocxistence in a hostile nuclear world.

Andropov believed that there was still hope for Sakharov and suggested in a 1968 report to the Central Committee that Sakharov be called in for "an appropriate conversation." However, Sakharov, a shy but fearless man, was already well beyond persuasion or threat. Two years later Andropov informed the Central Committee that it was "advisable to install secret listening devices in Sakharov's apartment." In April 1971 Andropov reported without a trace of irony: "Meeting regularly with anti-Soviet individuals, some of whom are mentally ill, SAKHAROV looks at the world around him mainly through their eyes. It seems to him that he is constantly subjected to provocations, surveillance, eavesdropping, etc."

The line on Sakharov was that his anti-Soviet stances could only be the result of bad influences upon him, especially that of his firebrand wife, Elena Bonner, who had been born into Communist "royalty" and grown up in luxurious apartments (though everything in them belonged to the state, as indicated by the small copper tag with a number on every piece of furniture). Her father was executed in the purges of 1937 and her mother was in the camps from that same year until 1954. Bonner was half Jewish, more than Jew enough for the KGB. Putin, who would let those close to him know that he took no pleasure in anti-Semitism, had no problem agreeing with those who expressed such opinions on the sound philosophical basis of—why spit against the wind? But, if only from the point of view of professional finesse, he did not like how the affair was handled, especially the "illegal" arrest and internal exile of Sakharov for protesting the Soviet invasion of Afghanistan in December 1979. "The Sakharov affair was crude," judged Putin.

Putin denies that he did any work for the Fifth Directorate in its task of suppressing ideological subversion. Though his image gained luster from his work in espionage, there was no upside in admitting to helping crush dissent, especially in the years immediately after the fall of the Soviet Union, when everyone was scrambling to provide themselves with some sort of democratic credentials. It is of course very much in the interest of Putin's enemies to prove he worked in the Fifth Directorate. But it's not only his enemies who hold that view. Putin's friend and KGB colleague in Dresden, Vladimir Usoltsev, who wrote an entire book, *Co-worker,* about their relationship, took it for granted that Putin had gotten all his unorthodox ideas from all the dissident literature he had read as part of his job of suppressing it: "Gradually it dawned on me that Volodya had acquired all his fancy dissident ideas back in Leningrad while working in the 5th." Putin, he says, showed particular esteem for the work of Solzhenitsyn, on whom he would bestow high state honors many years later.

Putin continues to deny having worked in the Fifth or having any dissident ideas, fancy or otherwise. Confiscated dissident literature, samizdat, no doubt circulated among KGB agents, sexy and forbidden as an errant issue of *Playboy.*

What's the truth? There was a brief period in the early nineties when Russia was on a spree of liberty and the KGB archives were opened up to scholars and antiseptic sunlight. That didn't last long, and it's a safe bet that nothing of the sort will be coming along again any time soon. Given that, probably the truest thing that can be said is that it doesn't matter greatly if Putin worked in the Fifth or merely collaborated with it from time to time or had in fact nothing to do with it. Though literature and life had already lent him a certain light ironic attitude, he was still defined by the virtue he valued most: loyalty. He was loyal to the KGB and its chief, Andropov. No matter what private sentiments he harbored, Putin would not have deviated an iota from KGB policy. He would have supported Sakharov's exile, the use of psychiatric incarceration as punishment, and even Andropov's ban on any public mourning for John Lennon in 1980. He was a company man.

And for that very reason he had to be proud and amazed when in November 1982 his boss became the boss of the whole Soviet Union. Andropov took the helm at a dark time. The invasion of Afghanistan had led to a boycott of the 1980 Olympic Games in Moscow. A civilian airliner, Korean KAL 007, was shot down after having strayed over Soviet territory, a U.S. congressman among the 269 victims. Reagan branded the USSR the "evil empire" and called for implementation of "Star Wars," a missile defense program that might have had little chance of success but which could bankrupt the Soviets if they tried to match it. Andropov began purging corrupt officials, which gave public morale a bit of a boost, but he mostly seemed interested in nabbing malingerers in bath houses and movie theaters, acting more like a truant officer than a tyrant enlightened with good intel.

Later it would emerge that Andropov was, like Dzerzhinsky, the founder of the security services, a bit of a poet. It could even be said that he created something of a unique literary genre—the brevity of life as mourned by one of its abbreviators:

> We are fleeting in this world, beneath the moon.
> Life is an instant. Non-being is forever.
> The Earth spins in the universe,
> Men live and vanish. . . .

There was even some poetic justice in Andropov's death after less than fifteen months in power. Dying of renal failure, he was like the

Soviet system, which could not purge itself of the poisons it se-creted. The hagiography machine went into immediate operation after Andropov's death. He was lent a cloying tragic aura and be-came the Saint Who Had Not Had Time to Complete His Mission on Earth. Someone else would have to do it.

Though whether or not Putin spent any time in the Fifth Di-rectorate suppressing dissent must remain conjecture, there is no question that he was viewed within the KGB as an intelligence agent who should be trained for the plummiest of assignments, service abroad.

And thus it was that in the Orwellian year of 1984 Major Vladi-mir Putin, now a married man, traveled again to Moscow, this time to spend a year at the Red Banner Institute, which had just been re-named the Andropov Red Banner Institute. This was the highest and most elite school, accepting only three hundred pupils a year and of such state significance that to even reveal its address was consid-ered treasonous.

One of the odder side effects of Gorbachev's glasnost and the greedy turbulence of the Yeltsin nineties was that many top KGB officers rushed to cash in by writing tell-all books about their clan-destine careers. Remarkably, most of them proved closet liberals just waiting for the chance to breathe free. Since these were top KGB officials, including one general, Oleg Kalugin, they all had studied at the Red Banner Institute. For that reason, we have a pretty fair idea of Putin's experience there after arriving in July 1984. The course was spartan and severe, with reveille at 6:45 a.m. and lights-out at 11:00 p.m. Classes were held six days a week, with students able to leave the institute grounds only between 3 p.m. on Saturday and 9 a.m. on Monday. Putin's wife would come to Moscow to visit him once a month, and he got back to Leningrad a couple of times during the year. Though a married man, a major in the KGB, and a student at the highest intelligence school, Putin had not lost any of his street-brawler ways. During one trip home, pestered by a punk in the Leningrad metro, he socked him so hard he broke his own arm. Putin was very worried, telling his friend Roldugin: "They're not going to understand this in Moscow. I'm afraid there are going to be consequences."

But there weren't any consequences for Comrade Putin, or Comrade Platov, as he was known in the school, where everyone's name was changed. In addition to studying German, he took a class in the structure of the KGB, which was labyrinthine. It consisted of nine chief directorates. The First Chief Directorate, dealing with foreign intelligence, was the one everyone wanted to work in and the one for which Putin was being groomed. That First Chief Directorate had four directorates of its own: "S" (illegal intelligence), "T" (scientific and technical intelligence), "K" (foreign counterintelligence), and "RT" (intelligence work carried out among foreigners on Soviet territory). But that was just the beginning. There were also two services, one for processing information received, the other for processing disinformation. These services were further subdivided principally by geography and importance into sixteen departments (actually fifteen, since the Thirteenth Department, perhaps out of superstition, did not exist). The United States and Canada were Department 1.

The lectures on U.S. and British intelligence were the most riveting because this was the enemy you had to know before you could go up against him. There was some time for the firing range and martial arts during the daily exercise hour. Some recruits would spend time with a Soviet parachute division learning how to jump from planes, hand-to-hand combat, survival in the wilderness. One officer reports shooting a grand total of three cartridges during his training, and for many even that was a waste of time. Of course tradecraft—brush contact, dead drops, eluding surveillance, and the use of espionage high tech—was essential, but in the end espionage was a mind game. It was the art of seducing someone into betrayal.

The person in charge of training and evaluating Putin was Colonel Mikhail Frolov. "I taught the art of intelligence. What does intelligence mean? It's the ability to come into contact with people, the ability to select the people you need, the ability to raise the questions that are of interest to our country and our leaders, the ability to be a psychologist, if you will." Putin himself would later, in conversation with a friend, describe himself as a "specialist in human relations."

Putin had won Colonel Frolov's interest and respect by appearing at a lecture in a three-piece suit on a ninety-degree day when even Frolov was wearing short sleeves. Frolov pointed him out as an example to the others: "Look at Comrade Platov, now!"

On the basis of that and other incidents Frolov "decided to try him out in the role of division leader. At the Red Banner Institute, division leader was not just some sort of illustrious title. A lot depends on the division leader. You need organizational abilities, a certain degree of tact, and a businesslike manner. Putin had all of that."

But there was a little more than that to being division leader. The main job of instructors like Frolov was writing the evaluations on which the students' future depended. But Frolov's own future depended on how accurate his characterizations proved. For that reason it never hurt to have a little extra inside information; providing it was one key task of the division leader and not one that would make him popular with his fellow students, any more than being held up as an example for wearing a suit on a scorching day.

Yuri Shvets, who would rise to major in the KGB and later author *Washington Station: My Life as a KGB Spy in America*, was also trained at the Andropov Red Banner Institute and says of Putin: "We had 'uncles' who wrote our references on graduation. They needed to know as much as possible and used 'elders' or the leaders of the groups, who reported to them. Vova [Putin] was a leader—a snitch. Everyone hated the leader."

Putin's kind words about collaborators and snitches in *First*

Person—characterizing them as indispensable people working patriotically "for the interests of the state"—may be both inadvertent sincerity and an ex post facto attempt to justify his own "snitching" as a group leader. In any case, though originally published in Russian newspapers, this section was not included in the Russian book version of *First Person*, because praising Soviet-era stoolies was still too sensitive an issue for many Russians.

Some of the students believed their dorm rooms were bugged, a KGB within the KGB.

Everything was a test and you never knew if you passed or failed. "You would be ordered to prepare a presentation on one topic and then the instructor would change the subject moments before you were supposed to make your presentation. . . . Would you panic? Would you become depressed? Did you have a sense of humor? If you were too serious, it was not good. If you were too carefree, it was not good. They applied pressure at all possible points and they were always totally critical. There was never any positive reinforcement. None."

There were also the odd moments of diversion. Dale Carnegie's *How to Win Friends and Influence People* was one of the most popular books in the institute library. And Vladimir Kuzichkin, author of *Inside the KGB: My Life in Soviet Espionage*, recalls: "It was from the James Bond films that we first learnt how the West saw Soviet intelligence officers. Bull necks, stupid faces, and solving all their problems with their fists and not their brains. That neither upset nor angered us. We were simply amused by it. 'The more primitive you imagine us to be,' we thought, 'the worse for you.'"

In the end it was time for Frolov to write his evaluation of Putin. It was quite positive but included some negative characteristics as well—"he was somewhat withdrawn and uncommunicative. By the way, that could be considered both a negative and a positive trait. But I recall that I also cited a certain academic tendency among his negative aspects. I don't mean that he was dry. No, he was sharp-witted and always ready with a quip." Perhaps most important for the long haul was the notation concerning Putin's "lowered sense of danger." It was a criticism Putin took very much to heart, saying: "I had to work on my sense of danger for a long time."

Despite these criticisms, Frolov recommended Putin for assignment. Putin would thank him fifteen years later by inviting Frolov to his inauguration as president in 2000.

In the end, a high-ranking commission would both examine the reports on a candidate and summon the candidate himself for an interview and, on that basis, decide what use the KGB would make of him. In Putin's case that decision was: FOREIGN INTELLIGENCE. EAST GERMANY, DRESDEN.

3

DRESDEN

Of course life in East Germany was very different from life in Russia. The streets were clean.

—LYUDMILA PUTINA (PUTIN'S WIFE)

Once known as the Florence of the Elba, rococo Dresden was fire-bombed by British and American planes in February 1945 even though the city presented very little value as a military target. The real motivations were revenge for the German bombing of civilian populations in England and also to hasten the end of the war, which in the event was less than three months away. Statistics on casualties vary wildly, from 150,000 (higher than the death toll of Hiroshima) to revisionist lows of around 35,000, based on the contention that the Nazis themselves had inflated the original figures to demonstrate that they were not the only ones to inflict savageries on the innocent. Some of those victims had an odd afterlife, as noted by the legendary chief of Stasi foreign intelligence, Markus Wolf: "We had the advantage of being able, for example, to use the identities of people killed in the Dresden bombings as covers for the agents we settled in the West." In any case, it is not statistics or posthumous exploitation that gives the true feel of the carnage but a line from *Slaughterhouse Five* by Kurt Vonnegut, who was there during the firestorm and wrote that there "must be tons of human bone meal in the ground."

A bit of a backwater, Dresden was not one of the most coveted foreign postings, but plummy enough considering that by 1984 KGB salaries there were supplemented by $100 a month in hard currency and East German stores offered such exotic luxuries as bananas. Western European cities might be more attractive, but Dresden was East Germany's third-largest city, and any German city was important. "As the Soviet Union's westernmost satellite, East Germany was the front line in the battle against capitalism. The protection of Soviet security and military forces stationed in East Germany against defection and Western espionage was as vital as the suppression of any anticommunist stirrings among the populace," writes John O. Koehler in *Stasi: The Untold Story of the East German Secret Police.*

Dresden's out-of-the-wayness offered other advantages to Markus Wolf, who said that intelligence work was "very boring . . . a banal trade of sifting through huge amounts of random information in a search for a single, enlightening gem or illuminating link, so I varied my routine by insisting on running ten or twelve agents personally. As far as I know I was the only chief of any of the world's principal intelligence agencies to do so. This gave me the opportunity to get out and meet them from time to time in safe houses in the Berlin suburbs or—what I preferred—in Dresden and other places where there were fewer Westerners."

Dresden was also the home base of the twentieth century's greatest atomic spy, Klaus Fuchs, who settled there in 1959 after serving nine years in a British prison for passing secrets to the Soviets. For many years Fuchs was deputy director of the Institute for Nuclear Research just outside Dresden, and Wolf would confer with him on scientific and technical questions.

"Blond, athletic, simpatico," as one colleague described him, Putin arrived in Dresden in late summer 1985 just as the USSR's new leader, Mikhail Gorbachev, was launching his brilliant, doomed career. Putin would be in Dresden for nearly all the Gorbachev years; for him glasnost and perestroika would always be more echo than experience.

Putin was not only assigned to Dresden, he was requested by Dresden. A section chief about to be rotated home who knew Putin from Leningrad had seen his name on a list of recent Red Banner Institute graduates and politicked for his assignment to Dresden.

Putin worked out of a two-story building at 4 Angelikastrasse directly across the street from Stasi headquarters. The KGB and the Stasi worked very closely together, too closely sometimes for the young, ambitious General Horst Böhm, head of the Dresden Stasi, who jockeyed for more leeway from their ally and conqueror, who had full rights to act as they would in the USSR with the one exception of not being able to arrest East German citizens. General Böhm would become especially incensed when KGB officers like Putin would poach ex-Stasi who were still being used by the Stasi.

Putin, for his part, was a bit shocked by East Germany, which he called "a harshly totalitarian country, similar to the Soviet Union, only 30 years earlier."

Simon Wiesenthal, renowned Nazi hunter, said that when it came to their own citizens, the Stasi were "worse than the Gestapo." The entire society was infested with agents and informers. According to very rough estimates, the USSR had 1 agent per 6,000 people, the Gestapo, 1 per 2,000, and the Stasi 1 per 166, which, if informers and part-time informers were included, came to something like 1 per 6.5, meaning it was statistically impossible to have a dinner party without at least one person being an informer.

Wiesenthal goes on to say of the Stasi: "They not only terrorized their own people worse than the Gestapo, but the government was the most anti-Semitic and anti-Israel of the entire Eastern Bloc. They did nothing to help the West in tracking down Nazi criminals, they ignored all requests from West German judicial authorities for assistance. We have just discovered shelves of files on Nazis stretching over four miles. Now we also know how the Stasi used those files. They blackmailed Nazi criminals who fled abroad after the war into spying for them."

Unlike in Leningrad, where he may have been involved in suppressing dissent in addition to counterintelligence, there is little question what Putin's assignment was in Dresden. He was in Directorate S, illegal intelligence, which, among its many tasks, prepared agents to penetrate the enemy with forged documents. According to Major Vladimir Kuzichkin, author of *Inside the KGB*, who worked in Directorate S himself, an *illegal* was "a Soviet citizen, a KGB officer holding military rank, who has undergone special training and who has been documented as a citizen of a foreign country." By contrast an *illegal agent* "can either be a Soviet citizen or a foreigner. He is not a KGB officer, he does not hold illegal rank, and has been brought into intelligence to do a onetime operation." Illegals could remain undercover for decades.

One of Putin's tasks was to find and screen candidates to be illegal agents, knowing it unlikely that many of them would qualify. Putin describes his work in the bland and general terms designed to reveal nothing: "The work was political intelligence—obtaining information about political figures and the plans of the potential opponent. . . . We were interested in any information about the 'main opponent, NATO.' . . . So recruitment of sources, procurement of information, and assessment and analysis were big parts of the job. It was very routine work."

Though Putin himself put a bland gloss on it, he was working in the part of foreign intelligence, Directorate S, that was the place where there might be a touch of action and danger, the only place that was even remotely Bondish, as one of Putin's colleagues would put it.

Directorate S had a special status both because of the successes it could achieve and the dangers it posed to Soviet foreign policy. As Christopher Andrew and Vasily Mitrokhnin write in *The Sword and the Shield*: "The records of Directorate S revealed some remarkable individual achievements. KGB illegals successfully established bogus identities as foreign nationals in a great variety of professions ranging from Costa Rican ambassador to piano tuner to the governor of New York."

But it was a high-risk game Putin was playing. KGB major Kuzichkin writes of the difference between espionage performed by members of the diplomatic staff and that carried out by illegals using forged passports of the host nation. The former have diplomatic immunity, whereas "if a KGB mission abroad should misfire and a political scandal ensue, intelligence officers can expect no mercy from the Politburo. . . . At best, a culprit may be thrown out of the KGB without a pension. At worst, criminal proceedings may be instituted against him."

Though Putin was adept at covering his own tracks and though most of the Dresden KGB's records were burned in the final days of East Germany, a bit is known about one major operation in which Putin was involved. If NATO was the "main enemy," the "main worry" was a Sudden Nuclear Missile Attack (SNMA) that would begin with Green Berets operating behind Soviet lines to thwart a Soviet response. It turns out that this at least was hardly extravagant Soviet paranoia. A May 2, 2015, *New York Times* article, "A Secret Warrior Leaves the Pentagon as Quietly as He Entered," on the retirement of Michael G. Vickers, undersecretary of defense for intelligence, states: "During the Cold War, Mr. Vickers was a member of the Green Berets assigned to infiltrate Warsaw Pact borders should World War III break out. His mission: Detonate a portable nuclear bomb to blunt an attack by the overwhelming numbers of Soviet tanks."

There were three Green Beret bases in West Germany, and it was the ambition of Directorate S to penetrate those bases. Putin was involved in searching through "mountains" of invitations from Dresdeners to relatives in West Germany to find any to people who lived near those bases. In any case, it all came to naught, not a single nibble worth mentioning. But success was always rare in any such operation. As one of Putin's coworkers put it, to recruit a single Western agent was success enough for a career.

One agent Putin ran did not turn out too well. Klaus Zuchold was a Stasi officer recruited by Putin over a five-year period, only formally joining the KGB after the fall of the Berlin Wall, when KGB penetration of Germany became more important than ever. Just after the two Germanys were reunited, Zuchold, fearing exposure, surrendered himself to German intelligence, revealing that he had been run by Putin, who was also personally running a senior police inspector in Dresden.

Zuchold had immediately been charmed by Putin's jokes about police, Jews, and the crude Russian soldiers who stole vegetables from Zuchold's garden. "Putin is a man of few words. He is impenetrable and he mostly lets other people speak. He gives away very little but is clearly very driven and determined to get what he wants: friendly and seemingly very open, luring people into opening up but always in control. Whenever we drank together he always made sure he was at least three glasses behind everyone else."

False modesty and professional ambiguity aside, Putin's downplaying of his work was also quite sincere. The KGB was increasingly becoming an organization that processed paperwork. One agent quipped that Soviet intelligence runs on paperwork alone and [its] "main advantage . . . resides in its newly acquired ability to exist without undercover agents." And, as one of Putin's own colleagues put it: "Our work was seventy percent paperwork and sometimes was unbearably boring."

KGB generals and liberal intellectuals rarely agree on anything, but such is Putin's power to unite people that he has even brought these disparate groups together in their derision of his abilities as a spy. In her biography of Putin, *The Man Without a Face*, Masha Gessen writes: "Putin's biggest success in his stay in Dresden appears to have been in drafting a Colombian university student, who in turn connected the Soviet agents with a Colombian student at a school in West Berlin, who in turn introduced them to a Colombian-born U.S. Army sergeant, who sold them an unclassified Army manual for 800 marks."

KGB colonel Sergei Tretyakov, who ran Russian intelligence operations in the United States from New York after the fall of the USSR and who attended the Red Banner Institute at the same time as Putin did, was aghast at the very suggestion that he might have had anything to do with Putin afterward: "Of course I did not. Not only because we worked in different regions of the world, but first of all because I was a successful officer working in the Center and Putin was never successful in intelligence and never had a chance to work in headquarters. He was always kept in a provincial KGB station in a low and unimportant position."

Putin is further belittled for receiving only one award, a bronze medal awarded him by the Stasi in 1988, and for only advancing one rank, from major to lieutenant colonel, in his more than four years of service abroad.

Putin, of course, doesn't quite agree with these characterizations of himself. Responding to the charge that Dresden was a provincial posting, he said: "Probably. Actually, from that perspective, Leningrad is also a province. But I was always quite successful in those provinces."

The bronze medal Putin was awarded was pooh-poohed by Markus Wolf, the Stasi intelligence chief, who said it was awarded to every secretary provided she didn't have any gross violations on her record. Bristling, Putin said Wolf was "entirely correct. . . . He just confirmed that I didn't have any gross violations in my record" and pointed out where Wolf was incorrect—in saying that Putin was awarded the medal simply for "services" when it had in fact been awarded for "outstanding services." Spies can be as vain as ballerinas.

Those who denigrate his rising only to the rank of lieutenant colonel neglect to mention that the KGB has two hierarchies—a military-style one rising from private to general, and a parallel one among case officers and administrators. For example, a senior case officer like Putin would have authority over someone with a higher rank if that person was working for Putin on a given operation.

Putin's promotions came more on the administrative side than on that of the more formal ranks. As he says: "I was a senior case officer. My next job was assistant to the head of the department. That was considered quite a good advance. And then I was promoted to senior assistant. There was nothing higher. Above me was the top managerial level, and we only had one boss."

The KGB in the late 1980s was ruled, as one officer put it, by "Lord Paperwork." There was no time for either spectacular successes or catastrophic failures—agents were too busy filling out forms and filing reports.

And if Putin had had any significant successes in Dresden they would have by their very nature remained secret. In espionage a known success is half a failure.

In those increasingly dreary years, Putin had three consolations: family, beer, and Gogol. He adored his daughters and every day would take Masha to the day-care center and Katya to the nursery. Things were a bit more complicated with his wife, Lyudmila, a good-looking blonde and former Aeroflot stewardess. Lyudmila is on record as saying that their first years together were "lived in total harmony . . . a continuous sense of joy, as though we were on holiday." In fact, there had been some problems right from the start—she found him even more reserved than most Leningraders, and he could be insultingly, infuriatingly late for their dates, an hour and a half being more or less the norm. Already in the KGB, he never told her that, saying he worked with the police. Lyudmila frequently had the feeling she was being probed and tested by Putin. It was the wife of one of Putin's friends who told her he was KGB, and a young man who appeared out of nowhere on the street declaring his love for Lyudmila may have been set up by Putin to check her reactions and her loyalty. He considered any housework beneath him and always imposed his will, to which, she says, she "always submitted." She wanted their second daughter, born in East Germany, to be called Natasha, but Putin said, "No, it will be Masha," and despite all Lyudmila's tears and pleas, Masha it was.

Not a natural cook and homemaker, she trembled inwardly awaiting his reaction to dinner. He'd never say anything. Finally, once unable to restrain herself, she asked: "How's the meat?"

"On the dry side."

His second consolation was the excellent and easily available German beer. He was buying his beloved Radeberg by the keg, and since it was only a five-minute walk from house to office he put on twenty-five pounds in no time.

And reading Gogol's novel *Dead Souls* was particularly piquant because the hero, Chichikov, goes about provincial nineteenth-century Russia buying up serfs who have died but are still on the census rolls and thus can be used as collateral until the next count is made. A good deal of the paperwork done by the KGB in the late 1980s was based on the reports of invented agents and was actually information gleaned from local newspapers. Gogol would have loved it.

As mentioned earlier, one of Putin's comrades in Directorate S has written a book about those Dresden years under the title *Co-worker*. Its author, Vladimir Usoltsev, was something of an oddball among KGB officers, for he had a Ph.D. in physics, a fondness for classical music, and a bent for literature. His book, though of some value as the only close-up of Putin from those years, must be taken with several grains of salt, since KGB agents are trained to have a utilitarian attitude toward the truth, or, to put it more bluntly, they are liars by trade. The author stresses that Putin was, as a type, completely ordinary but had a persona that could be quite charming, especially with older men, which later may have helped win Yeltsin's approval to replace him as president. Like everyone else he was a "conformist" who thought one thing, said another, and did yet a third. He was reserved but good-humored, and would easily pass the American political test of being a guy you'd like to go out for a beer with. He was hardworking, very focused, with a tendency to tardiness and untidiness with papers, of which there were so many. Later, as president, he would keep the pope waiting.

Directorate S was small, just six officers and their leader. As luck would have it, three of the six were Vladimirs, nickname Volodya. To keep things straight, Putin became Little Volodya because he was small compared to Big Volodya, the author of *Co-worker*. The third was, for obvious reasons, Volodya Mustache. In his memoirs Big Volodya compares their world to the cramped quarters of a spacecraft with an intimacy that could be cordial or "hellish."

Big Volodya and Putin became friends, drinking buddies, confidants. From time to time Putin would surprise his friend by displaying a "dissident" point of view. He disliked the anti-Semitism that in the KGB was as customary as a slice of herring with a shot of vodka. Putin spoke warmly of Jewish neighbors, teachers, trainers, fellow athletes. He was also very pro-Sakharov, who had just been released from six years of internal exile by Gorbachev in 1986. In this account Putin even supported Sakharov's position that the West should have military superiority over the Soviet Union, saying with ironic humor: "Don't forget that we don't have to be afraid of the West, but they have every reason to be afraid of us, and only the West's clear military superiority can make the totally unbridled leaders in the Kremlin see reason." He spoke that way only with Big Volodya—when others were around he took the standard anti-Semitic line that Sakharov was controlled by his Jewish wife, Elena Bonner. Still, even in those conversations Big Volodya thought he could detect a light irony in Putin's voice and expression.

Trained in jurisprudence, Putin was a staunch defender of Law. He also stood up for the market, the right of inheritance, and private property, which he called a "natural element of the human personality." Without coming out in favor of religion, Putin expressed the belief that science could never explain everything, which irked Big Volodya, a physicist by training, who noticed that Putin's secret childhood baptism seemed to mean a lot to him. Both Volodyas found Germans more civilized than Russians because they knew how to genuinely enjoy themselves, unlike Russians, who, as Putin put it, "if there's a holiday have to get dead drunk and punch someone in the face."

That wasn't always the case. One night, General Horst Böhm, the young, ambitious head of the Dresden Stasi, had too much to drink and suddenly opened up. He complained bitterly of the direction the USSR was taking under Gorbachev. Stalin, he said, was the incarnation of Communism, and his path should have been followed. Brezhnev tried but was too weak. Böhm himself did not long survive the collapse of East Germany. In early 1990, about to be called to testify in hearings about the future of the country, he was found dead of a bullet wound in his office. His death was ruled a suicide.

Putin's time in Dresden coincided almost exactly with the period of perestroika and glasnost in the Soviet Union. His experience of those powerful forces would have been quite different if he had been in Russia, but he might have been more hostile to them there. That doesn't mean the great changes passed him by in Dresden. In fact, developments were followed closely in Dresden both through West German magazines like *Der Spiegel* and *Stern* and in Soviet periodicals, which grew bolder by the week. A few of the Stasi were jealous— they might have bananas in East Germany, but Russians were getting something more valuable: real information and the chance to change.

What also quickly became clear was what Andropov had seen from his window in Budapest in 1956 when gazing at the security officers hung from lampposts: free discussion leads directly to sedition.

Forces too mighty to control had been set loose. The Berlin Wall would soon be breached. The Center, as the KGB called their Moscow headquarters, was not holding. Soon enough the acrid smell of defeat was in Putin's nostrils—the smell of documents burned in frantic haste: "We destroyed everything—all our communications, our lists of contacts and our agents' networks," says Putin. "I personally burned a huge amount of material. We burned so much stuff that the furnaces burst."

The unthinkable became commonplace. One day the East Germans are ransacking the Ministry of Security, the next they're surrounding Soviet KGB headquarters on Angelikastrasse. As Putin put it: "We were forced to demonstrate our readiness to defend our building." Putin went out and addressed the raging mob. Usoltsev says that Putin grabbed a Kalashnikov; Putin mentions only that he was accompanied by bodyguards. In either case, the defenders' "determination certainly made an impression on them, at least for a while."

But only a while. The crowd started becoming aggressive again. Putin called for military backup and was told: "We cannot do anything without orders from Moscow. And Moscow is silent."

A few hours later Soviet troops did arrive and disperse the crowd. But the incident was profoundly disturbing to Putin. "That business of 'Moscow is silent'—I got the feeling then that the country no longer existed. That it had disappeared . . . and had a terminal disease without a cure—a paralysis of power."

With a beer gut, two kids, and a used car, Putin returned to the USSR in January 1990. His prospects were few and bleak. Perhaps he could get into some sort of law collective. Or maybe drive a cab.

PART THREE

ASCENT

The lowest card that wins the current game is worth more than the highest that won an earlier one.

—BALTASAR GRACIÁN

4

RUSSIA'S FALL, PUTIN'S RISE

Blaming Russia for a lack of democracy is similar to complaining about not being able to buy alcohol in Saudi Arabia.

—JAKUB KOREJBA

In January 1990 when Putin returned home, the USSR was still the USSR, Leningrad was still Leningrad, and he was still KGB. None of that would last another two years.

Putin now became a member of the "active reserves," meaning KGB officers who "were put in place as active agents in business, media and the public sector. . . . The status of an agent on active reserve is considered a state secret." Putin returned to his alma mater, a choice that would prove smart and useful. As he says: "I was happy to go 'undercover' at Leningrad State University. I wanted to write my doctoral dissertation, check out the university, and perhaps get a job there. So, in 1990 I became assistant to the president of the university, responsible for international liaisons."

Landing that position was a good solution for Putin. It allowed him to work on his dissertation, some fifteen pages of which would later prove to be plagiarized from an American textbook. It gave him a foothold in viciously fast-shifting Leningrad, where gang wars were fought in the streets, sometimes with the Kalashnikovs and RPGs filched from the collapsing military and sold on the black market, and where ration cards for meat, eggs, butter, and other commodities would soon be introduced, creating an urgent air of wartime poverty and shortage. Most important, the job gave him a piece in the game, one that in time could be moved to a better position.

Putin, like everyone else, was winging it. The system was in a state of slow-motion free fall; the only questions were when it would land and with how much bloodshed. Putin had been offered a KGB post in Moscow, but turned it down for reasons of sentiment and practicality. He wanted to be near his parents, who were getting old, and also because he knew "there was no future to the system. The country didn't have a future. And it would have been very difficult to sit inside the system and wait for it all to collapse around me."

Life was becoming increasingly meaningless for Soviet people, Putin included. Putin's wife, Lyudmila, could see that he "had lost touch with his life's real purpose." Every day brought new revelations of crimes committed in the name of Communism, and the system could barely deliver basic goods and services. A grocery store might contain nothing but stale macaroni and large jars of homemade-looking apple juice. Russians started hoarding matches and salt as they always do when crisis approaches. Suddenly, there was a real threat of hunger.

The year before Putin had returned to the USSR, the country had come to a standstill, stunned by the spectacle of its first free elections for people's deputies to parliament. Andrei Sakharov was elected a deputy only three years after Gorbachev released him from internal exile in the closed city of Gorky. Another deputy of note was the dashing, charismatic law professor Anatoly Sobchak, who would work closely with Sakharov and future Russian president Boris Yeltsin on such previously unthinkable projects as investigating, and condemning, the use of military force against civilian demon-strators.

In May 1990 Sobchak became the chairman of the Leningrad City Council, essentially the mayor, a title that would become official the following year. It was clear to him that Leningrad would soon go hungry without some foreign trade. That meant he needed a motivated, effective person, one with a mastery of a foreign language and experience of living abroad, to advise him on foreign relations. Leningrad State University, where Sobchak taught law, had just such a person heading its own Foreign Relations Department: Vladimir Putin, who had attended Sobchak's lectures in the early seventies when he was a student, though there was no personal relationship at the time.

As a rule in Russia things move with either glacial slowness or lightning speed, and the latter predominated in those final months of the Soviet Union. Sobchak had Putin in for an interview and made up his mind in a matter of minutes, telling him he should start the following Monday. Putin was more than happy to accept the offer, but felt obliged to reveal that he was a KGB staff officer. After a long moment's thought, Sobchak said: "Screw it!"

This is Putin's version of events. There are others. Some would have it that Putin was dispatched there as his next assignment as an officer in the active reserves. Or, as Masha Gessen thought, Sobchak himself might have chosen Putin because he "knew that it was wiser to pick your KGB handler yourself than to have one picked for you."

In any case, Putin took the position and began working in Smolny, an elegant building that had been a school for young ladies of the nobility before the revolution and Lenin's headquarters during the revolution itself. He chose a picture of Peter the Great, emperor and reformer, to decorate his office.

Putin, however, remained worried that his KGB connections

could be used against him or against Sobchak. The only foolproof means against being outed was to out yourself.

Putin contacted the well-known filmmaker Igor Shadkhan, telling him: "Igor, I want to speak openly about my professional past so that it stops being a secret and so that no one can blackmail me with it." Shadkhan had just returned from grueling fieldwork filming in the Gulags of the far north and was more interested in resting than in working, but apparently Putin's ability to charm older men worked again, and it wasn't long before the interview was broadcast on Leningrad TV.

Looking beefy and deeply tired with dark, raccoonish circles under his eyes, confident but unpolished, Putin not only revealed the crucial information about himself, but also demonstrated that he had mastered the new vocabulary of the time. He called Communism "a beautiful but dangerous fairy tale" and said of the USSR: "As soon as the barbed wire was removed, the country began falling apart."

Sobchak did not regret his choice of Putin. "He was utterly professional. He worked very well with others, knew how to talk to them. He was decisive." Putin was on his way up.

It had been a smart choice to turn down Moscow for Leningrad. Putin knew how to operate there and was a Leningrader by temperament—aloof, cerebral, acerbic.

In a referendum in the spring of 1991 the people of Leningrad chose to restore the city's original name, St. Petersburg. To lead that newly named city into a very uncertain future they elected Anatoly Sobchak as mayor. As a sign that their political careers were now linked and in tandem, Sobchak immediately promoted Putin from adviser on international relations to head of that department. He went from an intellectual resource to an active player.

But Putin was not a month on the job before he and his country faced a crisis of the first order. In August 1991 the lurch and drift of the Soviet Union reached critical mass. A small group of high officials—among them the chairman of the KGB, the prime minister, the interior minister, and the vice president—attempted a putsch, placing Gorbachev under house arrest in the south of the country, where he was vacationing. It was the USSR's last attempt to save itself and it lasted barely three days. The whole affair was a very Russian mix of the sublime, the ridiculous, and the tragic.

The iconic moment for Russia came when Boris Yeltsin stood on top of a tank that was threatening the White House, as the Russian parliament building in Moscow was known. He called on the army and the people to stand up for freedom and to defy the putschists. Moscow's patriotic tarts lowered themselves down the tank turrets to distract any soldiers who weren't yet on the side of the people and freedom.

The mood of Moscow was one of elation, bordering on exaltation. Referring to the three young men, one of them Jewish, who had lost their lives in the struggle for Moscow, one Russian woman said to me in conversation: "There can never be anti-Semitism in Russia again now that a Jew has given his life for Russia's freedom!"

For Putin these were not days of exaltation but, he says, ones of agonized choice and self-definition. He was torn. The goal of the coup—"preserving the Soviet Union from collapse—was noble." That, however, was not enough. "As soon as the coup began, I immediately decided whose side I was on. I knew for sure that I would never follow the coup-plotters' orders. I would never be on their side. I knew perfectly well that my behavior could be considered a crime of office. That's why, on August 20, I wrote a second statement resigning from the KGB. . . . All the ideals, all the goals that I had had when I went to work for the KGB, collapsed."

The bond with Sobchak grew tighter in those tense days when people in Russia were making the choice that would decide their own future and the country's. In St. Petersburg, Sobchak played a role similar to Yeltsin's. "Speaking from the steps of the Winter Palace, he gave heart to the thousands who did not want to see the clock turned back," wrote the *Economist* in his obituary. "Deploying weapons no more violent than his personality and his command of language, he persuaded the commander of the armored troops moving on the city to withdraw."

But in the midst of trauma there was a certain grotesque levity. "Once I saw the faces of the coup-plotters on TV," says Putin, "I knew right away that it was all over." At the junta's one and only press conference, the "leader," drab Soviet vice president Gennady Yanayev, kept sneezing into a handkerchief. Dictators should not make their debut blowing their noses.

In an iconoclastic rampage Russians began tearing down the images of Soviet rule. The immense statue of Felix Dzerzhinsky, founder of the secret police, was torn from its pedestal in front of KGB headquarters on Lubyanka Square. Though heavy, it proved hollow. Some, but not all, of the statues of Lenin were toppled. One of Stalin was struck in the face with a sledgehammer. All of them were taken to a park near an art museum, the New Tretyakov Gallery, and strewn on the grass in a random fury.

No one had any idea what tomorrow would bring, though it was clear the USSR's days were numbered. What would the next Russia look like? Whose voices would be heard?

Wandering on the grass where the statues were strewn I saw an older man in glasses and a sweater-vest who looked like a retired shop teacher. When he opened his mouth to rant he revealed steel-plated teeth, common in the USSR: "They were nearly all kikes, the Communists. Lenin was part kike on his mother's side and the rest of him was Asiatic. And the capitalists are all kikes too, and now they're trying to finish up what the Communists didn't get around to doing. The kikes want the death of Russia!"

But there were other voices, equally passionate and brighter with intelligent hope. As winter and the fear of hunger crept into the cities, a TV producer I knew, a great battleship of a woman who issued opinions like salvos, said: "We are so happy, you can't imagine. We did something wonderful. We stood up for freedom. And now we are free. Yes, maybe there will be starvation this winter but at least we'll be starving as free people. We've starved before but we've never been free before."

Other stars besides Putin's were on the rise and moving with greater speed than his, though his, of course, would in time eclipse them all. Like him they came out of nowhere, a good sign, proof that Russia's long-suppressed ambitions and creative force had been loosed. For people alert to the moment and its possibilities there were three questions: how best to dismantle the old system; what to build in its place; how to get rich in the process.

Rules, law, and the rule of law were never very much respected anyway in Russia, which had "a décor of laws," as the dissident writer Andrei Amalrik put it. Proverbs spoke of the law as a cart that went where the driver wanted. In the transition between systems there were fewer rules and guidelines than ever. Clear-eyed ambitious men entered that vacuum with great energy. Everyone had stolen from the state when it was a going concern, and now that it had collapsed there was even less reason not to loot the ruins.

Others were more intent on dismantling the system than on exploiting the transition. One of those was Anatoly Chubais, who was born in 1955 and was thirty-six when the USSR fell. His father was a Soviet army colonel, a World War II vet, and a believer in Marxism who lectured on it to the troops. A lanky redhead, Chubais was drawn to economics, a subject that had been his mother's major, but she stayed home with the children and never practiced her profession. Chubais, who would quickly become known as "the most hated man in Russia" for the pain he inflicted on the country during the shock-therapy phase, did not himself come swiftly to his new worldview. In the beginning he was an economics Ph.D. student in Leningrad trying to figure out why command-and-control economies were always economies of shortage. He gradually came to the conclusion that only prices set by the open market could provide realistic and reliable information as to what goods and services were needed. But, once convinced, he had something of his father's Soviet steel in his convictions.

He was a natural for Mayor Sobchak's team and quickly became one of its top economic advisers, dealing with the attempt to create a Free Economic Zone in Leningrad. That was in 1990. By the end of 1991, Chubais had moved to the center of power, Moscow, and the highest echelons of President Yeltsin's government. He was appointed chairman of the Committee for the Management of State Property, which was in charge of privatizing state property. Chubais became the "architect of the largest transfer in history of state-owned assets to private hands," as David Hoffman put it in *The Oligarchs*, by now a classic text.

No one knew what they were doing, for two very good reasons. First, the people in charge of dismantling the Russian economy were mostly men in their early thirties who, apart from receiving an education, had not done very much at all, certainly nothing on the order of running large enterprises. Second, what they were doing was historically unprecedented. It also contradicted the Marxism on which they had all been reared and that held that Communism was the stage of development that came after capitalism, not vice versa. And so turning Communism into capitalism was as absurdly impossible as trying to turn fish chowder back into fish.

But Chubais and his ilk had strongly held attitudes, goals, and assumptions. The attitude was a visceral hatred and contempt for the system. "I hate the Soviet system. There is little in life I have hated like the Soviet system," said Chubais. The goal was the absolute destruction of the Soviet economy and thus the Soviet state by putting the USSR's assets in private hands. The assumption was that the laws of the market would sort things out. The inefficient would die away, the efficient would thrive. Private ownership and personal freedom were two aspects of the same thing. Russia would leap into both democracy and capitalism all at once.

The process would be modeled on the Polish experiment with "shock therapy." The first step was to free up prices so that they would reflect market realities and not the decisions of bureaucrats in the planning commission. As the Russians quipped bitterly, they got the shock but not the therapy.

Between 1990 and 1994 prices increased by well over 2,000 percent. By the hideous magic of inflation, $100,000 turned into $400. The stores were "pristinely empty," as Egor Gaidar, the other main leader of economic reform, put it. The farmers weren't delivering grain. "Why should they? To get some piece of paper that, out of habit, people still called money?"

Huge trucks appeared in downtown Moscow bearing potatoes from the countryside. People bought as much as they could, staggering away bent parallel to the ground by immense burlap bags. In apartments potatoes were everywhere—in cabinets, in closets, under beds.

Everything was for sale. Old women stood in the cold holding up a single knit shawl, like human stores. For people raised on socialist ideals, which considered property to be theft, there was a particular shame in the act of selling, not to mention the fact that these goods were often family heirlooms or simply all people had left in the world. Those with nothing to sell simply knelt on the freezing sidewalks and offered up their own pain and self-abasement. The younger women chose other strategies, equally desperate. Flocks of prostitutes chased every car that slowed in the downtowns of Russian cities. Many were nurses and teachers who could no longer feed their families on their meager salaries, if they were even paid.

In the street markets and flea markets treasures could be had for a song—amber necklaces, icons, rugs from Asia. You could buy Red Army uniforms from fur hats to high boots, medals for valor included. The currency was meaningless, life was meaningless, there was a whiff of Weimar in the air. Groups favoring black clothing and the hatred of Jews (and Masons) emerged quite naturally from that context of empty air and violent streets.

My reportage from the first post-Soviet winter of 1992 captures something of that time and place:

In Sophia, one of Moscow's better restaurants, you can feast on black caviar, sturgeon, and beef Stroganoff with vodka and coffee galore, tip extravagantly and still get away for under a dollar. The waitress apologizes. For reasons she can't begin to understand, there is no Russian vodka, only Smirnoff's, from America. Her teeth are chattering. The heat has gone off in the restaurant. All the waitresses and customers are shivering, even those who are still wearing their fur hats. And so at least there is practically no shock when we leave the restaurant and see through the whirling snow the statue of the poet Vladimir Mayakovsky, who blew out his brains in 1930, disappointed by love and revolution.

But for most that winter, shivering in a restaurant would have been an unimaginable luxury:

The schools now serve as distribution points for the food being funneled in from America. The pilferage rate is assumed to be high, though somewhat less than in other places. Schoolchildren are being issued milk and tinned meat—leftover rations from Operation Desert Storm, crumbs from the table of the conqueror. It is a gift that elicits both gratitude and a sense of humiliation among Russians. As parents they are glad that their children will have milk to drink, for milk is simply unavailable in Moscow. It might be because the farmers had to slaughter their cattle for lack of grain to feed them. Or there may be thousands upon thousands of gallons turning sour in idle freight trains somewhere. Nobody knows. Nobody ever really knows anything here.

Grateful as parents, they are mortified as Russians. They feel themselves part of a laughable failure—the idiotic dream of communism, which took tens of millions of lives and in return gave them two-hour bread lines in the icy cold.

Meanwhile, even at this early stage before the large state enterprises began to be auctioned for a song to insiders in sweetheart deals, there were still plenty of people fast on their feet who saw ways to make big money either from the falling value of the ruble—borrow cheap, repay even cheaper—or by buying up the vouchers that were issued in 1992 to every citizen in an effort to make Soviet serfs into shareholders. Factory managers and the party elite had already concocted schemes for gaining control over state property.

But a good percentage of the population simply couldn't cope with the new reality. The environment had shifted radically and they could not adapt. People demonstrated in the streets with signs reading: "Put the redhead behind bars." They meant Chubais.

There was a violent nostalgia for the Soviet past. For the democracy of poverty, cheap goods, brutal certainties. The extreme tensions in Russian society were expressed in the battle waged by the nationalists and Communists in parliament against the presidency of Boris Yeltsin. In mid-1993 the parliament declared itself the supreme power in the country, which now seemed on the verge on civil war. In response Yeltsin suspended parliament to protect, as he put it, "Russia and the whole world against the catastrophic consequences of the disintegration of the Russian state, against anarchy recurring in a country which has an enormous arsenal of nuclear weapons."

The rebellious deputies seized the White House. Well armed—five hundred submachine guns, six machine guns, two hundred pistols—the rebels' numbers shifting from 400 to 800. Outside, the building was ringed by supporters bearing the black-and-yellow flags of the nationalists and the red banners of Communism along with signs: "Revive the Communist Party of Russia," "Let's reveal the ethnicity of all those who were in the mass media!" (meaning Jews), "Blacks out of Moscow!" (meaning people from the Caucasus mountain region, often referred to as "blacks" or "black asses").

The sporadic violence came to a head on October 4, 1993, when Yeltsin ordered an attack. There was a fifteen-minute tank barrage followed by a mop-up action inside the building in which twenty soldiers and forty rebels were killed.

The ironies were heavy-handed even by Russian standards. Some two years before, Yeltsin had stood atop a tank in front of that same White House to save Russia from a putsch, and now he had ordered tanks to fire on parliament. The blackened front of that white building became a sort of tragic icon of its own.

In winter 1992 St. Petersburg was in a panic over a possible famine. The city council put Marina Salye in charge of food supplies, and it was she who introduced rationing and ration cards. Every resident of the city had the right to three pounds of meat per month, two pounds of processed meats, ten eggs, one pound of butter, half a pound of vegetable oil, one pound of flour, and two pounds of grain or dry pasta—if he or she could find any.

Salye, a geologist by profession, had spent much of her adult life far from the tense, polluted cities. Geology was a romantic profession that allowed for travel over all the vast yet still somehow claustrophobic territory of the USSR. Days of hard work in nature, nights of campfires, wine, guitars. Nevertheless, Salye proved totally adept at politics and quickly emerged as one of the leaders of the democratic movement in Leningrad. "With a cigarette dangling from her lips, she could lead a crowd up and down Nevsky, stopping traffic," as one of her political opponents described her.

Her attempt to feed her starving city would prove the misfortune of her life. She could not help but notice that an agreement to ship Russian raw materials—gas, oil, timber, metals—in exchange for food to a foreign concern had gone totally awry. The nearly $100 million of raw materials had indeed been shipped, but not a ruble's worth of food had arrived. Looking into the matter further, Salye discovered documents indicating that Vladimir Putin, as head of the Foreign Relations Committee, had entered into contracts with legally dubious companies. Working with a colleague, Yuri Gladkov, she collected more evidence and presented it to the city council, which concluded that the money had been stolen and recommended to Mayor Sobchak that Putin be dismissed.

Sobchak's response was to dissolve the city council. He wasn't about to impede Putin, whose achievements were obvious. "Judge his success—he was in charge of foreign investment, and by 1993 we had 6,000 joint ventures, half the total in Russia." Putin helped attract American firms like Coca-Cola, Wrigley, and Gillette. And foreigners enjoyed working with Putin. Graham Humes, an American who set up a charity in St. Petersburg, said of him: "I found him great to deal with compared with these other Russian bureaucrats who all wanted to fleece you. He was very intense; he controls everything in the room. You felt he wanted to be feared but didn't want to give you cause to fear him."

Putin succeeded in completing a project to lay fiber-optic cable to give St. Petersburg world-class international phone service. So what if $100 million disappeared? A thousand tons of gold also disappeared as the USSR was collapsing. Later on, Russia's chief comptroller at the time called the case "not radically more serious than what was going on in the rest of Russia. . . . It was just a typical case at the time." You hardly threw away one of your most gifted and dogged assistants over such a measly sum, such a typical case.

Like all important moments in Putin's life, his role in the missing hundred million is blurred with multiple ambiguities. Only three things are certain—the money disappeared, the food never arrived, and Putin had a hand in the paperwork. He does not seem to have benefited personally from the deal. His wife says that they returned from the GDR with a twenty-year-old washing machine that an East German friend had given them and which lasted them another five years. If Putin had been siphoning off some of the money from the food deal, he presumably would have found enough to buy his wife a new washer. The American Humes said he didn't want to "fleece you." Boris Berezovsky, the oligarch and kingmaker who would figure greatly in Putin's destiny (as would Putin in his), describes meeting Putin in the early nineties: "And what was absolutely surprising for me was that he was the first one who didn't ask for a bribe."

If he didn't get any money out of it, why would he have risked his high position in the new government?

It's possible that Putin was simply chumped—in Russia, swindling is an art form. Inexperienced in the ways of commerce, Putin may have unwittingly helped abet a scam. In the chaos of those years anything was possible. More likely, however, is that Putin knew some people would line their pockets with the money and he wanted those people in his own pocket for later use. It was a time when sudden and immense fortunes could be made, but it was also a time when sudden and immense power could accrue to those alert to the utility of secrets and favors. Putin preferred power.

Marina Salye tried to raise the issue again when Putin was running for president in 2000. In her version of events, she was made to understand that any such effort would simply cost her her life. She disappeared into a tiny village in northwest Russia far from Moscow.

There were no good years for Russia in the nineties, but 1994 seems particularly bad.

Something had changed in Russia after fall 1993 when Yeltsin ordered the tanks to fire on parliament. The society became more violent, precipitate, unhinged. In June of 1994, the oligarch Boris Berezovsky climbed into the backseat of his Mercedes. His driver and bodyguard were in front. As they left the courtyard a remote-controlled bomb in a nearby parked Opel exploded with tremendous force, decapitating the driver, taking an eye from the bodyguard, injuring seven pedestrians, and shattering windows a block away. Boris Berezovsky stumbled from the wreckage, badly burned but able to walk away.

There had already been fifty-two bomb blasts in Moscow alone by that June. The use of lethal force had become a part of business as well as of politics.

In July the giant pyramid scheme known as MMM collapsed, leaving millions penniless. The 27 percent plunge in the ruble's value on Black Tuesday, October 11, inflicted suffering on those who still had rubles left to lose. Two months later, on December 11, Russian troops were sent into Chechnya. To chaos, poverty, and desperation now war had been added.

After simmering for three years since Chechnya had declared its independence in 1991, hostilities broke out in late December between Russia and Chechnya, a war that would quickly prove "barbaric on both sides." In the Kremlin's eye oil-rich Chechnya was a lawless land with impudent aspirations to independence. But business mattered more than war.

To succeed in business in Russia during the 1990s three things were needed: capital, connections, and chutzpah. When Gorbachev tried to revive the economy, new, looser laws allowed for various cooperative-type enterprises, including financial ones that were essentially banks. Some people acquired capital by reselling goods bought abroad for fantastic profit. As one Russian exclaimed on selling a computer for 70,000 rubles: "It was my salary for forty-eight years!" Others dealt in cars, designer clothes, it almost didn't matter, since everybody needed everything. It wasn't that long ago that enterprises like these could have cost you prison time or, in some cases, death. Russians were well aware that the last time anything like this was attempted was Lenin's New Economic Policy (NEP), which flourished for a few years before ending very badly. That this could happen again no one doubted. The Communists could come back into power—with a vengeance. The Red attempt to seize power in 1993 had been quashed by tanks firing at the White House, but there was an election coming in 1996 that at the least would be bitterly contested, a Communist defeat by no means a certainty.

It was an odd atmosphere that prevailed in those days. A mix of Klondike Gold Rush and Feast in Time of Plague, a sense that anything was possible, calamity included. Though Russian gangsters were making small fortunes via extortion, protection, drugs, and casinos, the great fortunes would end up in the hands of educated men like Boris Berezovsky, who held a Ph.D. in mathematics, and Mikhail Khodorkovsky, who, before he became Russia's richest man and then its most famous prisoner, earned a degree in engineering. Though a few of the future oligarchs had street smarts, what they all had, and what made them all superrich, was knowing how to work the system. It really didn't matter which system it was—the crumbling Soviet system, the system for transitioning to capitalism, or the new rudimentary capitalist system itself—as long as there was some sort of system they would find some way of gaming it.

The image of Berezovsky stumbling away from the smoking

wreckage of his Mercedes is, in its way, an oligarch icon. It was a perfect example of Nietzsche's "What does not kill us makes us stronger." Only prison and death could stop those men in Russia who had dedicated their every waking moment to the acquisition of fabled wealth.

Berezovsky, born in 1946, an only child, a Jew, took Russian maximalism to the max. His applied-mathematics lab needed not only to flourish but to win the Nobel Prize. When he pursued wealth, only billions would do. Others said of him, "He uses every person to the maximum. That is his principle of life," and he said of himself: "Everything I do, I do to an absolutely maximum degree." If Berezovsky wanted to speak with you, he would wait on your doorstep for hours or follow you fully dressed into the shower at your athletic club. Short, dark-haired, dark-eyed, he vibrated with incessant nervous energy. If he ever had a moment's peace in his life, he would not have had the slightest idea what to do with it. "He was in one place one minute. And in another the next. He had a million phone calls. A million places where he was to arrive. Another million places where he promised to arrive but never went," recalled a colleague. He was insistent, infuriating, charming.

The USSR was officially based on so-called scientific socialism, and in the country's waning days its rulers hoped science would save socialism. A great deal of hope, trust, and credence were placed in institutes and labs, like Berezovsky's, which studied the mathematics of decision making. That plugged him into industry, specifically the auto industry, on a high level and allowed him to make a fortune by obtaining cars from the state with loans that soaring inflation allowed him to pay back with much cheaper rubles.

Berezovsky also wormed his way into the Kremlin by publishing Yeltsin's ghostwritten memoirs in a deluxe edition that greatly pleased the "author," who was even more pleased by the tremendous checks from the inflated, if not in some cases utterly bogus, foreign sales that Berezovsky routinely presented. Bribes disguised by vanity as royalties.

Now in the Kremlin's inner circle, Berezovsky could put his capital to good use. He gained a controlling interest in the national airline, Aeroflot, and the television broadcast company ORT, which gave him access to the burgeoning advertising revenue; but more important, it gave him political power because Russians got their news and views from TV, as they do to this day.

His two daughters attended Cambridge. He had a new, glamorous trophy wife. He had attained both significant wealth and significant power. Nothing could stop him.

The post-Soviet Russian government may still have had enough nuclear power to destroy the planet, but it couldn't pay its bills. Teachers, nurses, pensioners, weren't being paid. Inflation was still sky-high. And there were presidential elections coming in 1996. Yeltsin could easily lose. Already there was a powerful nostalgia for Soviet stability, which the Communist Party promised to restore.

Yelstin was increasingly seen as a fool, a has-been, a drunk. Gorbachev had alienated Russians by his clampdown on vodka; Yeltsin had alienated them by his overreliance on it. At the final ceremony for the withdrawal of Russian troops from Germany in August 1994, Yeltsin grabbed the baton from the Berlin Police Orchestra leader's hand and began vigorously conducting himself. Good for a laugh, but an uncomfortable one. His popularity rating was in the single digits and flirting with zero.

To win the upcoming election, Yeltsin needed money. A deal was worked out and given the rather innocuous name "Loans for Shares." The oligarchs with cash would loan the government money; shares in state-owned industries would be held as collateral. It was clear to all that the government would never be able to pay back the loans. And when the time came to auction off those shares held as collateral, the people currently holding them made sure the auctions were rigged in their favor, though a few face-saving forms were observed. Still, if an airport had to be closed to prevent unwanted prospective bidders from arriving, that airport would be closed.

Chrystia Freeland, who covered those turbulent times as Moscow bureau chief for the *Financial Times*, called Loans for Shares a "Faustian bargain" because the young and still committed reformers like Chubais knew the sale of the immense state enterprises to a handful of rich men would put an end to the free-wheeling capitalism they dreamed of. Chubais and Yeltsin consistently said: "We do not need hundreds of millionaires, but millions of property owners." But the choice was stark: either give the tycoons control of the economy or lose the election to the Communists. Chubais found an eschatological formulation: "Isn't it clear that there is one and only one question facing Russsia today: will there be a second coming of communism—or not?" A Red scare in Russia of all places.

The Communists' leader, a colorless apparatchik by the name of Gennady Zyuganov, had suddenly come to life and been the hit of the World Economic Forum in Davos in February 1996. He presented Western leaders and businessmen with an image of sober, serious dependability. To Chubais's horror, those Western leaders danced attendance on Zyuganov: "The world's most powerful businessmen, with world-famous names, who with their entire appearance demonstrated that they were seeking support of the future president of Russia, because it was clear to everyone that Zyuganov was going to be the future president of Russia." At Davos, George Soros warned Boris Berezovsky that if Zyuganov was elected, as he certainly would be, Berezovsky would "hang from a lamppost" and advised him to leave Russia.

But nothing energized Berezovsky like a good crisis. He made peace with his enemy Vladimir Gusinsky, who owned the other major TV network. Now the airwaves that had throbbed with criticism of Yeltsin's prolonged, expensive, and apparently unwinnable war in Chechnya began to sound the alarm of a Communist resurgence and to beat the drums for Yeltsin. Zyuganov, though taking advantage of the free television time due him by law and buying some in addition, preferred to communicate with his constituency in written form—poster, newspaper, leaflet. This was a throwback to Soviet times, but not entirely a foolish decision, since the Communist Party still had 500,000 members, a large percentage of whom could be mobilized for door-to-door campaigning. Better a personable youth delivering a leaflet to your door than yet another talking head on the screen.

But there were other deeply retro aspects to the Communist campaign. The evil stink of anti-Semitism was very much in the air. When Zyuganov spoke of "the cosmopolitan elite of international capital," which was using the United States to destroy Russia, everyone knew what he meant—the cabal of Jews that ran the world as described in the tsarist secret-police forgery *The Protocols of the Elders of Zion*. Yeltsin and company were not just political opponents but "the turncoats, destroyers and traitors of the Fatherland who currently rule in the Kremlin." But Zyuganov made practical proposals as well—rents would not exceed 15 percent of income, the army would be rebuilt, natural resources would be renationalized, but law-abiding, tax-paying privatized enterprises would, though with great distaste, be tolerated.

Like Berezovsky, Yeltsin was a man who could be energized by crisis. He came alive, regaining "his spark and charisma." He quit drinking and lost close to twenty pounds. Chubais was running his campaign Western-style, replete with "sound bites, daily photo ops and nervous advance men." He began dealing with the war in Chechnya and used some of the Loans for Shares money to begin paying long overdue salaries and pensions. What Yeltsin had that Zyuganov did not was a strong, clear, positive message. "Five years ago we chose freedom. There can be no retreat." And, as he said to voters: "I will ensure you freedom of choice, but the choice is up to you. Vote for a free Russia!" He reminded voters of what the "circles of Bolshevik hell" had been like: the camps, the hunger, the fear. It hadn't been that long ago either—people did not need much reminding. "I was under a communist regime once, and I don't want a replay of it," said the leader of one of Russia's most popular bands, the aptly named Time Machine. "Come cast your vote on June 16 so Time Machine can keep on playing."

Rock 'n' roll was on Yeltsin's side. How could he lose?

On June 16 he didn't lose, but he didn't win either. Yeltsin received 35 percent of the vote, Zyuganov 32 percent. The rest of the vote was split among other candidates. This was still a time when Russia was gloriously messy with its new democracy, dozens and dozens of parties competing, even the Beer Lovers won 428,727 votes. A runoff was scheduled for July 3.

In the meantime there had been another election—for mayor of St. Petersburg—which at first seemed mainly of local importance. Putin ran the election campaign for Mayor Sobchak, his boss and mentor. "Politicians like Sobchak are usually the last to learn their luster is gone," as Masha Gessen put it. And Sobchak was mostly luster to begin with. He had made some progress, with Putin's help, in attracting foreign business to St. Petersburg but had done very little for the people, to improve their daily lives, the ultimate measure of all politics. Corruption, crime, and a crumbling infrastructure were what people saw. And there was always some ambiguity about Sobchak, how much of his attachment to reform was genuine, or did that tall, telegenic man just wear democracy as if it were a well-cut foreign suit?

Defeated in the election, Sobchak would remain in office until June 12, at which point both he and Vladimir Putin would be officially unemployed. But no moves could be made until the presidential runoffs were held.

This time the results were clear and striking—54 percent to Yeltsin, 40 percent to Zyuganov. As Yeltsin's biographer Leon Aron said: "In the end he won because the election had, as he intended it to, become a referendum on democracy and communism, rather than on market reforms or the Russian version of capitalism."

If things had gone the other way—a Yeltsin defeat and a Sobchak victory—Putin would probably have remained in St. Petersburg, dabbling in democracy and corruption, at the margins of history.

But that's not what happened. Instead, Chubais, the much-hated chief of privatization and the successful manager of Yeltsin's reelection campaign, contacted Putin with a job offer—deputy chief of the Kremlin's Property Department. It was an important post, dealing with the $600 billion in property that Russia had acquired from the USSR. Putin would be "in charge of the legal division and Russian property abroad." He accepted and moved to Moscow.

It's probably axiomatic that no one gets to the top without fierce ambition, especially the top of the heap of Russian politics. But Putin himself could hardly have dared set his sights as high as he in fact rose, nor imagined how swift that ascent would be. A year after moving to Moscow he had become deputy chief of staff to the president; the next year he would be named director of the FSB, the successor to the KGB; and in the following year, 1999, he would be appointed prime minister, a post he did not hold for very long because, during his annual December 31 speech to the nation, President Yeltsin shocked the country by announcing that he was retiring prematurely, with Prime Minister Vladimir Putin to take the his place effective immediately.

Even for a man of ferocious ambition and killer instincts to rise from unemployed bureaucrat to president in the space of some three and a half years would be a dizzying achievement, but for a man of no particular outward ambition it assumes the sheen of legend. How did it happen?

First, neither Putin's uniqueness nor the scale and speed of his rise should be exaggerated. Stalin, Gorbachev, and Yeltsin all seemed to come from nowhere. And as vice mayor of St. Petersburg, Putin had been the number two man in Russia's number two city, not exactly nowhere. Still, it's a long way from there to the Kremlin.

Putin had already caught the Kremlin's eye when amazing Boris Berezovsky by not asking him for a bribe. In refusing that bribe, Putin won a reputation for both integrity and something worth more than integrity in the Russian political situation—the brains to know which bribes to take and which not to. Berezovsky was a man of great power behind the scenes, a "kingmaker"—better to have his respect than his rubles.

The Russia of the late nineties was ruled by "the Family," meaning Yeltsin's own family and a few others, like Berezovsky, who were allowed into that inner circle. Among the members of the Family none was more important than Yeltsin's daughter Tatyana. At one point she needed an apartment in St. Petersburg. The one that would be perfect for her was, unfortunately, being occupied by some important Americans and other foreigners. Putin made the problem go away.

When Sobchak lost the race for mayor of St. Petersburg, Putin was offered the chance to stay on as deputy mayor. But he had pledged not to if Sobchak was not elected, and he kept his word. Sobchak was not important to the Kremlin, but Putin's reflexive loyalty was duly noted.

In Moscow it looked like Putin was fated to forever remain the number two man, distinguished by his loyalty and ability, but without the drive and charisma to reach the top of any one governmental body, not to mention the government itself. He would be the deputy chief of the Kremlin's Property Department, then Boris Yeltsin's deputy chief of staff, and, later, one of three first deputy prime ministers in August 1999.

But in the meantime Putin had actually headed something. To the immense chagrin of his former colleagues, between July 1998 and August 1999, Putin served as director of what would soon be called the Federal Security Bureau, the FSB. That organization is often described as the successor to the KGB, which is not entirely accurate. Until the fall of the USSR the KGB was like a combination, at the minimum, of the FBI and the CIA. After the fall, those two functions were separated, and now everything connected with foreign intelligence is handled by the SVR, the Foreign Intelligence Service.

Putin claims to have been in no hurry to return to the closed, arcane world of the security services. He would not make any dramatic shake-ups during his tenure, but two developments of significance would occur in that year and a month. For the first time he tasted the pleasure of being the boss. Of course, there were still a few people above him, but it was a foretaste of the Kremlin, where, as he put it, "I control everybody."

The second development was more tied to specific events. The prosecutor general, Yury Skuratov, had launched a corruption investigation that was coming too close to Yeltsin and the Family for comfort. Ruin and prison were among the possibilities they were facing. Suddenly in March 1999 state TV broadcast footage of the prosecutor general cavorting in bed with two prostitutes. A short time later FSB chief Vladimir Putin also appeared on television to attest that experts from his organization had analyzed the video and ascertained its authenticity. This compromising material, known as *kompromat*, effectively put an end to the investigation and the prosecutor general's career. Yeltsin and the Family owed a debt of gratitude to Putin, who had exhibited not only loyalty but fierce, impressive effectiveness.

Yeltsin now understood that as long as he held power it would be possible to fend off attacks like that of the prosecutor general, but once out of office, he would be defenseless, easy prey. And that time was rapidly approaching. Conferring with Boris Berezovsky among others, Yeltsin began developing a plan.

In midsummer 1999 kingmaker Berezovsky was dispatched to Biarritz in the South of France, where Putin and his family were vacationing, to convince Putin to accept the post of prime minister. There two things impressed Berezovsky. One was "the very modest, absolutely simple apartment" where Putin was living. The other was Putin's lack of eagerness, confidence: "He wasn't sure he was capable." Neither money nor power seemed greatly to tempt him, and what else was there?

Of course, there may have been a dose of cool calculation in Putin's coyness. The post of prime minister was a stepping-stone to oblivion. Yeltsin was changing prime ministers every few months, at such a dizzying rate that, upon the appointment of Putin, the editor of the *Financial Times* asked his Moscow bureau chief: "Do I really need to remember this one's name?"

In the event, he took the position of first deputy prime minister, one he would hold for a bit less than five months. That was time enough for Yeltsin and Berezovsky to hold their magnifying glass over Putin.

He had already demonstrated strength, loyalty, and effectiveness. In addition, he was vigorous, unlike Yeltsin, who was suffering heart attacks and undergoing quintuple bypasses, and had the flushed, puffy look of those who are not long for this world. Putin was tough on Chechnya and knew how to use the security service to neutralize enemies. A bit colorless, a bit ordinary, but that might be just what Russia needed after extravagant Gorbachev and flamboyant Yeltsin.

But most important were Putin's strength and loyalty to keep the deal Yeltsin would offer—power for immunity.

Yeltsin's vital interests and Putin's chief characteristics aligned and clicked. A perfect fit.

And so it was that on December 31, 1999, on the eve of a new century, President Boris Yeltsin, in his annual address to the nation, asked Russians for their "forgiveness for the fact that many of the dreams we shared did not come true and for the fact that what seemed to us so simple turned out to be tormentingly difficult." And thereupon he handed Russia—its eleven time zones and its nuclear weapons, its thousand-year history and future fate—over to Vladimir Putin.

Lenin had famously said: "Any cook should be able to run the country." A cook's grandson would now have the chance.

5

THE RUSSIA PUTIN INHERITED
AND ITS SPIRITUAL ILLS

POST-TRAUMATIC POLITICS

Few lamented the demise of the Soviet Union more than Vladimir Putin; none benefited from it more.

The man who in his state-of-the-nation speech on April 25, 2005, called the collapse of the USSR the "greatest geopolitical catastrophe of the twentieth century" was propelled from an obscure KGB posting in East Germany to the leadership of twenty-first-century Russia by the very forces unleashed by that collapse. Had the Center held and the Soviet Union remained essentially intact, today Putin would be a KGB retiree with a thickening waist and thinning hair, out fishing on a quiet river or pestering his grandchildren with kisses. Instead, in one capacity or another, he has led the new Russia since the year 2000 and will continue to do so until 2018 at the very least, unless calamity intervenes again, this time not necessarily in his favor.

Though Putin's fate is singular, in some ways it resembles that of those who were born and grew up under the old Soviet dispensation and were forced to reinvent themselves when their world gave way around them. There was a no-man's-land between the last Soviet generation and the first real post-Soviet one. A woman who had done well in real estate told me her mother was continually berating her: "You help a fellow human being find a place to live and for that you take money!?"

Both in being nostalgic for the USSR and in facing the need to reinvent himself, Putin is ordinary. Russians sense that ordinariness and are comforted by it. That is of course especially true for Putin's main electoral demographic, older working-class types who do not live in central Moscow or St. Petersburg but on the outskirts and are strung out across the country's eleven time zones. A good many of those voters are even more nostalgic for the Soviet Union than Putin. They yearn for the cozy democracy of poverty, for cheap rent, cheap utilities, free schools, and free health care, and find the hurly-burly of the marketplace vulgar, alien, and confusing.

For Putin and everyone else the fall of the USSR came as a shock because no one saw it coming. For most people in the 1980s the USSR had always existed during their lifetime, and the opposition between the USA and the USSR was part of the architecture of reality, even its keystone. The United States and the USSR seemed interlocked, as if MAD stood not only for mutual assured destruction but mutual assured duration. The only likely end to the dynamic impasse of U.S.-Soviet relations was nuclear war. That was certainly easier to imagine than the Marxist fantasy of the withering away of the state or what in fact happened, the soft and largely bloodless implosion of the largest empire the world had ever seen.

The events of 9/11 were formative for the United States, or perhaps deformative is a better word. The Middle Eastern wars, the debate over drone strikes, Guantánomo, surveillance, torture, liberty vs.

security, everything that has bedeviled America since 2001, flows directly from that date and those incidents.

The fall of the Soviet Union was also formative in that way. Russians watched with a similar amazed horror as their own society collapsed with all the helplessness of a bad dream. First, it was the Soviet empire that was disintegrating, the nations that were never part of the Soviet Union itself, but always under Kremlin control. Those countries had only been in the Soviet dominion since the end of World War II and had never made any secret of their reluctance to be there, rebelling every twelve years—Hungary in 1956, Czechoslovakia in 1968, Poland in 1980. Later when he was criticized for giving away the farm, i.e., Eastern Europe, Gorbachev testily replied: "I gave Poland to the Poles. Who else should I give it to?" To that rhetorical question the imperialist answer is: "No one."

But to see cracks spreading through the edifice of the Eastern Bloc was one thing; to see them spread to the Soviet Union itself was quite another. Even the loss of the three Baltic states—Estonia, Latvia, Lithuania—could somehow be justified: culturally and historically they belonged to Europe and had initially been acquired as part of the dirty deal, the Molotov–Ribbentrop Pact, that Stalin struck with Hitler in 1939. But it was unthinkable that Kazakhstan could be lost, Kazakhstan with its enormous prairies and wheat fields, its oil, uranium, and gold, its launching platforms from which the Soviets had sent the first Sputnik, dog, and male and female cosmonauts, into space. Even more unthinkable was that Ukraine could be lost. Kazakhstan may have been conquered and settled by Russians, but, to the Russian mind, Ukraine *was* Russia. All Russian history flowed from Kiev. Every schoolchild learned: Kiev is the mother of Russian cities, Ukraine is Russia's breadbasket.

And the losses weren't only emotional and symbolic. Ukraine was rich in coal, industry, agriculture. It had the port where the Black Sea Fleet was stationed, it had the only shipyard where aircraft carriers were built. Even Kazakhstan might in the end be arguable. But Kazakhstan was lost. And so was Ukraine.

It all seemed impossible, incredible. But as Putin put it: "There's a lot that seems impossible and incredible and then—*bang!* Look what happened to the Soviet Union. Who could have imagined that it would simply collapse? No one saw that coming—even in their worst nightmares."

The loss was indeed catastrophic. The USSR's population had been somewhat over 300,000,000. Now Russia was down to half that, with its population continuing to fall for years, 170 people dying for every 100 babies born. The country was losing the equivalent of a San Francisco a year to alcohol, heart attacks, car wrecks, suicide.

The economic losses were immense not only in and of themselves, but in their consequences. The centralized command-and-control economy dictated where certain machines or parts were to be produced; many were concentrated in places that had now broken away. That system had never worked well anyway, and now that parts had to be not only shipped but imported, things only grew worse. The military losses were also immense. Both Tsarist and Soviet Russia had been known for their huge standing armies, but now there were 150,000,000 fewer people to draw from.

And over it all hung the malodorous air of farce and fiasco, defeat and disgrace. To make matters worse, the United States and the West were not only now the victors in the Cold War; they also wanted to take credit for the collapse of the Soviet Union. In his book *Heroes* British historian Paul Johnson epitomizes what was for Russians the West's unbearable preening and triumphalist self-love: "Three people won the Cold War, dismantled the Soviet empire and eliminated Communism as a malevolent world force: Pope John Paul II, Margaret Thatcher and Ronald Reagan." As if the writings of Solzhenitsyn, the actions of Sakharov, and the decisions of Gorbachev had not played the slightest part whatsoever. The actual physical losses—territory, population, agriculture, industry, space, and military—were horrendous enough, but the incessant crowing of the West was galling beyond measure.

In an ornate tsarist palace turned high-tech gym in St. Petersburg I had a conversation with a Russian gangster who, behind his very broad back, was called simply "Tank." But his mind was sharp and he liked to sprinkle the occasional English phrase into his conversation. He took a very Darwinian view of power and the relations between states—to the victor the spoils and to the loser bitter humiliation. Speaking of the Cold War in particular, he said: "You won, we lost. We have to bow down to you. You have the right to teach us how to live."

That same sense of humiliation, which Thomas Friedman has called "the single most underestimated force in international relations," was present in President Yeltsin's voice when he exclaimed to President Clinton: "Russia isn't Haiti!" *The Russia Hand* by Clinton's Russian adviser Strobe Talbott records Russian foreign minister Andrey Kozyrev saying in regard to the U.S. bombing of Serbia: "You know, it's bad enough having you people tell us what you're going to do whether we like it or not. Don't add insult to injury by also telling us that it's *in our interests* to obey your orders!"

After the pain and humiliation of losing Poland, Hungary, Czechoslovakia, and East Germany, after the pain and humiliation of losing all the Soviet republics, it would seem that the hideous course had been run, that there was no more loss that could occur, no further humiliation that could be inflicted.

But in fact the greatest dangers lay ahead. Russia itself was at risk. The cracks that started in the Eastern Bloc and broke the USSR into fifteen separate countries were now threatening the new Russian Federation itself. The centrifugal demon wasn't done yet.

The epicenter of schism was Chechnya. It was hardly a new

problem. The fierce mountaineers of the Caucasus—Chechens, Ingush, Dagestanis—had been resisting the Russians since the eighteenth century. That resistance flared into war in the mid-nineteenth century when a great leader arose. The Imam Shamil, a Dagestani, was able to unite the various tribes and nations of the Caucasus, becoming both their spiritual and military leader. Handsome in a fierce, severe way (to this day his picture, along with that of Jean-Claude Van Damme or Rambo, adorns the bedroom walls of many teenage boys in the Caucasus), he was a cunning and valiant leader, able to resist the tsar's armies for nearly thirty years until he was taken prisoner in 1859. The Russians treated him with honor and he died a white-bearded patriarch in the holy city of Medina in 1871.

But his fighting spirit lives on, especially among the Chechens, the Comanches of Islam. And Shamil's hometown of Gimry is kept under strict government control so that it does not become a sacred place and rallying point—all residents have a five-digit number that they must recite to police at checkpoints when entering or leaving town.

The outbreak of war in 1994 between Chechnya and Russia sent existential shock waves to the north. This wasn't just another tiny republic seeking vainglorious independence; this could be the beginning of Russia's unraveling, the secret sweet dream of the United States and NATO. That same year NATO launched airstrikes against the Bosnian Serbs. Strobe Talbott describes the reaction of the Russian hawks: "NATO's war against Belgrade over Kosovo was a warm-up for the one it would someday unleash against Moscow over Chechnya."

NATO bombing or invasion aside, the parallels with Yugoslavia were ominous. Putin was obsessed by what he called "the Yugoslavization of Russia," the breaking apart into ever smaller fragments. Chechnya, said Putin, "is a continuation of the collapse of the USSR." And it wasn't just Chechnya. "The entire Caucasus would have followed . . . and then up along the Volga River . . . reaching deep into the country." Putin was very clear about his "mission": "If we don't put an immediate end to this Russia will cease to exist."

America from time to time is troubled by the prospect of decline. But for all-or-nothing Russia decline is not an issue. Its very existence is always at stake. It is the default position of the Russian mind. A former legislator, Vladimir Ryzhkov, says: "Under Putin's police state we are headed for another Time of Troubles in the best case scenario, if not a total collapse of the Russian state." A museum director says that unless Russia creates a harmonious society within five generations "Russia will perish. Only the Duchy of Moscow will be left." A columnist wonders—Will Russia survive until 2024?

Very prevalent today, the idea of Russia ceasing to exist is nothing new. In 1836 Peter Chaadayev published the first of his *Philosophical Letters*. Like a good Russian aristocrat, he wrote them in French, and later on they had to be translated into Russian. In those *Philosophical Letters* Chaadayev despaired of Russia, which he said belongs to neither Europe nor Asia. It neither partakes of the dynamic of those great civilizations nor possesses a dynamic of its own. "We belong to that number of nations which do not seem to make up an integral part of the human race, but which exist only to teach the world some great lesson. The lesson which we are destined to give will, naturally, not be lost; but who knows when we shall find ourselves once again in the midst of humanity, and what affliction we shall experience before we accomplish our destiny?"

In a move that predated Soviet abuse of psychiatry by a century, Chaadayev was declared insane and forcibly placed under medical care, his papers seized.

A paradigm emerged from Chaadayev's ideas. Cut off from the West by the Mongol conqueror and by obscurantist tsars, Russia had missed all the developmental stages of civilizational progress—Renaissance, Reformation, Counter-Reformation, Enlightenment.

The lack of any developmental dynamic meant that progress came from above, from the omnipotent ruler, the tsar. It was a country held together by power, religion, and fear—in Chaadayev's excellent phrase "a realm of brute fact and ceremony."

Russia's inherent shakiness was sensed not only by Russian philosophers, but by travelers to those parts in the nineteenth century. "Russia may well fall to pieces as many expect," noted the dashing British intelligence officer Arthur Conolly, who often traveled through Central Asia in native guise, using the name Khan Ali, a pun on his own. Not only is he credited with creating the term "great game," he played it to the hilt until he was beheaded in Bukhara in 1842 at the age of thirty-four.

For the anti-regime intellectuals of the late nineteenth and early twentieth centuries, the destruction of Russia was something they not only sensed but actively desired. One of the major poets of that period, Alexander Blok, claimed he could actually hear the empire collapsing. Blok, who hailed the sinking of the *Titanic* in 1912 as proof that Nature was still mightier than man and his arrogant works, longed for an elemental revolution that would sweep away all the cant and rot, making a place for a new and better civilization to arise. Deeply disillusioned by the actual revolution that took place, he died in 1921, no longer able to hear history in the making because, as he said, "all sounds have stopped."

In Russia the sense of shaky enterprise, the tendency to build structures that collapse, is balanced by a genius for survival. A Russian hacker with the handle "Lightwatch" put it like this: "The Russians have a very amusing feature—they are able to get up from their knees, under any conditions, or under any circumstances."

Russia withstood and outlasted the invasions of Genghis Khan, Napoleon, Hitler. Russia survived its own tyrants from Ivan the Terrible to Joseph Stalin. It survived the implosion of its state structure during the Time of Troubles in the early 1600s, again in 1917, and yet again in 1991.

Those events have inspired great works of art—the opera *Boris Godunov* about the Time of Troubles, *War and Peace* about the invasion of Napoleon, *Life and Fate* about World War II. And those works of art have in turn inspired further acts of heroic survival by Russians, and have spread the fame of Russian fortitude throughout the world. It seems to have always been there. In the mid-900s the Arab traveler Ibn Miskawayh called them "a mighty nation . . . with great courage. They know not defeat, not does any of them turn his back until he slays or be slain."

Even one of the American Mafia families took inspiration from Russia when going to war against the other families. As Salvatore "Sammy the Bull" Gravano, underboss to John Gotti, put it: "Fuck the battle. You learned that from the Russians. Yeah, they were dogs, they kept backing up. They let them Germans come right into their country. They made them freeze their asses off, run out of supplies, and then they destroyed them. So it's not the battle, it's the war."

The principal Russian holiday is Easter, not Christmas. Of course, that is as it should be, because the rising of Christ from the dead is the central mystery and promise of Christianity. (How all that was reduced in the West to bonnets, bunnies, and eggs is a mystery in itself.) The Russians do not wish each other Happy Easter but exchange passionate affirmations: "Christ is risen!" "Truly He is risen!"

The myth of rebirth is central to the work of the Russian philosopher Nikolai Fyodorov (1829–1903). Said to be the only person in whose presence Count Leo Tolstoy ever felt humble, Fyodorov was an inspiration to Konstantin Tsiolkovsky, the father of Russian rocketry and thus of the Soviet space program. Fyodorov's main idea was that Christianity and science were not at all at odds, but in fact were destined to work together for the greatest of all possible goals, the resurrection of everyone who had ever lived, the rescue of our ancestors from hated death.

The myth of rebirth also animates the Russian body politic at its moments of crisis. No invasion is too great not to be withstood and ultimately repelled, no collapse of the state from within can lead to permanent diminishment or ruination. What explains this? Is it the inbred hardiness of people who have endured centuries of harsh winter? Is it the cunning, also developed over centuries from dealing with the severities of invasion and tyranny? Is it simply a straightforward response to the straightforward Darwinian imperative: Do or Die? It is all of these, but there is also something else.

The source of Russia's ability to overcome any trauma has been the cluster of values, images, and ideas that gave the nation its irreducible identity. But now there is a void at the core of the collective psyche. For the first time in its more than thousand-year history, Russia is without icons.

A Russia Without Icons

The Russians were iconoclasts even before they had icons.

In 988 Grand Prince Vladimir of Kiev, "a fundamentally good man who led a life of lechery and murder," had a spiritual awakening and decided to convert his people from paganism to one of the three great religions in that part of the world. According to the ancient Chronicles, a mixture of legend and history, Vladimir dispatched envoys to see what those religions had to offer. The loss of Israel did not make Judaism seem a fortunate enterprise. Islam's prohibition on alcohol made it out of the question, for, as Vladimir himself remarked in a two-line poem:

> *The Russian cannot bear to think*
> *Of a life devoid of all strong drink.*

However, his envoys reported from Constantinople that the beauty of the cathedrals was such that "we knew not whether we were in heaven or on earth." So, beauty won the day. Or at least beauty coupled with realpolitik, for it made more economic and military sense for Vladimir's domain, Kievan Rus as it came to be called, to ally itself with Byzantium, the great power in those parts.

But before Christianity with all its beliefs, rituals, and icons could be fully implemented, the old paganism had to be done away with. In that belief system life was a struggle between the Dark God and the Bright God, but there were many lesser deities as well, chief among them Perun, god of thunder and lightning. Grand Prince Vladimir "directed that the idols be overthrown and that some should be cut to pieces and others burned with fire. He thus ordered that Perun should be bound to a horse's tail and dragged . . . to the river. He appointed twelve men to beat the idols with sticks."

In all this can be observed several tendencies that would persist through the centuries: Change comes from the top down. Ideology tends to be imported. Not only must new sacred images be introduced, but the old ones must first be desecrated and destroyed.

The tenacious persistence of cultural forms in Russia is at times nothing short of amazing, as James Billington observed in his classic *The Icon and the Axe*: "Just as the iconostasis of a cathedral was generally built over the grave of a local saint and specially reverenced with processions on a religious festival, so these new Soviet saints appeared in ritual form over the mausoleum of the mummified Lenin on the feast days of Bolshevism to review endless processions through Red Square."

And in 1917 Vladimir Lenin showed himself little different from Grand Prince Vladimir of Kiev when it came to a passion for iconoclasm. Lenin, who actively hated the very idea of God, persecuted both the symbols of Christianity and its priests, who were imprisoned and executed in large numbers. In his book *Soviet Civilization*

Andrei Sinyavsky describes "the Bolsheviks' extravagant acts against sacred objects, as when they did not just remove the icons from a church but used them to make floors for the village baths without even sanding off the saints' faces. Or when they lined them up against a wall and shot at them, as if, for these atheist resisters of God, the icons were living beings."

In 1931 Stalin ordered the demolition of Moscow's Christ the Savior Cathedral, built in the mid-1800s to commemorate the victory over Napoleon. It was to have been replaced by a Palace of Soviets, much larger than the Empire State Building and topped with a 260-foot statue of Lenin. However, after the demolition of the cathedral, the ground proved too marshy to support such a grandiose edifice, and for years the gaping hole was left empty. Later, Khrushchev hit on the idea of turning it into the world's largest outdoor swimming pool, which fit nicely into the totalitarian cult of mass sport, if not rising to the iconic heights of the original concept. It was only after the fall of the USSR that the Christ the Savior Cathedral was rebuilt from scratch at enormous expense by Moscow mayor Yuri Luzhkov. And so it was into that long-suffering, much-manipulated, and symbol-drenched cathedral that one day in 2012 three young women, their faces concealed with balaclavas, began singing a discordant song of protest against Putin, a punk prayer. They were immediately arrested and almost as immediately became famous as members of Pussy Riot. Though they were quite sincere in protesting the suspect coziness of church and state, they had also inadvertently entered a labyrinth of symbols that led, as do so many things in Russia, to prison.

A desacralization and desecration of images had also occurred when the Soviet regime began falling in the late 1980s. Statues of Lenin—though not all of them—were torn down, and of course he himself, so to speak, remains in his mausoleum on Red Square.

Immediately to the left of Lenin's tomb is Stalin's grave and the bust with its oddly crafty eyes. Stalin too had been embalmed and entombed alongside Lenin in the mausoleum until 1961, when Khrushchev, as part of his anti-Stalin campaign, ordered the body removed under cover of night, then buried. Stalin's body was then placed under a concrete slab, just to be on the safe side. Who knows, maybe the corpse had even been dragged by a horse and beaten with sticks.

The collapses of Tsarist Russia in 1917 and of Soviet Russia in 1991 were greatly different. Though Lenin was caught by surprise by events, having despaired of seeing any revolution in his lifetime, he and the other far-left revolutionaries had one enormous advantage: they knew what they wanted to be rid of and what they wanted to replace it with. The Bolsheviks had a worldview, a theory of politics, government, economics, foreign policy; they had a flag and a color—red, the color of flame, blood, and revolution; they had songs that could move the masses, they had artists itching to use the instruments of modernism to create a new art for all of society and not just one for an elite of connoisseurs. They had a philosophy of life and a theory of history as a progressive dynamic evolving through contradiction toward social justice for all. The state would gradually wither away as people achieved ever higher levels of consciousness, a vision described by Leon Trotsky in the concluding words of his book *Literature and Revolution*:

> Man will become immeasurably stronger, wiser and subtler; his body will become more harmonized, his movements more rhythmic, his voice more musical. The forms of life will become dynamically dramatic. The average human type will rise to the heights of an Aristotle, a Goethe, or a Marx. And above this ridge new peaks will rise.

In 1991 there was no Lenin waiting in the wings. Instead of the drama of violent armed clashes, there was only a void that only grew the more it was fed.

The questions about this period are myriad: Did the United States do too little to help in the critical early nineties? Or, on the contrary, did the United States interfere too much and propose solutions that were ill-suited for the reality of Russia? Or was there in fact very little that any outside nation could do, since Russia's resurgence, like its demise, would largely be a matter of its own making?

One thing is, however, certain. No one had a vision for post-Soviet life apart from generalizations about constitutions, human rights, and free markets. But what actual policies to pursue, what flag should be saluted, what anthem sung, what holidays and heroes celebrated, what icons should be smashed and which new ones created, no one had the slightest idea.

Survival needs no justification, but tribulation is always easier to bear in the name of something higher. For Russians that has traditionally been what they themselves call "the Russian Idea," meaning a sense of national identity and purpose crystallized into a specific vision and a way of life. The Russian Idea also has a a quasi-mystical nationalistic aura about it, "the conviction that Russia has its own independent, self-sufficient and eminently worthy cultural and historical tradition that both sets it apart from the West and guarantees its future flourishing," wrote Tim McDaniel in *The Agony of the Russian Idea*.

The Russian sense of national self, like the history that produced it and the history it produces, clearly tends toward the extremes rather than to cluster around some middle point. The country's greatest twentieth-century philosopher, Nikolai Berdyaev, wrote in his book *The Russian Idea*:

The Russians are a people in the highest degree polarized: they are a conglomeration of contradictions. One can be charmed by them, one can be disillusioned. The unexpected is always to be expected from them. . . . In respect of this polarization and inconsistency the Russian people can be paralleled only by the Jews: and it is not merely a matter of chance that precisely in these two peoples there exists a vigorous messianic consciousness. . . . Never has Russia been bourgeois."

And another philosopher, V. M. Mezhuev, put it another way: "We are not suited for moderation and measure, which are the marks of rationality."

In the view of these two philosophers the Russian collective psyche keeps its balance by going from one extreme to the other, rather than by seeking a midpoint. This makes Russia both fragile and tenacious, able to survive any ordeal, but unable to construct states that do not sooner or later implode. To some extent, it is precisely that fear of the tendency to fly off to extremes that causes Russians to create rigid hierarchical states that in time ossify and break apart to release the very forces they were created to contain.

Out of the thousands of signs, markers, and symbols of a national identity, anthem and flag have to rank high. A piece of decorated cloth, a few minutes of music, might not seem important in and of themselves, but their lack, or, as in Russia's case, their presence in a stunted form, is indicative of a profound malaise, a failure to achieve integrity, that touches every schoolchild who must salute the flag and sing the national anthem.

The Bolsheviks had a flag and a song. Post-Soviet Russia really has neither. Instead of creating a flag as new as the new Russia, the government adopted a tricolor from the late tsarist period. From top to bottom it is white, blue, and red. Whether there's any subliminal significance to the counterrevolutionary white being on top with the revolutionary red on the bottom is anybody's guess. To provide some aesthetic/emotional continuity the music of the Soviet anthem was kept, but the words were rewritten. Lenin was now tossed out as Stalin had been in an earlier rewrite. God, however, is back.

But these are very new and still raw "traditions." It means that parents and children will have grown up saluting different flags, singing different anthems.

There is a similar problem with holidays. Victory Day, May 9, celebrating the defeat of Nazi Germany, and New Year's are the only holidays that provide some kind of continuity with the Soviet past. Though a large portion of the population is Russian Orthodox, many Russians aren't religious, and there are also ten to fifteen million Muslims in Russia, not to mention Jews and Buddhists. No holiday with a religious tinge can become truly national.

For schoolchildren there's not only the problems of flag and anthem but the problem of what history they're taught. As it used to be said with a more sinister tone in Soviet times, it's even harder to predict the past than the future.

The question remains—how to integrate the Soviet past into the post-Soviet present, what sense to make of it. "Russia should not repent for Soviet history," said Duma Speaker Sergei Naryshkin. Others would vehemently disagree.

Principally, the issue revolves around the image of Stalin, an icon that has been neither utterly smashed nor quite restored to a place in a new pantheon.

The Germans "lucked out" with Hitler. He was so evil, so destructive, and so unsuccessful that it was easy to reject him completely. But the Russians were not so lucky with Stalin.

Tomes have been written comparing the two great dictators, but in the end what matters most is their differences. The main difference is that in World War II Hitler lost and Stalin won. That meant suicide for Hitler and the Nuremburg trials for his high command. For Stalin, it meant the spoils and honors that come with being the victor, not least of which was a seat on the United Nations Security Council.

Russians are of course aware of the cost of Stalin's Gulag, which the historian Norman Davies says "accounted for far more human victims than Ypres, the Somme, Verdun, Auschwitz, Majdanek, Dachau and Buchenwald put together."

But Stalin himself knew such comparisons carry little weight, supposedly saying: "One death is a tragedy, a million is a statistic."

Stalin's terror ended with his death, but his achievements live on after him. Those achievements include the industrialization of Russia, the defeat of the Nazi invader, making his country an atomic superpower. One of the worst mass murderers in history had atomic weapons for five years and never came close to using them. The crisis occurred with his successor, the more liberal, humane, anti-Stalinist Nikita Khrushchev.

There are other of Stalin's achievements that continue to elicit admiration: the Moscow Metro, a wonder of the world, and the many solid residential buildings, which were much better constructed than those of his successors, especially Khrushchev. Perhaps the best recommendation for a building is that it was constructed in Stalin's time by German POW slave labor.

Even the seven sisters, the Soviet wedding-cake high-rises that dominate the Moscow skyline, which seemed grim and overbearing in Soviet times, have now acquired a sort of retro imperial chic. In fact at least two of the more daring new buildings shaping the contemporary Moscow skyline deliberately echo their shape.

Stalin's name still has magic power whether it is invoked with hatred or respect. In 1956 Khrushchev banned Stalin's name from the national anthem. Later, to be on the safe side, all the lyrics were removed, and for more than twenty years the Soviet Union's national anthem was a song without words. When the new version appeared in 1977 the lines

Stalin reared us on loyalty to the people.
He inspired us to labor and heroic deeds.

had been airbrushed out. That would have seemed to be the end of that, but then in 2009 the elegant Kurskaya Metro Station finished its redo to its original Soviet purity, and, lo and behold, the lines airbrushed from the anthem had reappeared in large golden letters along the top of the interior wall, instantly generating controversy between those for whom Stalin's name only signified suffering and those who preferred the uplift of imperial grandeur.

Word magic, the making and breaking of verbal icons, is also widespread in Russia. St. Petersburg was changed to the less German-sounding Petrograd (same meaning—Peter's city) during World War I, then to Leningrad in 1924 when Lenin died, then back to its original name in 1991 with the fall of the USSR. In a nice twist, the new St. Petersburg is also the capital of Leningrad province, which they haven't gotten around to renaming yet.

Right after the fall of the USSR, Moscow cabdrivers had to consult bulky volumes to find out the new names of Soviet streets, which had in turn been changed from their names in Tsarist Russia. "They even changed Chekhov Street back to its prerevolutionary name," said one cabdriver plaintively. "What did Chekhov ever do to anybody?"

By the time Putin assumed office in early 2000, neither in words nor in images had post-Soviet Russia found any new icon to guide it into a future that looked hazardous at best.

Not only had enormous power been bestowed on Putin; he had also been charged thereby with resolving enormous tasks. He had to restore stability, strength, and status to his country. No easy tasks, but these were mostly tangible, solvable with time, money, and skill. But Putin was also faced with somehow curing the spiritual ills from which Russians and he himself suffered—the anxiety and suspicion generated by the country's post-traumatic condition, and as well the lack of any clear vision of cultural values, national aim. Putin could not of course hammer out new icons for Russia, but good leadership could help create the matrix from which those new icons could yet arise.

Presented with immense power and daunting tasks, Vladimir Putin had been given a shot at greatness.

PART FOUR

CORE ISSUES

*Without Ukraine, Russia ceases to be
a Eurasian empire.*

—ZBIGNIEW BRZEZINSKI

The empires of the future are the empires of the mind.

—WINSTON CHURCHILL

6

OIL: A WASTING ASSET

The key to the fate of Russia is the fate of Russian oil.

—THANE GUSTAFSON

Amazingly, reassuringly, suspiciously, Russia had followed its new Constitution. Putin, as prime minister, had automatically replaced President Yeltsin when he stepped down. Putin was then elected president in the elections the Constitution mandated take place within three months.

And so, on May 7, 2000, in the gilded and blue-silk moiré splendor of the Kremlin's St. Andrew Hall, once the throne room of the tsars, Vladimir Vladimirovich Putin, his hand on the Constitution, took the presidential oath of office, which in its entirety ran: "I vow, in the performance of my powers as the President of the Russian Federation, to respect and protect the rights and freedoms of man and citizen, to observe and protect the Constitution of the Russian Federation, to protect the sovereignty and independence, security and integrity of the state and to serve the people faithfully."

Putin was open about his statist views from the start. The "rights and freedoms of man and citizen" had less timbre for him than the "security and integrity of the state."

In *First Person*, his 2000 autobiography—actually a mix of interviews with journalists and oral history reminiscences by his friends, teachers, and family—Putin was quite clear how he viewed the state: "From the very beginning, Russia was created as a super-centralized state. That's practically laid down in its genetic code, its traditions, and the mentality of its people."

Though there were some liberal economists in Putin's inner circle, like Alexei Kudrin, who served as minister of finance from 2000 to 2011, most, some estimates range as high as 40 percent, were security types, preferably ex–Leningrad KGB. One colleague from Dresden, Sergei Chemezov, would head up Russia's weapons export. This was not only loyalty, but calculation—Putin knew these types, how to read them, how to use them.

Three moves he made in the summer of 2000 should have been enough to indicate his bent and dispel some of the hopeful haze around his election. In July he summoned the oligarchs to the Kremlin and laid down the law: You can keep your money, but pay your taxes and keep your nose out of politics. Subsequent events would reveal that not everyone got the message.

The second move was one he did not make—not quickly returning from vacation in Sochi to deal with the crisis of the Russian nuclear-powered attack submarine *Kursk*, which had gone down in Arctic waters. Putin was extremely reluctant to seek foreign aid to rescue the sailors, still alive but dying a slow, hideous, and unnecessary death. None of this played well on television.

Yeltsin's election in 1996 and Putin's own election in April 2000 had convinced him of the power of television, a lesson that was only negatively reinforced by the poor coverage he received during the *Kursk* disaster. The oligarch Boris Berezovsky's TV Channel 1, sometimes called ORT, was especially unrelenting in its criticism of

Putin. In his third move of clear significance, Putin summoned Berezovsky and said quite matter-of-factly: "ORT is the most important channel. It's too important to be left outside government influence. We made a decision . . ."—meaning the state would be taking control of ORT and resistance would be not only futile, but criminal. It didn't matter in the least that Berezovsky had been instrumental in Putin's rise.

Soon enough the conversation grew emotional, ranging from self-pity to rage, with Putin asking: "Why are you attacking me? Have I done anything to hurt you?"

"Volodya, you made a mistake when you stayed in Sochi. Every station in the world . . ."

"I don't give a fuck about every station in the world," interrupted Putin. "Why did *you* do this? You are supposed to be my friend. It was you talked me into taking this job. And now you are stabbing me in the back."

By the end of the year, rightly fearing prison, Berezovsky left Russia, never to return. Living in England, he would expend considerable energy trying to prove that the three explosions of apartment buildings in late 1999 that were blamed on Chechens were in fact a secret police operation designed to create an atmosphere of alarm and help the tough-talking Putin get elected. That Putin's reign began under the shadow of deceit and homicide has not yet been proved, nor will it likely ever be.

Like most of the other oligarchs, Berezovsky had no real business acumen. Though he lived high on the British hog for a decade, his fortunes took a severe turn for the worse in 2012 when he lost a costly court battle, and in the following year, faced with mere diminishment, all-or-nothing Berezovsky chose nothing, hanging himself in a bathroom locked from the inside, though doubts flicker even around this incident.

But it was not Putin's seizure of the media, his suppression of dissent, or even his invasions and incursions that would matter most in his own fate and Russia's but, as will become quite clear, his failure to diversify the economy away from its dependence on gas and oil. The roots of that problem go back a century. In Russia all stories are old stories.

For centuries Baku's "fountain of oil," as Marco Polo called it when passing through in the 1270s on his way to China, had been used for lighting and as "an unguent for the cure of cutaneous distempers in men and cattle." It wasn't until the late nineteenth century that Baku's first gusher came on. Things developed at a breakneck pace. Between 1898 and 1902 Imperial Russia's oil fields were at the peak of their production, having surpassed those of the United States to lead the world.

The possibilities for fast and enormous wealth attracted people like John D. Rockefeller, the Rothschilds, and the Nobel brothers (they of dynamite and the Prize), who constructed the world's first pipeline and oil tanker. But it was not only international capitalists who were drawn to the oil fields of Baku. Just as the Russians were overtaking the United States, a twenty-two-year-old Georgian who had been radicalized while studying to become a priest, arrived on the scene. Mixing metaphors from his seminary and political lives, Joseph Stalin said that the strikes he organized in Baku were his "revolutionary baptism in combat."

He and his fellow organizers succeeded all too well. By the end of the failed 1905 revolution two-thirds of the oil wells in Baku had been destroyed.

Though names like Standard Oil and Rockefeller were in Communist mythology synonymous with rapacious exploitation, it turned out that Soviet Russia's oil fields could not be put back into operation without foreign help. In the early 1920s, Lenin had to come to terms with the severity of the havoc wrought by the First World War, the revolution, and the civil war. To bring back some of life's daily necessities and pleasures, Lenin introduced NEP, the New Economic Policy, which allowed small business to reemerge and flourish. Foreign experts were allowed in.

Lenin's moves, though ideologically distasteful, were successful. Goods reappeared on the shelves of stores and the oil began flowing again both in the older fields and in the new ones opened up with advanced Western technology. One of those helping out was Frederick Koch, grandfather of today's notorious Koch brothers. As the story goes, an invention of his for refining gasoline from crude oil was effectively squashed by the major U.S. oil companies, which attacked him with patent-infringement lawsuits that took him more than a decade to win.

In 1928 Koch signed a $5 million contract to construct fifteen refineries in the USSR in Baku and other oil-producing regions like Chechnya. The young Mr. Koch left the USSR with two things: a small fortune of $500,000 (around $7 million in today's dollars), which would serve as the basis for the future Koch empire, and a fierce hatred of Communism that led him to become one of the founding members of the John Birch Society. Whether he perceived the irony of his entrepreneurial efforts being crushed by naked capitalism at home and handsomely rewarded by Stalin's Russia is doubtful to say the least.

By the end of the 1920s, however, Soviet farms and factories were producing enough for Soviet citizens, and NEP was done away with. The little stores were closed, and small business became a criminal activity overnight. The foreign oil specialists were paid off and sent packing. Lenin was dead and there was a new man in the Kremlin, the former oil-field strike organizer Joseph Stalin.

By 1929, with his archrival, Leon Trotsky, in exile and the capitalist world in a shambles, Stalin moved to reshape the Soviet economy into the centralized control-and-command model that persisted until the USSR collapsed under its own weight in 1991. Stalin forced the peasants onto collective farms. Those who displayed reluctance or resistance, and those who were considered well-off and therefore by definition exploiters, were shipped to Siberia and Kazakhstan by cattle car. Millions of Ukrainian peasants who were considered especially recalcitrant—conservative by their peasant nature, nationalistic because of being Ukrainians—were simply starved to death by artificially created famines. All food was confiscated; villages were cut off at the beginning of winter and the corpses were collected come spring. Many Ukrainians would later welcome Hitler's armies simply because they could not imagine anything worse than Stalin.

Like all the rest of industry, the oil industry came under greater centralized control. The measures of performance were, inevitably, quantitative. For example, when it came to drilling, it was not the amount of oil that was discovered that would prove the standard of measure, because it might be years before that number could be calculated. In the here and now what could be precisely determined was the number and depth of holes drilled, which more often than not led to landscapes pocked like moons.

Nevertheless, oil was found, pumped, refined. In any case, the world market for oil was weak throughout most of the thirties because of the Depression. The USSR was exporting more timber than petroleum.

Germany became one of the USSR's main customers for oil, especially after the surprise Molotov–Ribbentrop Pact of 1939, which pledged nonaggression and, secretly, agreed on the dismembering of Poland and the Baltic states. Time would reveal that Stalin had in effect been selling Hitler the gas for his tanks and trucks to invade the Soviet Union. When attacking in June 1941, Hitler knew his blitzkrieg had to succeed because he could never win a war of attrition against the USSR unless, that is, he had the grain of Ukraine and the oil of Baku.

September 25, 1942, was the date set for the capture of Baku's oil fields. A few days before the attack Hitler's generals presented him with a cake whose frosting depicted Baku and the Caspian Sea. (There are twenty seconds of black-and-white film of all this.) Greatly amused, Hitler took the "Baku" slice for himself though supposedly also saying: "Unless we get Baku's oil, the war is lost."

In July, aware that an attack on Baku was coming, Stalin summoned Nikolai Baibakov, who oversaw Soviet oil production. According to Baibakov's obituary in *The New York Times*, "Stalin pointed two fingers at Mr. Baibakov's head. . . . 'If you fail to stop the Germans getting our oil, you will be shot,' Stalin said. 'And when we have thrown the invader out, if we cannot restart production, we will shoot you again.'" As the *Times* notes laconically: "Mr. Baibakov accomplished both missions." And so Baibakov not only was not executed once or even twice, but outlasted Stalin and all the other bastards great and small, only dying in 2008 at the age of ninety-seven.

From the end of the war to the end of the USSR, a stretch of only forty-six years, the oil industry was much like the country itself— mighty, cumbersome, fatally flawed. The Baku oil fields, damaged during the war, never regained the production heights achieved before the war. But vast new fields were discovered in the Volga-Ural region and later in West Siberia by teams of intrepid geologists out "feeding the mosquitoes." Paranoia about contact with foreigners was in part what drove the relentless hunt for new oil fields. Instead of acquiring the knowledge and technology that would have maximized output, but which would have required foreign technicians and specialists on site to demonstrate how the equipment worked, exploration was unceasing. There were always more fields, more oil over the next ridge. *Rossiya bolshaya*, Russia is big, as the Russians like to say.

The USSR's main use for oil was for domestic purposes, Moscow always prizing independence from a hostile capitalist world. But Moscow needed that world too because Russia, which before the revolution had been the world's greatest exporter of grain, had become by the late 1970s the world's largest importer. In 1963 Khrushchev had spent a third of the country's gold to buy grain. The collective agriculture forcibly imposed by Stalin was a failure. As the head of a collective farm once said to me: ". . . collective farming could have worked. It worked in Israel. . . . But it couldn't be done by force and decree." Storage and distribution were also significant problems, up to a third of a year's crop lost to spillage and spoilage.

Sales of oil on the world's open market became increasingly important and paid for meat, grain, and machinery that the USSR imported. Gas and oil also had their political applications. The Kremlin's aid to Cuba, to take one example, came largely in the form of oil. This was pretty much the situation until 1985, when Mikhail Gorbachev came to power. Perestroika, his plan to rebuild the system, assumed there was still something left worth rebuilding. One of Gorbachev's first acts in office was to fire the long-term director of Gosplan, the agency that planned and regulated the entire Soviet economy, everything from nails to rocket ships. That director was none other than Stalin's lucky and tenacious oil commissar Nikolai Baibakov, who had remained loyal to his old boss, saying of Khrushchev's secret speech denouncing Stalin in 1956: "Maybe there were individual acts of repression but what Stalin was denounced for, that never happened." The "maybe" is a particularly nice touch.

And "maybe" Gorbachev could have rebuilt the Soviet economy or enough of it to form a new union composed of Russia, Belarus, Ukraine, and northern Kazakhstan, as Aleksandr Solzhenitsyn proposed in his 1991 book *Rebuilding Russia*. But there were too many forces opposed to that—the failed and costly war in Afghanistan; the nationalistic aspirations of the smaller states, whose efforts at withdrawal had a sort of avalanche effect; and the wisdom, or the weakness, not to use force against the opposition as the Chinese chose to do on Tiananmen Square in June 1989, those protesters in part inspired by Gorbachev's presence in Beijing at the time.

But as much as anything it was oil that did Gorbachev in. It was $50.11 a barrel in 1985 when he took office, but fell more than 50 percent, to $24.71, during his first full year in power. And the price stayed in the twenties from 1986 to 1991 except for two years: 1987, when it was $31.68, and 1990—$35.62. There is some but insufficient evidence that William Casey and the CIA, working with OPEC, engaged in a clandestine campaign to bring down the price of oil and the Soviet Union with it. That there is insufficient evidence does not of course prevent many Russians from insisting that the conspiracy was all too real and, moreover, was the forerunner of today's efforts to weaken and subvert Putin's Russia through the use of NGOs and by funding movements like the Orange Revolution in Ukraine. Even a reform-minded high-ranking official like Egor Gaidar could write:

The timeline of the collapse of the Soviet Union can be traced to September 13, 1985. On this date, Sheikh Ahmed Zaki Yamani, the minister of oil of Saudi Arabia, declared that the monarchy had decided to alter its oil policy radically. The Saudis stopped protecting oil prices, and Saudi Arabia quickly regained its share in the world market. During the next six months, oil production in Saudi Arabia increased fourfold, while oil prices collapsed by approximately the same amount in real terms.

As a result, the Soviet Union lost approximately $20 billion per year, money without which the country simply could not survive."

The Politburo was in a panic over those $20-billion-a-year losses from the fall in oil prices, and, contrary to what was generally thought, the USSR did not hold $36 billion in gold reserves but only $7.6 billion because of Khrushchev's extravagances in buying grain. There really was no need for theories about cunning conspiracies. The Union of Soviet Socialist Republics was broken and broke.

A joke of the 1990s offers the following definition of Russian business: three guys steal a case of vodka, sell it all, and then go get drunk on the proceeds. And truly in that decade there was something drunken about all Russian life from the street to the Kremlin, where the first freely elected Russian president, Boris Yeltsin, a burly Siberian with a W. C. Fields nose, became more of an embarrassing boozer with each passing year. Still, President Bill Clinton did say: "Yeltsin drunk is better than most of the alternatives sober."

Clinton must have had a quite low opinion of those alternatives given Yeltsin's behavior one night at Blair House, the vice president's official residence. "Yeltsin was roaring drunk, lurching from room to room in his undershorts . . . demanding, 'Pizza! Pizza!'"

In the nineties crime lords arose out of nowhere, suddenly rich, powerful, and well armed with all the weapons the country was awash in. At one point Yeltsin declared they controlled 40 percent of the economy. Gangs shot it out on the streets. At one of their favorite hangouts, the still trendy Aist (Stork) restaurant in central Moscow, the diners looked on in horror as a gangster rolled a grenade like a bowling ball along the floor toward a rival's table. (A dud, as it turned out.)

Though Russian gangsters were making small fortunes via extortion, protection, drugs, and casinos, the great fortunes would end up in the hands of educated men like Berezovsky, who held a Ph.D. in mathematics, and Mikhail Khodorkovsky, who, before he became Russia's richest man and its most famous prisoner, earned a degree in engineering.

Khodorkovsky was born in 1963 in Moscow, the only child of a mixed marriage, his father Jewish, his mother Russian. In a sense that left him being neither fish nor fowl because Jews trace lineage through the mother and Russians through the father. People like Khodorkovsky had the choice of having their internal passports marked either "Russian" or "Jewish," which was considered a nationality. There were any number of advantages in choosing "Russian," though they only went so far, as a famous joke illustrates: A friend comes running into Moishe's apartment all excited, saying: "Moishe, down on the square they're beating up Jews!" Moishe replies grandly: "What do I care? My passport is marked 'Russian.'" "Moishe, they're not punching them in the passport, they're punching them in the face!"

A little prince in a dingy apartment, Khodorkovsky grew up adored and protected by his parents, who chose never to air anti-Soviet sentiments when their child was around. Khodorkovsky, who as a little boy wanted only to be a factory manager when he grew up and was nicknamed "the Director" by his classmates in kindergarten, proved adept at working the first system he encountered—the Young Communist League, the Komsomol. Founded right after the revolution in 1918 for people between fourteen and twenty-eight, the Komsomol had two basic purposes—to harness the energy of the young into clubs and supervised events like dance and sports, and to help make good little Soviet citizens out of them. It was also an organizational structure for the politically ambitious to climb, a transition between the Pioneers (Communist boy scouts) and the Communist Party itself.

By the time Khodorkovsky joined the Komsomol in the late 1970s there were precious few true believers left. Membership was a purely practical matter, a cynical choice. Moved by ambition, cool calculation, and his own natural zeal, Khodorkovsky thrived in the Komsomol, building a good reputation and strong connections that would stand him in very good stead later on. He graduated from the Mendeleev Institute of Chemical Technology in 1986, the year after Gorbachev had come to power. Fate, in the guise of institutionalized Soviet anti-Semitism, did him a favor by denying him a job in the defense industry. He took advantage of the greater economic freedom under Gorbachev to try his hand at business; his first enterprise was a flop, but he caught on quick.

His first serious success came from working the Soviet financial system, in which there were three kinds of money—foreign or "hard" currency; regular cash (or "wooden rubles" as they were sometime derisively called), which was used to pay salaries; and noncash rubles, which existed on the books of various enterprises and institutions but were difficult to transform into usable, spendable money. Those with a small-time-hustler mentality went into the black market for hard currencies, paying much more than the absurdly low government-set rate. Those who thought bigger like Khodorkovsky saw that a handsome profit was to be made by turning noncash rubles into real cash rubles, then ultimately changing them into hard currency, i.e., dollars or, as they were affectionately known, bucksy and greeny.

Using the connections he had built up during his Komsomol years, Khodorkovsky convinced them to let him handle their noncash rubles to increase their organizations' real wealth while of course cutting himself and his associates in for a healthy piece of the action. The money flowed, fueling Khodorkovsky's various other enterprises, which included construction and importing computers that could be sold for a 600 percent profit. There was a great headiness to it all, an odd combination of cool, sober calculation and the elation of sudden wealth.

By the end of 1988, taking advantage of new laws on co-ops, including financial co-ops (i.e., banks), Khodorkovsky, at the age of twenty-five, had his own bank called Menatep. The old saying that a man with a gun can rob a bank but a man with a bank can rob a country definitely applies to the Russia of those days. Menatep, like the other new banks that had sprung up in profusion, routinely violated government restrictions on hard currency. But as David Hoffman puts it in *The Oligarchs*: "The gradually collapsing Soviet state had no way to keep track of the fleet-footed easy money boys."

The people holding positions of power in the slowly sinking Soviet state had a vital interest in maintaining good relations with the new class of young bankers. In the final years of the USSR fortunes in hard currency and gold belonging to the Communist Party simply vanished without trace. There is some suspicion that Khodorkovsky's bank was involved in this diversion of wealth as part of a hand-washes-hand relationship. Khodorkovsky himself always vigorously denied any such relationship while at the same time maintaining: "A bank is like a waiter. Its business is to cater to its clients independently of their political beliefs or affiliation with this or that camp."

The last thing anybody cared about in the Russia of the late 1980s was moral or legal niceties. The state, the sole owner of everything, had always been seen as a fair target to be ripped off—some lumber, bricks, electric cable, whatever you could get away with. Now, however, whole enterprises and institutions could be ripped off from the state. It was a matter of degree, not kind.

Though akin geologically, gas and oil are quite different economically and politically. Oil is much more valuable than gas and easier to transport—it can be shipped by tanker, train, or pipeline. Gas can be sent only by pipelines unless there are in place the complex and costly systems for liquefying it at one end and deliquefying it at the other. Russia had little capacity for that in the nineties. Though worth less than oil and more difficult to transport, gas would nevertheless prove a formidable instrument in the political arena, since Europe was hooked on Russian natural gas to heat homes and run industries.

Oil is the big moneymaker. In time it along with gas would account for some 50 percent of Russian federal government revenue. Balancing the budget was entirely dependent on the price of oil. It was a dangerous situation and everyone knew it, but in the chaos of the nineties you used what you had at hand, and getting through the month was more critical than planning for any future.

A second fundamental difference between gas and oil in Russia was that the Ministry of the Gas Industry had transformed itself into a corporation called Gazprom. Shares in Gazprom could be sold, but the state would remain the majority owner. The more complex oil industry quickly subdivided into ten or so separate entities, which meant that they, unlike Gazprom, could easily be privatized.

In 1995 the Russian government was hurting for money. Nobody was paying their taxes, especially those who had become suddenly and exorbitantly rich. The government's principal source of revenue, oil, had sold for an average of $21.07 in 1994 and wasn't doing much better in 1995 at $22.03. This all set the stage for what Marshall Goldman in his book *Petrostate* describes as "the biggest and most controversial transfer of wealth ever seen in history," which elsewhere in the book he terms more succinctly "a massive scam." That transfer, blandly known as Loans for Shares, was brilliantly simple and worked like this: the banks would loan the state money with state enterprises as collateral. Fine, except for one thing: "Everyone knew from the beginning that there was little likelihood that the state would be able to collect the taxes it needed to repay the bank loans. How could it when the oligarchs themselves and their companies, as well as their banks, were among the largest tax delinquents?"

And so the state would have to auction off its holdings to pay off its loans.

As for the auctions, almost all of them turned out to be rigged. Foreigners and most other viable bidders were excluded from the bidding. With the number of bidders sharply limited, it is no wonder that in virtually every case, the auction winner turned out to be the bank running the auction itself, or its straw or accomplice, and for a price that barely covered the amount of the loan. It was part of the Loans for Shares scheme that allowed Mikhail Khodorkovsky and his Menatep Bank to end up as the owners of Yukos . . . bidding a mere $309 million. (Not pocket change but cheap for even a poorly operating oil company. It soon had a market value of $15 billion.)

Scammed though it was, the state was not entirely a fool either. Yeltsin and his team had good reason to go along with Loans for Shares aside from the revenue stream it produced. Privatizing the oil industry would break up the "red directorship," the party bosses who controlled the industry and were not about to go gently into history's good night. The support of the oligarchs was essential to Yeltsin in the 1996 elections, in which it was feared that an already weary, cynical electorate would veer hard left to the Communist Party.

Khodorkovsky was a man with a tendency to get religion. Beneath his placid, "corporate" exterior, he had a deep need to find something to which he could dedicate himself utterly. He became an apostle of the gospel of wealth. Suddenly it was obvious—the most glorious thing in the world was to be gloriously rich. Khodorkovsky even went so far as to say that there had to be something wrong with a person who did not aspire to be an oligarch. Yet he was not oblivious to the transformations that had occurred within himself, which he could regard with distance and irony: "If the old me met the new me, he'd shoot him."

But Khodorkovsky was undergoing other changes as well, some exactly those hoped for and predicted by the young team around Yeltsin busily dismantling the old command-and-control Soviet economy. Because of its own internal logic, ownership engenders a desire for law and order to protect property. Pride of ownership can in turn engender a desire to maintain and improve what is owned. This is, of course, far from automatic—many in Russia were content to rip off and resell and the devil take the hindmost. Most were not like the American robber barons whose extravagant wealth was at least based on the building of something—steel mills, banks, railroads. But Chubais and Yeltsin really believed in the market, in its power, over time, to shape mentality and behavior.

Khodorkovsky was someone who reacted in the very way the reformers hoped. He saw his newly acquired oil company, Yukos, as a challenge to his powers to envision and enact. A maximalist in the best Russian tradition, he strove to build the biggest, most efficient, most Western and transparent oil company in the country. He was loyal and generous to those around him, but woe to anyone who got in his way. At Yukos headquarters he had closed-circuit TV secretly installed to monitor the workers and abruptly fired a third who had been found not up to snuff. Later, there would be rumors and innuendos about Yukos-sponsored violence, but no evidence was ever brought forward, nothing ever proved.

Khodorkovsky faced many obstacles, not least of which was himself. The veteran Siberian oilmen could only snort with contempt at a city slicker with aviator glasses and a lounge-lizard mustache. He changed his look to something more modern and corporate, losing the mustache and switching to transparent-framed glasses. He fired some of those old-timers and won some over. He had come into the oil business just as it was hitting bottom. Production in 1996 was just about half what it had been in the peak Soviet year of 1987. Urals crude hit a low of $8.23 a barrel on June 15. This, however, also had its good side—the price for exports was now quite competitive, and since little oil was consumed at home, most of production could be exported in return for hard currency.

After the financial crisis of 1998 oil prices began an almost linear upward surge. Though Khodorkovsky's fortunes as the head of Yukos were of course bound up with the price of oil, he still charted his own course. He broke cleanly with the Soviet past, refusing to have his company play the paternalistic role of providing social services like housing, hospitals, and schools. He brought in Western technology and specialists. He used computers to control the flow of oil and revenue, which had been haphazard, to say the least, under the Soviets.

During the financial crash of 1998, which essentially bankrupted the country, Yukos survived for two reasons—the improving cash flow it had from its newly streamlined computer-monitored production system, and Khodorkovsky's creative reneging on his own financial obligations. Like many other banks in the country, Khodorkovsky's Menatep went belly-up during the crisis, but not before he had switched its few remaining assets to a financial entity he owned in St. Petersburg. The Western banks that had loaned Khodorkovsky tens of millions of dollars were left holding the bag. A bewildering labyrinth of offshore shell companies guaranteed that he would always be several steps ahead of his creditors. Other, less subtle tricks were also used: in May 1999 a truck containing 607 boxes of Menatep documents somehow ended up in the Dubna River.

But Yukos was the end that justified the means. A year and a half after the financial crisis of 1998 its income had doubled and it costs fallen sharply. By the end of 2000 Yukos was holding $2.8 billion in cash.

But other things had also changed by the year 2000. Vladimir

Putin had completed his unlikely rise to power, "a suave cop who had lucked into a big job" as Strobe Talbott, deputy secretary of state under Clinton, had described him. Russian society was sick of the turmoil and larceny of the Yeltsin years. There was a palpable yearning for law and order. The bloom was definitely off the idea of democracy and privatization, foreign-enough-sounding words to a Russian ear anyway.

Not only was there a sentiment against the 1990s and its disappointments, but a doctrine had emerged in the late nineties that would in time put Khodorkovsky and Putin on a collision course. In those years there was an odd confluence in the thinking of Putin and the security types for whom order and control were paramount, and of liberal economists, who wanted a free market. At that point no contradiction was seen between a strong state and a free market. On the contrary, only a strong state could guarantee the regularity and tranquillity needed for markets to function. And there could be no state power if the state did not control the country's natural resources.

As Putin said: "Russia will not soon become, if ever, a second edition of the USA or England. . . . In our country the state, its institutions and structures have always played an exceptionally important role in the country's life and people. For the Russian people a strong state is not an anomaly, not something to be struggled against, but on the contrary a guarantor of order, the initiator and chief moving force of all changes."

In late July of 2000 the newly elected president of Russia, Vladimir Vladimirovich Putin, invited twenty-one oligarchs to the Kremlin to deliver his message: Keep your money, pay your taxes, stay out of politics. Khodorkovsky, one of those present, was probably not much impressed by Putin. He was short and had some of officialdom's grayness about him, and his ascent seemed more a matter of dumb luck than of smart moves. Putin would soon prove perilous to "misunderestimate."

By 2000 oil prices had doubled since hitting bottom in the years 1996–98. The government was deriving increased income from taxing sales rather than profits, which the Russians were masters at concealing. And then again the Kremlin had to ask itself: why tax oil companies when you could own them?

Yukos was growing richer all the time and its CEO, Mikhail Khodorkovsky, was increasingly an irritant for Putin on every level, from the personal to the political. He did not show the respect due a president. He took the wrong tone. Something haughty and dismissive entered his demeanor, especially when China and its voracious appetite for energy were concerned. Khodorkovsky wanted to build a pipeline to China, and to Putin's objections he replied, in front of others: "Vladimir Vladimirovich, you do not understand the importance of developing relations with China."

Khodorkovsky was by then the richest man in all Russia; he met with heads of state and other prominent figures like Dick Cheney and Bill Gates; he could say what he thought when he wished. Foreign advisers then and later would be astounded and appalled by his overweening pride. Writing of the pipeline-to-China project, Marshall Goldman, usually one preferring graphs to exclamations, said: "What arrogance. Khodorkovsky and Yukos were acting as if they were sovereign powers." If that is what an American professor thought, what could the heavyweights in the Russian government and oil industry have been thinking? We know the answer. Sergei Bogdanchikov, the head of the state-owned oil company Rosneft, said of Khodorkovsky and those around him: "Three days in Butyrki Prison and they'll understand who's the king of the forest."

Khodorkovsky himself was not oblivious to the dangers he faced, saying: "There are worse things than going to jail."

It took a little more than three years for the showdown with Putin to play out—from that initial meeting in the Kremlin to Khodorkovsky's arrest in October 2003. In that time Khodorkovsky had made two moves which caused his supreme self-confidence to morph into reckless hubris. Without so much as informing Putin, he began negotiating with Chevron to merge and form the world's largest oil company. If Khodorkovsky's deal with Chevron went through, it could provide him with a moat of defense and security—the Kremlin might go after a Russian company, but it would think twice before going after the Chevron-Yukos merger. There was one outstanding and time-consuming detail in the negotiations—Yukos's share in the merger. Chevron's CEO, Dave O'Reilly, offered 37.6 percent. Khodorkovsky would not budge from his demand of 43.5 percent. That difference of 5.9 percent would cost Khodorkovsky ten years in prison.

In the meantime Khodorkovsky had also been doing precisely what Putin had expressly warned the oligarchs against—meddling in politics. Khodorkovsky backed opposition leaders, bought the votes of members of the parliament, and even hinted to the German magazine *Der Spiegel* in April 2003 that he himself might have ambitions to be president or prime minister. As his own mother would reportedly say later: "He forgot what country he lived in."

Typically, the KGB gives warnings, and Putin was old-school KGB. In the best Russian tradition he quoted from the national poet Alexander Pushkin at a Kremlin press conference while discussing Khodorkovsky and the oil companies' attempts to buy influence in the Duma. "Some are gone and some are far away," quoted Putin, hinting that arrest, exile, even execution, could await those who defied the Kremlin.

The hints weren't taken, the allusions went uncaught. On October 25, 2003, Khodorkovsky's private plane, on which he was the sole passenger, made a refueling stop in Novosibirsk. Masked men armed with automatic weapons, a unit of the elite antiterrorist Alpha Brigade, stormed the plane, handcuffed Khodorkovsky, and placed a hood over his head. Two hours later he was flown to Moscow to begin his odyssey of Russian prisons. Putin had reminded Khodorkovsky what country he was living in and who was the king of the forest.

"Give us the man and we'll make the case" was an old KGB saying. Khodorkovsky was charged with tax evasion, fraud, embezzlement. Since the verdict was a foregone conclusion, no great care went into finessing the details of the case. Certain of them were simply absurd—in some years the taxes Khodorkovsky was accused of evading exceeded the total revenue earned. Khodorkovsky was sentenced to eight years in Prison Colony YaG-14/10, near the Chinese border, founded in 1967 to mine uranium.

The meaning of the Khodorkovsky affair was clear to all—anyone who challenged Putin's authority in word or deed was subject to severe penalty. The era of privatization was definitively over. The state would now be the major player in oil as it already was in gas. In an auction worthy of the oligarchs themselves, Yukos ended up the property of the state oil company Rosneft.

There was no general sympathy for Khodorkovsky among his fellow businessmen, some of whom now quickly prepared to leave the country before their turn came. And of course the masses greeted the news with a sardonic grin. A few members of the dissident intelligentsia like Andrei Sakharov's widow, Elena Bonner, spoke out in defense of Khodorkovsky, considering him a political prisoner because the law had been selectively used as an instrument of repression against him and sharply condemning Amnesty International for not coming to his aid. Others, like Boris Kagarlitsky in his book *Back in the USSR*, took a more jaundiced view: "It was exactly because the directors of Yukos did not differ from the tenants of the Kremlin that the ruling clique considered them to be really dangerous. And therefore took stringent measures. Khodorkovsky is a political prisoner only in the medieval sense, as when great lords and princes were jailed in the Bastille or the Tower of London after failed plots."

A rising tide of oil prices had lifted all boats, Khodorkovsky's, Putin's, Russia's. Putin of course deserves no credit for the price rise, though before a battle Napoleon would say, "I know all my generals are good, but tell me which are the lucky ones." And by arresting Khodorkovsky and incorporating most of Yukos into state-controlled Rosneft, Putin did assure a torrent of revenue for the state, some portion of which was well used and wisely saved, though billions of course were "reprivatized."

The figures are impressive. Thirty percent of the country lived in poverty in 1999, only 13 percent by 2008, the end of Putin's second term. Real incomes rose 140 percent and GDP per capita went from $5,951 in 1999 to $20,276 in 2008. The dollar value of the Russian stock market in 2000 was $74 billion and by 2006 it was $1 trillion. For the first time in its history Russia had a middle class.

At this point Putin was still taking the sound advice of his economics minister, Alexei Kudrin, who had pushed hard for a sovereign wealth fund as protection from any future calamity. Even Khodorkovsky writing from prison had said: "Putin is probably not a liberal or a democrat, but he is more liberal and more democratic than seventy percent of the population."

Showing a surplus, Russia was paying its bills and its debts. In fact, the five years between Khodorkovsky's arrest in 2003 and 2008 were very good years indeed for Putin, buoyed as they were by the rising price of oil, which on July 11, 2008, peaked at an all-time high of $147.27. Putin had control of gas, oil, and television, which for him meant control of Russia. Pipsqueak dissident intellectuals would be allowed a few newspapers, a radio station, the Internet, none of which was widespread or powerful enough to make much of a difference. Putin had been reelected in 2004 with some 71 percent of the vote, a figure that reflected his control of the airwaves and his genuine popularity, not to mention the self-interest of those prospering under his rule.

At the time of Putin's reelection, the state depended on the sale of gas and oil for 30 percent of its revenues. By 2013 that percentage would rise to 41 percent. It was clear to all that Russia was too beholden to oil. There had been no choice but to use what you had at hand when the task was to stabilize the country and revitalize the economy. Essentially that had been achieved in Putin's first term, ending in 2004. With his domestic rivals safely disposed of, that would have been the ideal moment for Putin to take stock and make changes, to begin the only solution for Russia's long-term viability—a diversification of the economy.

In 1999, before he was president, Putin published an article, "Russia on the Threshold," in which he criticized the Soviet system's "excessive emphasis on the development of the commodities sector and defense industry." Writing some ten years later, future president Dmitri Medvedev took a more emotional tone when speaking of Russia's "humiliating dependence on raw materials." Medvedev, whatever his weakness, was adept at stating the questions of the day in plain, clear Russian, unlike Putin, who went from abstract bureaucratese to vulgar street lingo without skipping a beat. "Should a primitive economy based on raw materials and endemic corruption accompany us into the future?" asked Medvedev. The answer to that question was obviously no, and the answer to the eternal Russian question of What is to be done? was also simple—diversify. But how, into what? Use Russia's highly educated population to make the high-value-added smart products that are the great wealth creators of the early twenty-first century.

And in fact Putin saw just such a solution—nanotechnology. First theorized in 1959 in "Plenty of Room at the Bottom," an article by the madcap Nobel laureate Richard Feynman, nanotechnology has been defined as the "ability to see, manipulate and manufacture things on a scale of 1 to 100 nanometers. A nanometer is one-billionth of a meter; a sheet of paper is about 100,000 nanometers thick." This is the level of molecules and atoms. In 2007 the Russian government allocated $7.7 billion for the development of nanotechnology over the next eight years. Often called Russia's most hated man, the survivor of four assassination attempts, former privatization chief Anatoly Chubais, his signature red hair less vivid with age, was chosen to head up the nano project, with the actual work done by the prestigious Kurchatov Institute, which had played a critical role in the development of the Soviet atomic bomb. "Nanotechnology is an activity for which this government will not grudge funding," said Putin. "The only question is that this work should be well organized and effective, yielding practical results." There were many possible practical applications, with, as Putin stressed, "super-effective weapons systems" not least among them.

Hopes ran high. "Nanotechnology will be the [foundation] for all institutes in a science-driven economy," proclaimed Mikhail Kovalchuk, director of the Kurchatov Institute and described by *Wired* magazine as "expansive to the point of dreaminess." "Nanotechnology will be the driving force of the Russian economy," he added, "if it can overcome the legacy of the recent past." An enormous if.

Like a third-world country leapfrogging from pay phones to cell phones, Russia would, to use a Soviet expression, "overtake and surpass the West."

The Soviet educational system was a formidable machine that mass-produced engineers and scientists. The hard sciences like physics and mathematics—unlike, say, history and economics—had posed no challenge to Marxist ideology. This is not entirely true either, for some sciences, like cybernetics, were for a time viewed as inherently bourgeois, and under Stalin genetics was effectively hijacked by a charlatan named Lysenko, who preached that acquired characteristics could be inherited, leading the great nuclear physicist Igor

Tamm to publicly challenge him by saying, "If that is so, why are women still born virgins?"

The hard sciences also of course had their very practical applications—Sputniks, Kalashnikovs, H-bombs—and were always well supported, the luminaries numbering among the elite. That changed with the fall of the Soviet Union. Science was barely funded by a government that could itself barely make payroll. The brain drain was so severe that it even became a national security issue for the United States, which began paying Russian nuclear scientists to stay at their jobs in their own country and not sell their expertise to rogue nations like Iran and North Korea.

In the new dispensation defined by mere survival at one end and get-rich-quick at the other, science wasn't sexy and didn't pay. Wanting to change that, nanotech head Chubais declared at a video conference with eight technical institutes: "As the industry expands to annual sales volumes of 900 billion rubles [$28 billion], which is our target, we will need 150,000 positions to be filled." One hundred people had graduated with degrees in nanotechnology in the previous year, 2008. Chubais did not mention where the other 149,900 specialists were going to come from. Like Kovalchuk, he too seemed to be suffering from a certain "dreaminess." Questioned about his progress by Putin in April 2009, he replied: "The prospects make one dizzy!" He did go on to list some areas in which some initial work had been done, satisfying Putin, who agreed that these "technologies have brilliant prospects. . . . Now, I see you are really making progress."

Fast-forward to 2013 and a grand scandal à la russe. Of the original $5 billion to $7 billion of state money, $40 million had vanished into shell companies, and another $450 million was spent on a silicon chip factory that proved inoperational. All told, something like $1.5 billion had gone down the rabbit hole. The joke about nanotech was, the more money you invest in it, the smaller the result. Russians who still hated Chubais from the shock-therapy privatization campaign of the early nineties were now calling for his head. Putin defended him, though tepidly, saying ineptitude was not theft, while also hinting darkly that some of Chubais's aides and employees had been CIA operatives seeking to disrupt scientific progress in Russia.

Rusnano, as the state-controlled organization is officially known, was also hit hard by the sanctions imposed after the annexation of Crimea and the incursion into Ukraine. Alcoa withdrew from a project to produce wear-resistant nano coating for drill pipe to be used in harsh environments like the Arctic's. That was a double loss for Russia because it hurt not only the nano but also the petro sector, which needs foreign expertise and investment because Russia's fields are now "browning," meaning all the easy oil has been taken.

The failure of nanotech, thus far at least, finds its explanation in a saying by former prime minister Viktor Chernomyrdin, known for his savvy malapropisms: "We were hoping for better but got same as always."

The real fault, however, is Putin's. In 2004–8, with oil prices at their highest and no real enemy on the horizon, he had a unique opportunity to transform Russia from a petrostate into a sleeker, smarter twenty-first-century economy, one that was knowledge-based. Such an economy would have required more highly educated people and would have created greater wealth among a greater number. And that dynamic combination of conditions—education, wealth, a sense of being a stakeholder—could have been the matrix out of which, by its own mysterious laws of development, a new sense of national identity could have emerged, delivering Russia from the zombie-like state it has been in since the fall of the USSR. Helping to craft a transformation of that magnitude would have meant crafting himself a major place in history, possibly even one alongside the other two great Vladimirs—Grand Prince Vladimir of Kiev, who brought Christianity to the country, and Vladimir Lenin, who brought it Communism. But he didn't.

For Putin to have risked transforming Russia from a petrostate into a twenty-first-century diversified economy would have created a hazardous transition in which his own grip on power could have been lost. Power would have had to be delegated and decentralized, endangering Putin's position at the apex of the "power vertical." His various constituencies from pensioners to power elite must feel secure and must receive their accustomed share of the wealth. Such a system runs on loyalty and corruption. It has been said of Russia that the system is not corrupt but rather corruption is the system. And that is because no one feels a stake in the system, which inspires no sense of solidity, dependability, longevity—it can all be gone in the blink of history's eye. And Putin's chance to truly reform his country was also gone in the blink of that same eye.

Oil is termed a wasting asset because, once used, it can never be replaced. Still, some substitutes can be found. It is time that is the ultimate wasting asset. And the one Putin so wrongfully squandered.

7

THE HEART OF THE MATTER: UKRAINE

*In geopolitics, the past never dies, and there
is no modern world.*

—ROBERT D. KAPLAN

"You have to understand, George," said Putin to Bush at the 2008 NATO summit in Bucharest, "Ukraine isn't even a real country."

It is not only Putin but millions of other Russians, from workers to intellectuals, who share that sentiment. Discussing Russians and Ukrainians, even former president Mikhail Gorbachev said: "It might not be a scientific fact but we are one people."

That attitude has two very different aspects—one is a mélange of history, mythology, and emotion, while the other is cool, practical, pure geopolitik.

For generations it was drummed into every Russia schoolchild's head that Kiev is the mother of Russian cities. In fact, Russia's two great foundation myths are centered on Kiev and Ukraine. The ancient Chronicles report that around 860 the forever-warring Russian princes sent an envoy to the Vikings with the following plea: "Our land is vast and rich, but there is no order in it. Come and rule over us." The second sentence—"Come and rule over us"—is disingenuous. In all probability, the Vikings had already conquered the country, and the chronicler was using verbal sleight of hand to turn invasion into invitation.

The other foundation myth concerns the conversion of Grand Prince Vladimir of Kiev to Eastern Orthodox Christianity in 988. Vladimir himself was baptized in Crimea, and more than a thousand years later Putin would use that fact as one of his justifications for the annexation of that territory, calling that land "sacred." When word went out for the mass baptism of his subjects in Kiev, Vladimir made himself quite clear on the point: "If anyone does not come, let him consider himself my enemy."

Had it not been for Genghis Khan's Mongol Horde that overran the lands of the Eastern and Southern Slavs in the early 1200s, it might well have been a Ukrainian leader confiding to President Bush: "You know, George, Russia is not even a real country."

The some 250 years between Vladimir's baptism and the violent arrival of the Mongols is claimed by both Ukrainians and Russians as their happy childhood. Subsequent miseries may have cast too bright a light on the whitewashed walls and golden cupolas of ancient Kiev, yet contemporaries describe the city as architecturally splendid. The art of icon painting swiftly reached a high level. Bards with stringed instruments sang epics that still read well on the page. An enlightened system of laws was in effect, with fines playing a greater role than corporal punishment or incarceration. A Kievan princess married King Henry I of France and, proving the only literate one in the family, began signing her name to official documents to which the king would append his royal, analphabetic mark.

The main problems were discord among the princes—no order in the land—and the still only intermittent raids from the horsemen of the Central Asian steppe.

Speaking of Bukhara's rulers, "they must be very sinful," said

Genghis Khan, "otherwise God would not have sent a punishment like me down upon" them. The Mongols' usual MO was to offer a city the chance to surrender, and in return for 10 percent of their wealth and their sworn obedience, the people's lives and their city would be spared. But sometimes the Mongols would simply destroy a city without even first making any such offer so that the terror of that example would spread like prairie fire. That appears to be what happened to Kiev, which was torched and sacked. A victory feast was arranged—still alive, the captured Kievan princes were laid out on the ground, then covered with planks and rugs on top of which banquet tables and benches were placed. The Mongols then held their victory feast to the music of screams and breaking bones.

Much of the surviving population fled north to other cities or into the forests, where the Mongols lost their advantages of horsemanship and marksmanship with their long and excellently engineered bows (even their arrows were notched in such a way as to make it impossible for the enemy to reuse them.)

The Mongols disliked forests and cities. Genghis Khan, who said that he "hated luxury," thought a Mongol best off either in the saddle, using his stirrups, a Mongol invention, to fire more accurately, or in an encampment of yurts on the open steppe. That is how Crimea was originally settled by Tatars, a tribe allied with the Mongols. The Russians preferred the term Tatar, so the years of Mongol domination are called the "Tatar yoke." Under Stalin the entire Tatar population of the Crimea was exiled en masse to Siberia for supposed treason, and it took the Crimean Tatars the better part of twenty years to get back home. They are now suffering under Russian rule in annexed Crimea and have been involved in partisan-like tactics, e.g., the destruction of four electricity pylons in late November 2015 that put the entire Crimea in the dark. In Russia all stories are old stories, the problem is they won't stay old.

A mystic who worshipped the Eternal Blue Sky, Genghis Khan

was quite tolerant when it came to local religions, having none of the iconoclasm of the Kievans themselves. He was known as much for his tolerance as for his savagery. Gibbon, in his *The History of the Decline and Fall of the Roman Empire*, said of Genghis Khan's tolerance: "The Catholic inquisitors of Europe who defended nonsense by cruelty, might have been confounded by the example of a barbarian, who anticipated the lessons of philosophy and established by his laws a system of pure theism and perfect toleration."

That "perfect toleration" meant that the Orthodox Church now began to play a role as the keeper of historical memory, especially in the Chronicles compiled by monks, and as a haven of uplifting beauty amid the scorched earth. In Soviet times the Russian Orthodox Church would again offer a sanctuary of beauty amid the brutalist gray-cement architecture of advanced socialism. And it is now one of the pillars that supports the House of Putin.

The Mongols dominated Russia for something like two and a half centuries (1240–1500) but continued to pose a serious danger well after that. St. Basil's Cathedral in Red Square, the very symbol of Russia, was built in the 1550s by Tsar Ivan the Terrible to commemorate his victory over the Tatar stronghold of Kazan in 1552.

Apart from the words for money and customs control, the Mongols left little trace in Russia's culture or language, but they changed its history and mentality. The force of the Mongol invasion shifted the center of Slav civilization from south to north. Eventually Moscow, until those times a tiny settlement of no importance whatsoever on the bend of a muddy river, emerged as the new power center under the various Ivans of the sixteenth century, the fourth of whom, known as the Terrible, was also the first to assume the title of tsar. The south languished over the centuries to such an extent that when Catherine the Great entered on her grand tour of her newly acquired lands in Ukraine and Crimea in the late eighteenth century she was simply shocked by Kiev, calling it "abominable."

Moscow and Muscovite Russia were the historical success stories, of that there can be no doubt. The southern lands were called *ukrainia*, meaning "borderlands." The Mongol domination taught Russia the lesson that Putin summed up laconically as "the weak get beaten." The state must be strong and centralized; top-down one-man rule was the most effective model. The state alone could provide security and order. The state was a fortress, a kremlin, to which people fled in time of attack. And if attack came once, it could come again. From any direction, any nation—humanistic France, scientific Germany. A case could be made that after the Mongol invasion and rule all Russian politics were post-traumatic.

The Mongols left the Russians with a culture of invasion. The driving force of Russian civilization became the avoidance of and preparation for the next invasion. This has induced suspicion and conservatism, xenophobia, paranoia, and an imperialism that seeks to buffer the heartland with as much territory as possible.

In an invasion-minded culture special attention is paid to the enemy within, the traitors who would open the gates to the enemy. The free city-states like Novgorod that resisted Moscow's centralizing will were subjected to intense, focused cruelty. Ivan the Terrible created the *oprichniki*: black-clad horsemen answerable only to the tsar, their symbols the dog's head that sniffs out treason and the broom that sweeps it away. They were the world's first secret police, the archetype and granddaddy of them all, including the KGB that Vladimir Putin so longed to join in his youth.

Russia became imperialistic as a defense against invasion, not that any nation worried overmuch about justifying its land grabs back then. Harried by Swedes, Lithuanians, and Poles from the north and west, steppe tribes and Turks from the south and east, Russians considered every acre of land won not only possession but protection. Russia became a nation-state and an empire at the same time; imperialism was thus fused with its very sense of identity.

Inevitably, there would be some people who saw no place for themselves in the new Russia forming around Moscow. Some of the more adventurous sorts joined the expeditions to the east, Siberia, where the natives were few and far between and easy to subdue. But most of the freebooters and free spirits who rejected Kremlin rule and, later, the imposition of serfdom headed south to the wide-open spaces of the steppe, the grasslands they called the "wild fields." The weather was better, the black earth richer, and Moscow's arm could not yet reach that far. People lived a life something like that of the early Romans, every man a farmer and a soldier. They won the respect of the fierce Turkic-speaking nomadic tribes they encountered in battle, who called these transplanted northerners "free warriors," Kazaks (Cossacks), a name they took on for themselves. A heterogeneous bunch, their numbers included "escaped serfs, indebted nobles, defrocked priests, pioneers, fortune-hunters, fugitives of various sorts."

By the mid-1500s, the time of Ivan the Terrible, Mongols were no longer the problem. Poland was the problem. Having combined with the then good-sized Lithuania to form a commonwealth that stretched from the Baltic to the Black Sea, Poland routinely trounced Russia and put Moscow to the torch on more than one occasion.

Poland was part of the Catholic West, even calling itself *antemurale Christianitatis*, the outer wall of Christendom, protecting Europe from savages like Mongols and Russians. Poland went through the developmental stages of European civilization, participating vigorously in the Renaissance, the Reformation, the Counter-Reformation, and the Enlightenment. The Mongol invasion not only had cut Russia in two, north and south, but had cut it off from Europe and its great fugue of development. Leonardo da Vinci had lived and died before Ivan the Terrible was even born.

Polish domination over much of Ukraine had deleterious effects.

The Ukrainian elite adopted "the faith, language and manners of the ruling Poles," Ukrainian becoming the "language of serfs and servants."

But the Cossacks rebelled against Polish rule, rising up periodically against the Poles and the Jewish middlemen who were used by the ruling classes to collect rents and debts, thereby deflecting anger onto them. The greatest Cossack rebellion of all, the 1648 uprising, was led by Hetman (Chieftain) Bohdan Khmelnitsky, who slaughtered Jews and Poles in great numbers, making him a heroic freedom fighter to this day in Ukraine, while for Jews he remains a figure of biblical evil like Haman.

A few years into the uprising Khmelnitsky was deserted by his Tatar allies (steppe politics also made for strange bedfellows) and faced a stark choice: defeat by the Poles or alliance with Muscovite Russia.

In January 1654, in a small town near Kiev called Pereyaslav, Hetman Bohdan Khmelnitsky formally swore Ukraine's allegiance and union with Moscow. For many years the Ukrainian national anthem asked:

> Oh Bohdan, Bohdan,
> Our great Hetman,
> Why did you give Ukraine
> To the wretched Muscovites?

Except for the briefest of intervals in the twentieth century during times of war and upheaval, Ukraine was not so much ruled by Russia as it had become an integral part of it. It was "to Russians what Ireland and Scotland were to the English—not an imperial possession, like Canada or India, but part of the irreducible centre, home."

Ukraine was a county, not a country. The Ukrainian language almost died out like Gaelic. In any case, the Russians considered it only an amusing dialect spoken only by yokels. A classic quip has it that a language is a dialect with an army and a navy. But for the eastern Slavs, for whom language and literature assumed an especial importance, that quip might be amended to read: A language is a dialect with an army, a navy, and a great poet. Russia, Poland, and Ukraine all got their great national poet at roughly the same time: Russia's Alexander Pushkin (1799–1837), Poland's Adam Mickie-wicz (1798–1855), and Ukraine's Taras Shevchenko (1814–61).

Shevchenko, who would turn the patois of servant and serf into poetry, was himself born a serf and soon orphaned. He seemed fated to a life of dreary and anonymous labor. But he had a passion for drawing and would exercise it with whatever was at hand, a lump of coal, a stick of chalk. Taken to St. Petersburg, he drew copies of the statues in the Summer Garden. His talents were noticed and encour-aged by other artists and writers, Ukrainian and Russian alike. They took up a collection, and in 1838, when he was twenty-four, they bought his freedom for the sum of 2,500 rubles. Shevchenko was delighted, even giddy, with his new freedom, cutting a chic swath in St. Petersburg nightlife in his new coat, for which he had paid 100 rubles, and thus we know that the exact worth of the freedom of a human being in the Russia of that time was twenty-five coats.

Now he devoted more time to his poetry, "an odd mixture of pas-toralism, xenophobia and self-hatred. His themes are the beauty of Ukraine's landscape, her lost Cossack greatness and her shame in la-boring under the Russian and Polish yokes. Though Russians, Poles (and, embarrassingly, Jews) all get short shrift, most of his bile is directed at the treachery and complacency of the Ukrainians them-selves."

Success and excitement were immediate. The Ukrainians had their poet.

Shevchenko now moved between St. Petersburg and Kiev, where in 1846 he joined an underground discussion group that espoused the abolition of serfdom and a democratic confederation of Slavs headed by Ukraine. As was nearly always the case in both Tsarist and Soviet times, such groups were infiltrated and betrayed by an informer. Shevchenko was arrested in 1847 and dispatched to St. Petersburg. There, in a rare honor, he was interrogated by the head of the secret police, Count Alexei Orlov, who concluded: "Shevchenko has acquired among his friends the reputation of a brilliant Ukrainian writer, and so his poems are doubly harmful and dangerous. His favorite poems could be disseminated in Ukraine, inducing thought about the alleged happy times of the Hetman era, the exigency of a return to those times, and the possibility of Ukraine's existence as a separate state."

Socially, creatively, amorously, Shevchenko had enjoyed life to the fullest in his nine years of freedom between his liberation and his arrest. He would spend the next ten years in exile near the border with Kazakhstan. In his own hand Tsar Nicholas I, so absolute a monarch that he considered criticism sedition and praise impertinence, added a note to the paperwork on the poet's exile: "Under the strictest surveillance, prohibited from writing or painting."

But as Tsar Nicholas himself had once exclaimed: "I don't rule Russia, ten thousand clerks do!" And the local clerks and officials in Shevchenko's place of exile on the Ural River were only too glad to have their provincial boredom alleviated by welcoming a celebrity into their midst. Shevchenko painted and wrote without much intrusion at all, and was able to live in private quarters and wear civilian clothes.

After ten years of exile, Shevchenko was freed by the new, more liberal Tsar Alexander II on condition that he register with the police and "not misuse his talent." With his typically Ukrainian walrus mustache and Astrakhan hat, Shevchenko once again became a fixture on the St. Petersburg literary scene, appearing at readings with luminaries like Dostoevsky and Turgenev.

In his most famous poem, "Testament," he asks to be buried on the steppe but declares that he will not leave his grave for heaven and will "know nothing of God" until Ukraine has risen up against the tyrants, watered its rivers with their blood, and finally joined "the family of the free."

On March 10, 1861, he died after a night of caroling and carousing at the age of forty-seven.

Shevchenko's life was a drama of freedom gained and freedom lost, then freedom gained again, that would become every bit as iconic to his fellow countrymen as his work itself. In his youth he had felt that both he and Ukraine were doubly unfree, as serfs and as subjects of a foreign master, the Moskali, as the Russians were called with hatred and disdain. All the serfs of the Russian empire were freed around the time of Shevchenko's death in 1861 (two years before the slaves in America), but that did not change Ukraine's subject status one whit. The dream would remain national liberation. Freedom, however, proved as elusive for Ukraine as it had for Shevchenko.

In the four years between the fall of tsarism and the establishment of Communist rule in 1921, Ukraine made three failed attempts at securing its independence. After the last tsar, Nicholas II, abdicated in February 1917, Ukrainians by the tens of thousands took to the streets holding banners of blue and yellow, the national colors, and pictures of Shevchenko. An independent government was formed and lasted a year until internal squabbling and Red artillery put an end to it. A second attempt was made in the western city of Lviv, whose fortunes had changed so often that it had four names—Lviv (Ukrainian), Lvov (Russian), Lwow (Polish), and Lemberg (German)—causing the locals to say: "We don't travel to Europe. Europe travels to us!" The attempt at forming an independent government in Lviv failed in much less time, falling victim to a shortage of cohesion and an excess of enemies. Guerrillas would, however, fight on for years.

Out of their diplomatic depth, the Ukrainians got very short shrift at the peace talks in Versailles, unlike Poland, which was better equipped diplomatically, more European, and viewed as a better buffer against any new dangers from the east. So newly independent

Poland got a part of western Ukraine, and the rest of the country would in time fall under Moscow's control and become a Soviet republic. It all left a very bitter taste.

But no doubt Ukraine would have been more than content with the defeats and indignities it suffered in those years if it had even a moment's foretaste of the nightmares soon to come.

The Soviet twenties were relatively tranquil. Lenin allowed the return of small enterprise, which brought goods back to the shops and added some color and variety to daily life. The arts flourished, there being too many other immediate problems for the authorities to deal with. Meanwhile, practically unnoticed, described by some later as a "gray blur," Joseph Stalin, the former strike organizer of the Baku oil fields, was gradually rising through the party's ranks, taking on the tedious tasks that the other, more romantic revolutionaries felt were beneath them but which allowed him to grant favors and build constituencies. Lenin died in 1924, possibly nudged along by Stalin, who was in charge of his medical care. By 1929 Stalin's archrival for power, Leon Trotsky, had been exiled from the country. The shops were closed, the artists silenced, or worse, instructed.

Officially, the Soviet Union was the land of the workers and the peasants as symbolized by the hammer and sickle. The truth, however, was that while the workers tended to be progressive, "politically conscious," to use a term of the time, the peasants tended to be recalcitrant and reactionary, especially the wealthier ones known as "kulaks," meaning "fists." The Russian peasants were bad enough, but the Ukrainians were even worse. Not only were they greedy, benighted, and obstinate, they were nationalistic as well, preferring an independent Ukraine to one still dominated after centuries by Moscow and the Moskali.

Stalin and the Stalinists saw themselves as social engineers. A class that obstructed progress was ultimately no different from an outcropping that impeded the flow of a river needed for hydroelectric power. The solution was the same in both cases: remove the obstacle.

The Russian peasants were forced to collectivize in the early thirties, moving from small family plots to large collective or state-run agricultural enterprises. A special solution was created for the peasants of Ukraine—artificial famine, known in Ukrainian as the Holodomor, "murder by hunger." The peasants' food stocks were confiscated, roads were blocked at the beginning of winter, and in the spring the bodies were simply collected, with no damage done to property.

Because of the dishonesty of Soviet statistics and the execution of many statisticians in Stalin's time, we don't have a very exact number of how many Ukrainians perished during the Holodomor. As an example of shifting Soviet statistics, until the time of Gorbachev the figure for Soviet war dead was twenty million, a number that had acquired the tragic charisma of the six million Jews. Suddenly, and without even much fanfare, the official number was changed to twenty-six million. Where had that New York's worth of the dead been all those years?

Some of the same holds true for the Holodomor as well. Making use of census data and the statistics that weren't prohibited, like the production of various shoe sizes, scholars have constructed a general numerical picture of five million victims in Ukraine. Whatever the exact number, there is no doubt that the Holodomor qualifies as one of the great crimes of the twentieth century, that is to say of all history. The fact that this crime is largely unknown in the West and the wider world makes the pain of its memory all the keener.

In June 1941, some ten years after the millions of Ukrainians were starved to death, Hitler's armies attacked the USSR with a three-pronged blitzkrieg strategy of taking Leningrad, Moscow, and Kiev. But Leningrad held off the invaders in what would become a nine-hundred-day siege; Moscow, reinforced by an early winter and Siberian troops, halted the onslaught on the outskirts of the city; Kiev fell. Many Ukrainians went over to the German side on the assumption, reasonable but wrong, that nothing could be worse than Stalin.

The Germans, however, failed to capitalize on Ukrainian sympathy. Erich Koch, head of the Reichskommissariat Ukraine, considered Ukrainians *untermenschen*, "niggers" fit only for "vodka and the whip."

For all the bad blood between Moscow and Kiev, less than ten years after the end of the war, to mark the three hundredth anniversary of the union of Ukraine and Russia, Nikita Khrushchev made Ukraine the magnificent and meaningless present of Crimea. The gift had no more significance than taking money from one pant pocket and putting it in another. Ukraine's "ownership" was largely nominal. It was all one Soviet Union ruled by Moscow, and that Soviet Union would last forever, or at least until the attainment of the ultimate goal of Marxism—the withering away of the state. Still, just to be on the safe side, the city of Sevastopol, where the Black Sea Fleet was stationed, would remain under control of the city of Moscow. The only problem, of course, was that the state did in fact wither away, not in some unimaginably distant future in which people had evolved enough to live without laws and police, but a mere thirty-seven years later, and it didn't so much wither away as suddenly collapse like a building stripped from within by thieves.

On December 1, 1991, more than 90 percent of Ukraine voted for independence from what one legislator called "probably the worst empire in the history of the world," though one might ask how bad an empire could be if you could vote your way out of it.

Impoverished, corrupt, ill-prepared for the real rigors of statehood, Ukraine was now, whether Putin or any of his ilk liked it or not, a real country, a state. Not only that, with its some 4,500 nuclear missiles, Ukraine had suddenly become the world's third-largest nuclear power, in a league with Russia and the United States, far ahead of

China, England, and France. Ukraine, however, did not possess operational control over the missiles—the launch codes remained in Moscow. Still, the nuclear warheads or nuclear material could be reconfigured into other sorts of weapons, and if nuclear material fell into the wrong hands there could be serious trouble, as would become all too apparent in November 1995, when Chechen rebels planted cesium-137 in a large Moscow park, then alerted the media.

According to the 1994 Budapest Memorandum, Ukraine would surrender its nuclear weapons to Russia for dismantlement. In turn, Russia, the United States, and the United Kingdom pledged to "respect Ukrainian independence and sovereignty within its existing borders" and to "refrain from the threat or use of force against Ukraine." The memorandum was, however, not binding like a treaty, as subsequent events would amply demonstrate.

At first Ukraine seemed to have a good chance. It had coal, iron, and the fabled "black earth." The people had the positive, life-affirming energy of the sunny south, as John Steinbeck noted when traveling through back in 1948: "The people in Kiev did not seem to have the dead weariness of the Moscow people. They did not slouch when they walked, their shoulders were back, and they laughed in the street."

But things went bad soon enough. Though the economy righted itself after a long, nasty bout of inflation and a 60 percent drop in GDP in the nineties, Ukraine was still failing at its two principal tasks—state-building and nation-building. The east and west of the country, which had been in agreement about seceding from the USSR, soon found themselves increasingly at odds, splitting along the fault lines of cultural allegiance either to Moscow or toward Kiev, meaning Europe and the West. With a little luck Ukraine might have developed into something like Bulgaria, a largely invisible European country, a destination for adventurous vacationers. There were, however, forces afoot that would make Ukraine the most important country in Europe.

Chief among them was what might be called "Gorby and the angry inch." Though its implications are blurred with denial and duplicity, there is a generally agreed upon version of the event itself. In a 1990 conversation between Soviet leader Gorbachev and American secretary of state James Baker, Baker promised Gorbachev that if he pulled Soviet troops out of East Germany and permitted the peaceful reunion of the two Germanys, NATO, in return, would not move "one inch east."

NATO, of course, moved not inches but hundreds of miles east. This was effectuated by granting membership to three former Soviet republics—Estonia, Latvia, and Lithuania—and seven former Eastern Bloc countries—Poland, Hungary, the Czech Republic, Romania, Bulgaria, Slovakia, and Slovenia between 1999 and 2004. George Kennan, U.S. ambassador to the USSR and author of the containment doctrine that guided U.S. policy throughout the Cold War, called NATO expansion "the most fateful error of American policy in the post-Cold-War era" and foresaw its leading to a resurgence of "nationalistic, anti-Western and militaristic tendencies in Russian opinion."

But of course there were other factors and forces here besides NATO expansionism. The former Soviet Bloc countries were only too happy to take cover behind NATO's shield. Having suffered centuries of Moscow's domination, their desire for freedom and security was only natural. And among those nations there was also a strong sense that the democratic Russia of the nineties was a passing illusion, or as Estonia's president Lennart Meri, saw it, Russia was a malignancy in remission: the Yeltsin era was at best a fleeting opportunity to be seized before Russia relapsed into authoritarianism at home and expansionism abroad.

What gave those formerly Warsaw Pact nations their sense of security was Article 5 of the NATO charter, which states: "The Parties agree that an armed attack against one or more of them in Europe or North America shall be considered an attack against them all."

This meant that the United States and Europe were in the rather odd position of having to risk nuclear armageddon to defend Slovenia.

And of course none of this went over well in Moscow, where Baker's promise had been taken seriously. The obvious rejoinder here is: Next time, get it in writing, pal, or perhaps Samuel Goldwyn's immortal line that a "verbal agreement isn't worth the paper it's written on."

But the obvious rejoinder from Gorbachev and company could be: We were dismantling a nuclear empire and facing one crisis after the other, and did not have the time for all the niceties. Not only that—one's word counts for a great deal in any dealings with Russians, and true partners don't need everything on paper. As Gorbachev himself put it in a recent interview: "The Americans promised that NATO wouldn't move beyond the boundaries of Germany after the Cold War but now half of central and eastern Europe are members, so what happened to their promises. It shows they cannot be trusted."

In the view from the Kremlin, Russia had essentially been out-flanked from the Baltic to the Black Sea by March 2004, when seven former Soviet Bloc nations were admitted into NATO. To lock that ring tight only one more country was needed: Ukraine. So when the Orange Revolution broke out in November 2004 in protest against the rigged presidential elections, Putin could not fail to notice that it came on the heels of the latest round of NATO recruitment in March. Apart from the geopolitical dangers Ukraine's Orange Revolution would subject Russia to, there was also the danger of its spreading across the border, a bad example being infectious, as the Russian saying goes.

Ukraine's elections were reheld and a liberal president was elected. His administration, would, however, prove both so corrupt and inept, so riddled with factious infighting, that by the time the next elections were held in 2010, Viktor Yanukovich, who had won the rigged elections and lost the fair, would now, in an irony of democracy, be fairly elected to the presidency in what would prove a disastrous choice.

Ukraine was a calamity waiting to happen. It had had the same number of post-Soviet years as, say, its neighbor Poland, which was thriving, whereas Ukraine was almost a failed state. The country's east and west abraded against each other like tectonic plates. As usual, there was plenty of wisdom after the fact, with Gorbachev, for example, declaring: "Ukraine is in many ways due to the mistakes of the breakup of the Soviet Union. Once they decided to dissolve the union, they should have agreed on territories and boundaries." He was referring to what Solzhenitsyn had termed the "false Leninist borders of Ukraine," although they could in addition be termed "false Khrushchevian borders," for it was he who so cavalierly made Ukraine a present of Crimea.

Russia's street politicians saw the split coming in Ukraine. Asked in 2008, "If Ukraine were to move into NATO, what do you think the Russian reaction would be?" Aleksandr Dugin, the founder of the International Eurasian Movement, replied: "I think that the Russian reaction would be to support an uprising in the Eastern parts and Crimea and I could not exclude the entrance of armed forces there." A *Moscow Times* article of April 8, 2008, "Putin Hints at Splitting Up Ukraine," reported that at the same NATO conference where Putin remarked to Bush that Ukraine was not a real country, Putin also "threatened to encourage the secession of the Black Sea peninsula of Crimea and eastern Ukraine, where anti-NATO and pro-Moscow sentiment is strong."

Even the *National Geographic* magazine, whose prose is usually as anodyne as its pictures are vivid, entitled an April 2011 article on Crimea "A Jewel in Two Crowns: Russia's Paradise Lost Belongs to Ukraine—and That's Where the Trouble Begins."

All the same, Putin himself was surprised by events in 2014. When the fissures began splitting the surface of Ukraine, he was busy with the concluding ceremonies of the Winter Olympic Games in Sochi, which had been a resounding success, though some opposition figures like Boris Nemtsov would take Putin to task for the corruption involved in, at $50 billion, the most expensive Games in history. Still, there had been no problems with Chechen terrorists or gay demonstrations as feared, and the Games had accomplished what they had been designed to do—remind the world that Russia was resurgent, a major player again.

What really surprised Putin was how rapidly and radically events developed in Ukraine. One moment he is offering the lordly sum of $15 billion as a loan to prop up President Yanukovich and to keep the country from sliding into the Western camp; the next moment Putin is offering that same president refuge in Russia as Yanukovich flees his country, leaving behind a trail of carnage and vulgar luxury. Of course, Putin had designs on Crimea and eastern Ukraine, and no doubt his planners had worked out various scenarios to cover the foreseeable possibilities, but it is also clear that the events of late February were neither at the time nor in the manner of his choosing.

There is a point where geopolitics becomes existential, Darwinian, and, for Putin, the situation in Ukraine was one. Forget all the icons and cupolas and Cossacks—this was a matter of life and death. No Russian leader could allow his country to be outflanked from the Baltic to the Black Sea. He would be seen as weak. And Putin knows what happens to the weak.

The sage of Cambridge Tip O'Neill's remark that all politics is local even applies to Moscow, where Putin's principal role is Lion Tamer of the Kremlin. Though he has to a large extent defanged and declawed the oligarchs, who make public and servile protestations of their loyalty, that does not mean that they cannot harbor grievances or hatch intrigues. He must also balance the needs and ambitions of the security and military leaders, not to mention those of the gas and oil industry on which the country's economy depends.

Putin, a paranoid if not by nature then by profession, found himself being outflanked by a hostile military alliance that also manifestly seeks to drastically reduce his economic lifeline of gas and oil, all of which puts him in supreme jeopardy in the infighting of the Kremlin. To have failed to understand this was a cardinal sin on the part of the West. A February 2, 2015, *New York Times* article entitled "Britain and Europe Sleepwalked into Ukraine Crisis Report Says" states: "Britain and the European Union made a 'catastrophic misreading' of President Vladimir V. Putin and 'sleepwalked' into the Ukraine crisis, treating it as a trade issue rather than as a delicate foreign-policy challenge, British lawmakers said . . . in a scathing report. . . . The European Union had failed to appreciate the 'exceptional nature' of Ukraine."

The West was surprised not only by the importance of Ukraine to Russia, but by the violence of the Russian response. So intent on building a new world order based on the rule of law, the West somehow missed the obvious fact that Russia was still a country where the rule of law counted for very little, another way of saying that the law of the jungle prevailed.

When discussing their country's behavior, Russians will often say with a wistful, self-mocking irony: "Whereas in civilized countries . . . ," meaning as opposed to in Russia. Murder is an instrument of politics by other means in Putin's Russia. The KGB renegade Alexander Litvinenko is murdered with radioactive polonium in London, the harshly critical journalist Anna Politkovskaya is gunned down on Putin's birthday while returning home with her groceries, the lawyer Sergei Magnitsky is put to death by abuse and neglect in prison after purportedly committing the very crimes he attempted to expose, and the opposition leader Boris Nemtsov is shot dead in sight of the Kremlin while walking home from a date. Putin's critics are frequently killed, his supporters never.

Until the Ukrainian crisis the civilized West and Darwinian

Russia were able to coexist in an uneasy equilibrium of interests. Russia's authoritarianism lite kept any of the various assassinations and injustices from tipping the balance to the breaking point. Business was done. Russian gas and oil were bought, the French contracted to build Mistral assault carriers for Russia. There were independent newspapers, a radio station, Ekho Moskvy (Moscow Echo), and a web TV station, Dozhd (Rain). And Russians had the right that human-rights champion Andrei Sakharov considered the most important of them all—the right to leave the country. Some suggested that Putin's new, modern, twenty-first-century authoritarianism would, unlike the Soviet Union, much prefer to be rid of anyone who was at odds with the system. All the same, it remained possible to believe that Russia just might be zigzagging its own way to its own version of a free society, as George Kennan had predicted.

Still, Putin had long been suspicious of the West's intentions toward Ukraine. He knew full well that if he were in charge of Western intelligence he would use all those pleasant and neutral-sounding NGOs to gradually draw Ukraine into the Western camp, and the EU. Membership in NATO could come later. And even without any such malign intent it is still all part of one process. As Fiona Hill, former national intelligence officer for Russia and Eurasia, put it: "The E.U. operates in a completely different framework, when you pool sovereignty and have the same temperature gauges, the same railway gauges and do lots of other boring things that have a profound impact. Once you do this you don't come back. Russia looked at places like Estonia and Poland and said we can't let this happen to Ukraine."

The fog of war has been particularly thick in Ukraine, and truth as always was the first casualty—it was in fact assassinated. Putin has maintained deniability from the start, employing tricks and tactics that have been called "hybrid warfare," meaning a newfangled combination of proxies, volunteers, propaganda, and lies. But it's nothing so new either. In 1921 the British foreign secretary and "arch-Russophobe" Lord Curzon wrote to Georgy Chicherin, the Soviet commissar for foreign affairs: "When the Russian government desire to take some action more than usually repugnant to normal international law and comity, they ordinarily erect some ostensibly independent authority to take action on their behalf. . . . The process is familiar, and has ceased to beguile."

Except for its command of English, that letter could have been written today.

Murky as the situation remains, a few things are clear. First, the Crimea will remain part of Russia. The leading opposition figure, the valiant anticorruption muckraker and often-jailed Alexei Navalny, who took 27 percent in his 2013 run for mayor of Moscow, has said he wouldn't return Crimea if he became president: "Despite the fact that Crimea was seized with egregious violations of all international regulations, the reality is that Crimea is part of Russia" and "will remain part of Russia and will never again in the foreseeable future become part of Ukraine." Like Putin and Gorbachev, Navalny doesn't "see any kind of difference at all between Russians and Ukrainians," a sentiment, that, tellingly, is almost never voiced by Ukrainians.

If the leader of the government and the leader of the opposition are agreed on the status of Crimea, we can be sure that any negotiations contesting Crimea's status will be a nonstarter. The West will ultimately make a sharper distinction between Crimea and east Ukraine, continuing not to recognize Crimea's annexation and to apply sanctions to companies in Crimea or doing business with it. If, however, Russia complies sufficiently with the Minsk agreements, and proves a compellingly necessary partner in international affairs like the fight against ISIS, the sanctions imposed in connection with Ukraine will gradually be lifted. Though like China no fan of "splittism," Russia was glad to see cracks appear in Western unity with the exit of Britain from the European Union. The Russians can ask why the UK's referendum was legitimate and Crimea's was not.

Meanwhile the sanctions are still in force. Those sanctions have caused Russia genuine pain, hurting Russian businesses big and small, delaying exploration for oil in the Arctic, pushing millions into poverty, depriving the better-off of their European vacations and French cheeses. Though they offer no immediate emotional satisfaction, sanctions do work, as shown by Iran coming to the negotiating table in 2015. Still, it shouldn't be forgotten that the sanctions cut both ways. The French had to return the 1.2 billion euros to the Russians for the Mistral assault carriers and also had to pay out some 2.5 million euros a month for their maintenance. By 2016 the Italians had lost upward of $10 billion because of the sanctions.

Russia will be satisfied with some low level of continued turmoil in eastern Ukraine because NATO will not offer membership to countries with frozen conflicts and border disputes. Ideally for Putin the rebels will bite off a bit more territory to create a land bridge to Crimea, which can now only be supplied by sea or air without risk of obstruction. A bridge to link the Russian mainland and Crimea is under discussion with China as the probable contractor, but it will take years and cost billions, a cost that may be offset by the gas and oil deposits off the Crimean shore.

The lasting consequence of the Ukrainian adventure was the revelation that Russia is a Darwinian society that will not play by the West's rules, because, by its very nature, it cannot.

Breaking with the West over Ukraine, Russia veered in two directions—north to the Arctic and east to China.

PART FIVE

NORTH- AND EASTWARD

. . . With escalating terrorist threats at home, including in the Chinese heartland, and Uighur militants working with extremist groups like the Pakistani Taliban and the Islamic State, the imperative to stabilize China's entire western periphery has increased.

—ANDREW SMALL

8

RUSSIA'S MECCA: THE ARCTIC

The Arctic has always been Russian.
We will surrender it to no one.

—ARTUR CHILINGAROV

In late 2015 Dmitri Rogozin, deputy prime minister in charge of space and defense, tweeted the following: "The Arctic is Russia's Mecca." A flamboyant type, Rogozin has been known to say what others cannot or dare not. He first gained notoriety when he headed up the faux opposition party Rodina (Motherland), which produced a racist film spot, "Let's Throw the Garbage out of Moscow," showing dark-skinned men from the Caucasus leering at pure Russian women and littering the streets with watermelon rinds until a couple of real Russian men walk over to put things right. Rogozin was one of the first seven people to whom Obama's sanctions were applied. His response: "Tanks don't need visas." He speaks four languages and has a Ph.D. in philosophy.

When it comes to the importance of the Arctic for Russia's future Rogozin is hardly alone in voicing such maximalist sentiments. Addressing the next generation of Russians at a youth camp outside

Moscow, Putin said of the country's future: "Our interests are concentrated in the Arctic. And of course we should pay more attention to . . . strengthening our position [there]." When serving as president, Dmitri Medvedev frequently said that the Arctic must become a "main resource base" by 2020. The problem now is that after the break with the West over Crimea and Ukraine, the Arctic becomes both more essential to Russia's future and, without Western investment, equipment, and expertise, much more difficult to exploit.

Calling the Arctic "Mecca" implies that the Arctic will save Russia not only economically, but spiritually as well. The identity that failed to crystallize in the decades after the fall of the USSR will finally coalesce around a great new national enterprise where heroic boldness, economic feats, and patriotism will merge. For grandeur and complexity the Arctic project is often compared to the mastery of outer space, and from the societal point of view, it has the advantage of allowing many more people to participate.

Russia made its Arctic intentions fully explicit on August 2, 2007, when Artur Chilingarov, scientist, polar explorer, and politician, startled the world by descending to a depth of some fourteen thousand feet in a submersible and planting a titanium Russian flag on the seafloor beneath the North Pole. His courage was admirable. Chilingarov was sixty-seven at the time. There was no guarantee that he would find his way safely back to the hole on the surface, and the submersible could not break through the ice on its own. In quite un-Soviet fashion, the entire proceedings were broadcast live.

Staking a claim by planting his nation's flag like explorers of old elicited derision closely followed by alarm. "This isn't the fifteenth century. . . . You can't go around the world and just plant flags and say 'We are claiming this territory,'" mocked Peter MacKay, Canadian foreign minister at the time.

But the Canadians changed their tune quickly, dispatching their prime minister to the Arctic. As a senior official put it: "The Russians sent a submarine to drop a small flag at the bottom of the ocean. We're sending our prime minister to reassert Canadian sovereignty." (From the wording, it wasn't clear if they were also sending him to the bottom or whether a photo-op stroll on an ice floe would suffice.) Upon his arrival he announced the establishment of two new military bases in the region to defend that sovereignty.

Beyond the politics and the posturing a lot is at stake. The Arctic is warming twice as fast as the rest of the planet and is now ice-free long enough that its vast deposits of oil, gas, and precious minerals could conceivably be extracted. Passages for shipping have been opened up over Russia and Canada, which reduces distance, time, and costs by significant amounts. Potentially, the melting will make enormous fish stocks available for commercial harvesting. All this makes the Arctic a place worth exploiting and worth fighting for.

Most of us have maps rather than globes, which are already acquiring a sort of retro chic like typewriters. Maps are slightly absurd, of course, as are any two-dimensional representations of three-dimensional phenomena, especially when it comes to depicting Earth as a whole. A globe, when viewed from above, is a much better guide to the relative presence and proportion of the five Arctic countries—the United States, Canada, Russia, Denmark (as the foreign-affairs representative of Greenland), and Norway. It is there where all the lines of longitude converge in zero that the fate of Putin's Russia will play out sometime in midcentury.

The Arctic is an ocean surrounded by continents, unlike Antarctica, which is a continent surrounded by ocean. The Arctic was discovered by Phoenician sailors, who named the region after the northern star they had followed, called "Arktos" by the Greeks, meaning near the Great Bear (constellation Ursa Major). The larger Arctic Circle, which includes the northernmost parts of the five Arctic states, has bear—most famously, polar bear—musk oxen, reindeer, caribou, foxes, wolves, hare. The teeming plant and animal life under the ice sheet of the Arctic Ocean includes plants, plankton, and fish.

The ice that forms the polar ice cap in the Arctic Ocean is frozen sea water and is usually ten to thirteen feet thick, though some ridges reach heights of sixty-five feet. The ice cap is about the size of the continental United States and has typically lost about half its size with the summer, but quickly reacquired it with the coming of winter.

But recently something has happened. Over the last fifty years about 50 percent of the Arctic ice cap has melted away. As Scott G. Borgerson, international affairs fellow at the Council on Foreign Relations, put it in "Arctic Meltdown: The Economic and Security Implications of Global Warming":

> The Arctic has always experienced cooling and warming, but the current melt defies any historical comparison. It is dramatic, abrupt, and directly correlated with industrial emissions of greenhouse gases. . . . The results of global warming in the Arctic are far more dramatic than elsewhere due to the sharper angle at which the sun's rays strike the polar region during summer and because the retreating sea ice is turned into open water, which absorbs far more solar radiation. The dynamic is creating a vicious melting cycle known at the ice-albedo feedback loop.

This loop is defined as "the process whereby retreating sea ice exposes darker and less reflective seawater which absorbs more heat and in turn causes more ice to melt."

The breakup of Arctic ice has sent polar bears southward and onto land. There they have encountered grizzlies fleeing north from Canadian mining and construction sites. Mating, they have produced a new hybrid now known informally as the "pizzly" or nanulak, which combines the Inuit word for polar bear, *nanuk*, with the word for grizzly, *aklak*.

In a paradox both obvious and painful, it was the burning of fossil fuels that caused the climate change that is melting the Arctic ice cap, thereby making its vast deposits of oil and gas accessible now for the first time. The U.S. Geological Survey and Norway's Statoil jointly estimate that the Arctic contains one-fourth of the world's remaining oil and gas deposits. The territory claimed by Russia alone holds up to 586 billion barrels according to the Russian Ministry of Natural Resources. The world consumes something like 90 million barrels of oil per day and so the estimate for the Russian deposits could keep the entire planet chugging along for almost eighteen years. At $50 a barrel that's almost $30 trillion worth of oil.

Geological surveys also indicate that the Arctic seafloor, shallow at many points, also contains abundant high-grade copper, zinc, diamonds, gold, silver, platinum, manganese, and nickel.

The fishing stocks represent another bonanza with 25 percent of the world's whitefish, from the cod in the Barents Sea to the pollack in the Russian Far East. The Atlantic has been so fished out of cod that the great fishing town of Gloucester, Massachusetts, is practically moribund. In addition, "polar invertebrates represent a valuable resource for the chemical and pharmaceutical sectors as they are used in the production of analgesics and other types of medication, as well as for food and drink preservation."

Estimates of the wealth the Arctic holds clearly vary widely, even wildly. Partly this is simply due to a lack of information. It's been said that we know more about the surface of Mars than about the Arctic Ocean's floor. Still, two things seem fairly certain. One is that even the most conservative estimates of the gas and oil deposits make them attractive except in the worst of markets. The other is that the melting of the Arctic ice cap has opened the fabled, long-sought Northwest Passage across the top of Canada to commercial shipping, making it a "trans-Arctic Panama Canal," as Icelandic president Ólafur Ragnar Grímsson has called it. Russia's equivalent, the Northern

Sea Route (NSR), has itself already been compared to the Suez Canal, with which it intends to compete. Not all the money is to be made underwater.

There are several advantages to these two major new shipping routes. Shorter is cheaper. The Northern Sea Route reduces a voyage from Hamburg to Yokohama from 18,350 kilometers to 11,100. The story is much the same with Canada's Northwest Passage. Previously a ship traveling from Seattle to Rotterdam would have to pass through the Panama Canal. The direct Northwest Passage route cuts 25 percent off the distance, with commensurate savings in fuel and labor costs, though insurance costs can run higher.

The shorter routes also mean carbon dioxide emissions are reduced. The pirate-infested Strait of Malacca and Horn of Africa can be avoided. Supertankers that are too large for either the Suez or the Panama Canal and thus must sail about the Cape of Good Hope and Cape Horn will enjoy even greater reductions in time and distance.

But there are already problems. Canada claims full jurisdiction over the Northwest Passage as part of its territorial waters, which allows them to charge other nations for passing through them. The United States and the EU dispute that claim and are also against Russia's charging for passage through the Northern Sea Route. There are also maritime border disputes between the United States and Russia.

Those disputes may all be settled peacefully as was one between Russia and Norway over a 175,000-square-kilometer area in the Barents Sea. Originally over fishing rights, the dispute expanded to include the gas and oil deposits, which could run to thirty-nine billion barrels. That dispute lasted several years but was settled amicably in September 2010. Russia needs Norwegian assistance in drilling in the Arctic, and Norway has the most experience in such climatic conditions.

"The Arctic . . . is just an ocean . . . governed by the law of the sea," said Norwegian foreign minister Espen Barth Eide. In the simplest

terms that means that the treasures of the Arctic Ocean and any disputes arising over them are the exclusive business of the five nations
with an Arctic coastline. Germany, however, contends that the rapid
and dramatic climate changes occurring in the Arctic will affect
everyone and therefore are everyone's business.

Though the five Arctic countries can resolve their disputes multilat-
erally or even bilaterally, as Russia and Norway did, there are nevertheless two bodies for airing and resolving differences. The Arctic
Council is an intergovernmental body with eight permanent members
(the five Arctic Ocean states plus the Arctic Circle states Sweden, Finland, and Iceland). Germany has permanent observer status, to which
China also now aspires. Six native peoples also have permanent observer status. The council does not have the power to enact or enforce
laws, but has produced the council's first binding pact delineating the
Arctic Ocean for research-and-rescue operations.

The most serious problems relating to boundaries and sovereignty
are currently dealt with by the United Nations Convention on the
Law of the Sea (UNCLOS). UNCLOS has already defined and de-
lineated the power of any nation bordering a sea: within 12 nautical
miles of its coastline a nation exercises sovereign rights and may arrest
foreign ships entering those waters without permission. A nation's
Exclusive Economic Zone (EEZ) extends 200 nautical miles. Within
the EEZ, the coastal state has exclusive rights over the economic resources of the sea, seabed, and subsoil to the exclusion of other states.
The real troubles begin with the continental shelf, which is the seabed
and subsoil areas that can be shown to be an extension of the land of a
given country. The continental shelf can extend 200 nautical miles and
in some cases up to 350 if it can be demonstrated to be part of the
"natural prolongation of the soil."

Two enormous problems arise here. Russia aggressively claims the
continental shelf, which includes the underwater mountain ranges
known as the Lomonosov Ridge and the Mendeleev Ridge, as the

natural prolongation of Russia's land. This vast territory (465,000 square miles or about three Californias) includes the North Pole, one reason that the titanium flag was planted there in 2007. If Moscow's claims for the continental shelf are approved, Russia will not only be the largest country on earth but the largest underwater as well.

Russia's first claim on this territory was rejected by the Commission on the Limits of the Continental Shelf as being insufficiently demonstrated. In August 2015 it submitted a new claim. Denmark and Canada also claim part of it as belonging to their continental shelf.

Another major complication is that the United States is not yet an official signatory to the Law of the Sea Treaty. The motion died in the Senate in 2012 with Republicans declaring that "the treaty's litigation exposure and impositions on U.S. sovereignty outweigh its potential benefits." Former presidents George W. Bush and Bill Clinton have been strong supporters of the treaty. Then defense secretary Leon Panetta has said: "Not since we acquired the lands of the American West and Alaska have we had such a great opportunity to expand U.S. sovereignty." By not being a signatory to the Law of the Sea, the United States does not have official claim to its territorial sea, Exclusive Economic Zone, or continental shelf.

Republican senator Richard Lugar, addressing the Senate Committee on Foreign Relations, said that the Law of the Sea had been "designated by the Bush Administration as one of five 'urgent' treaties deserving of ratification." He added:

As the world's preeminent maritime power, the largest importer and exporter, the leader in the war on terrorism, and the owner of the largest Exclusive Economic Zone off our shores, the United States has more to gain than any other country from the establishment of order with respect to the oceans. . . . The Commander-in-Chief, the Joint Chiefs of Staff, and the United

States Navy, in time of war, are asking the Senate to give its advice and consent to this treaty. Our uniformed commanders and civilian national security leadership are telling us, unanimously and without qualification, that U.S. accession to this treaty would help them do their job.

Lugar also noted that Russia was already making "excessive claims in the Arctic."

The Russians, of course, don't see their claims on the Arctic as excessive but as just and justified. And indeed there is considerable historical basis for the Russians to feel a special relationship with the Arctic. There is no question that they were the forerunners of scientific exploration in the region, establishing a tradition of intrepid researchers who set up their research stations on ice floes that could suddenly break apart, as described in this Soviet report from November 1954:

A crack in the ice passed through the camp. Most of them were asleep and only the man on watch heard the noise. Suddenly a blow was felt and the floe shuddered. Everyone woke up quickly and ran out of the tents. All went to pre-arranged places for "ice alarm." The crack passed between the tents of the meteorologists and started visibly opening. It passed beneath the tent housing the magnetic instruments. The edge of the tent hung over the water, but tent and equipment were saved. In ten to fifteen minutes the floes had parted and there was open water 50 m. wide between them.

As Britain's leading expert on the Russian Arctic, Terence Armstrong, says in *The Russians in the Arctic*: "This sort of thing was not a rare occurrence." He points out that through their "boldly conceived expeditions, the Russians have made themselves the undisputed experts on the whole central Arctic region . . . ," adding that almost "everything that is known about the circulation of water in the Arctic Ocean . . . was discovered by Russian work."

Not only did the Russians explore the High North, they exploited it, which also means investing in it. Twenty percent of Russia's landmass, the Arctic Circle, accounts for something like 20 percent of the country's GDP and exports. None of the other five Arctic Ocean powers have any cities of notable size in the Arctic Circle. Nome, Alaska, the United States' largest Arctic city, usually has a population of just under 4,000. Russia, on the other hand, has eight of the ten largest cities in the Arctic Circle, Norway having the other two. Murmansk, the largest, had a population of 500,000 in Soviet times, though it has fallen almost by half in the years since.

The last city founded by the tsars, in 1916, Murmansk was a principal target of the 1918 U.S. invasion to keep Russia war materiel from falling into German hands. American soldiers are buried there. During World War II the "Murmansk run" became legendary as British, Canadian, and American ships kept an embattled Soviet Union supplied with food. German U-boats torpedoed eighty-five merchant ships and sixteen Royal Navy warships. Churchill called this "the worst journey in the world."

For Russians the Arctic is associated with the heroic and the hellish—sometimes the two have even been combined. Daring rescues of explorers and scientists trapped by ice provided patriotic fodder for Soviet newspapers and newsreels. In 1937, due to exceptionally severe conditions, twenty-six Soviet ships were forced to winter at sea, frozen in place. This might have been good luck in disguise because 1937 was the very apex of Stalin's Terror, and it was safer to be trapped in Arctic ice than home in your bed.

The Arctic was not only an arena of heroic exploits but a scene of ecological crimes. There were 138 nuclear tests—land-based, underground, underwater—in the Arctic between 1955 and 1990. Fourteen nuclear reactors were simply dumped into Arctic waters along with nineteen vessels containing radioactive waste. The K-27 nuclear submarine was scuttled in 1981 in thirty meters of water whereas international convention requires three thousand. In some places, like Andreeva Bay, nuclear waste leakages from a site containing thirty-two tons have rendered the waters "completely devoid of life."

But that may not be the gravest danger: "A Russian Academy of Sciences study indicates decades' worth of nuclear reactor and radioactive waste dumping in the Kara Sea by the Russian Navy—as well as fallout from Soviet-era nuclear tests—could cause heightened levels of radioactive contamination when major Arctic oil drilling projects ramp up. . . . Studies show that when the drill bit hits the ocean floor, there is a danger of disinterring a vast portion of the Soviet Union's irresponsible nuclear legacy . . . which threatens to contaminate at least a quarter of the world's Arctic coastlines."

But drilling presents other dangers—as well as some intriguing possibilities—apart from the release of radioactive wastes. Russian scientists, attempting to foresee and forestall some of the effects of climate change and drilling, have been working on the melting permafrost and have recently discovered more than twenty previously unknown and possibly dangerous viruses. One of them, termed a "giant" virus because, at a length of 0.6 microns, it can be seen under a normal optical microscope, is known as *Mollivirus sibericum* and has been frozen in ice for thirty thousand years.

Not all the viruses are potentially harmful. In fact, one of them, officially known as Bacillus F and more informally as "the elixir of life," shows mind-boggling promise. First, scientists noticed that Bacillus F "didn't show signs of aging," said Dr. Anatoly Brushkov, head of the Geocryology Department at Moscow State University. "My colleagues and I cultivated the bacteria and started studying them more closely. . . . We started injecting mice with a solution containing Bacillus F and their lifespan increased by up to 30 percent."

As the lab head, Vladimir Repin, put it: "Imagine an old mouse living the last of its average 600 days. We injected it with the solution, and suddenly it started behaving like it was much younger. All the vital signs returned to normal." Another of the lab's scientists said, "Experiments have already resulted in mice restoring their fertility and beginning to reproduce again."

The true treasures of the North may not be the obvious ones of gas, oil, and gold.

In private, members of an ethnic group will often say things about themselves that they would not tolerate being said publicly, especially by someone not a member of their group. By themselves Russians will often remark on their carelessness, their bent for the slapdash. This, however, is usually viewed with more affection then disdain, seen as a result of the maximalist Russian spirit, which cannot be bothered with mere fussy detail.

In an article entitled "Carelessness as a Russian National Trait," Michael Bohm, a former editor of *The Moscow Times*, lists eight horrific examples, including the crash of a Proton rocket in July 2012 because the velocity sensor was installed with the plus and minus poles reversed. The rocket carried three satellites worth $75 million, and they were not insured. Within Russia planes crash much more frequently than they do in other advanced nations, though Aeroflot's international flights are world-class and its safety rating is higher than American Airlines'. The sinking of the *Kursk* nuclear attack submarine in August 2000, Putin's first crisis, was caused by leaving on board cruise missiles that should have been removed to shore during training exercises and by proceeding with the testing of torpedoes that were leaking acid. One of those torpedoes exploded on board, causing a cruise missile to explode. This, and a long list of similar incidents, caused Prime Minister Dmitri Medvedev to declare sloppiness "a national threat."

Nothing is more portable than culture, and the Russians have brought theirs with them to the Arctic. In Soviet times that meant the dumping of radioactive wastes directly into the sea regardless of the depth. In post-Soviet times that mind-set has taken different forms. The sinking of the Kolskaya oil rig in December 2011 is a perfect example.

Everything was done wrong and everything went wrong. The captain had called his wife to say that their "mission is suicidal. . . . It was prohibited to transport oil rigs in those waters between December 1 and February 29." In mid-December, tugged by an icebreaker, the rig was traveling from the waters off the Kamchatka Peninsula in the Russian Far East and was carrying sixty-seven people, which was fourteen more than its crew; both Russian and international regulations stipulate that only skeleton crews be on board when rigs are being towed—sixty of the sixty-seven should have been on the icebreaker. Instead, the rig was packed like an "inter-island ferry in Indonesia." The captain, who had attempted to resign but not been permitted to, was among the fifty-three casualties when the rig capsized and sank in heavy seas on December 18, 2011, in the Sea of Okhotsk, where the water temperature was 33 degrees, meaning any survivors had only thirty minutes before freezing to death.

In a Voice of America article, "Russia Moves into Arctic Oil Frontier with a Lax Safety Culture?" longtime Russia watcher James Brooke says the sinking of the Kolskaya rig "involved the kind of stunning incompetence that most nations would rule criminal."

Brooke adds: "Some men, in what can only be described as superhuman feats of strength, donned wetsuits and managed to swim far enough in the freezing water to avoid getting pulled down in the deadly whirlpool created by the massive, multi-ton structure as it sank 1,000 meters to the ocean floor."

Russia's culture of carelessness produces the very conditions that elicit its cult of heroism; the two are linked in a self-perpetuating pattern.

There was no pollution from the sinking of the Kolskaya oil rig, but a catastrophic oil spill remains the main danger to the Arctic. Many experts would agree with Simon Boxall, a specialist in oil spills from the University of Southampton in England who helped analyze BP's Deepwater Horizon spill in the Gulf of Mexico and is quite straightforward on the subject of Arctic drilling: "It is inevitable you will get a spill—a dead cert."

There are two particular problems with an oil spill in the Arctic. Hundreds of boats were available in the Gulf of Mexico to aid in the cleanup, which would hardly be the case in the Arctic. To complicate matters, says Boxall, the Arctic presents "a completely different type of environment. In temperate climes, oil disperses quickly. Bacteria help. In the Arctic the oil does not break down this way—it can take decades before it breaks down. Nature will not help us." The rule of thumb is that what took five years in the Gulf of Mexico will take more than twenty in the Arctic.

Visiting the Arctic in 2010 and helping attach a tracking device to a sedated polar bear, Vladimir Putin announced: "We are planning a serious spring cleaning of our Arctic territories." That has remained largely an empty promise. In fact, rapid exploitation has been the order of the day, a project that includes what has to rank as one of the Worst Ideas in the World—the Russians are planning to supply their exploitation projects with floating nuclear power plants!

The prospect of these floating nuclear power plants (FNPPs) has elicited reactions that range from "floating Chernobyls" to "fairly proven hardware, derived from those used on the icebreakers." Other observers, like former Soviet submarine captain and atomic safety inspector turned antinuclear campaigner Alexander Nikitin, worry about earthquakes and their aftereffects. "If a working floating nuclear reactor were dashed against the shore in a tsunami, it would mean an unavoidable nuclear accident." For his troubles Nikitin has been arrested several times for treason and espionage, the first time coming in 1996, when Yeltsin was still president. Though never convicted—a good sign—he has spent considerable time in pretrial detention.

Luckily, the lightly enriched uranium the FNPPs will use will not make them an attractive target for criminals or terrorists.

The first FNPP, soon to be operational, is called the Academician Lomonosov; not coincidentally, the extended continental shelf that Russia claims as an extension of its mainland is also named after Mikhail Lomonosov, an eighteenth-century polymath of peasant origin. The floating reactors will be able to supply electricity, heat, and desalinated water to a city of 200,000. They will be refueled every three years and serviced every twelve, and have a lifespan of forty.

Fifteen countries from China to Argentina have already expressed interest in leasing FNPPs.

The vast blank whiteness of the Arctic can, it seems, take any projection—from wealth rising from the sea like some god of ancient myth to tsunamis lashing floating nuclear power plants toward cities through waters black with spilled oil. Yet it's also possible that both of these dramatic extremes will be avoided by the most common result of human endeavor—failure.

The gas and oil deposits may prove smaller than anticipated or more difficult and expensive to extract. The price of oil may stay low for a long time. And in the meanwhile breakthroughs in energy— fusion, superpowerful batteries—may make oil less necessary as fuel. The sea lanes over Russia connecting Asia and Europe may also not prove as lucrative as hoped. The dangerous unpredictability of the weather will impose strict limits on the shipping season, and many believe the main traffic will consist of raw materials being shipped out of the Russian Arctic rather than commercial traffic between Tokyo and Rotterdam. It wouldn't take more than a few serious accidents for shippers, and insurers, to have second thoughts about the route. There have already been close calls. Two tankers, each loaded with thirteen thousand tons of diesel fuel, collided in July 2010, though the Russians dismissed the incident as a mere "fender bender."

There are even pessimists when it comes to the possibility of a bounty of fish revealed by the shrinking ice cap. An *Economist* article, "Tequila Sunset," warns that a "warming Arctic will not . . . be full of fish. It will simply be an ice-free version of the desert it already is." The reason for this is that "global warming . . . may increase ocean stratification. This is the tendency of seawater to separate into layers, because fresh water is lighter than salt and cold water heavier than warm. The more stratified water is, the less nutrients in it move around."

The greatest failure that could occur in the Arctic is, however, war. Henry "Hap" Arnold, commanding general of the U.S. Army Air Forces and the only U.S. officer ever to hold five-star rank in two military services (Army and Air Force), predicted the following: "If there is a Third World War the strategic center of it will be the North Pole." Arnold was no doubt basing his thinking on the fact that the shortest distance between the United States and the USSR for strategic bombers was over the North Pole, and whoever controlled the Arctic would have a vital advantage. It wasn't long before ICBMs made the North Pole less important, but that in turn made it all the more important for nuclear subs. Just as the United States was shocked by Sputnik in 1957, the Soviets were shocked by advanced U.S. nuclear subs like the *Nautilus*, which transited the Arctic Ocean in 1958, and the *Skate*, which surfaced at the North Pole in 1959.

A resurgent Arctic is part of a resurgent Russia. Putin has declared, "We have no intention of militarizing the Arctic," but that statement is contradicted by other official statements that define the Arctic as a vital interest and main strategic base in the twenty-first century, by military doctrine dedicated to maintaining Russia's national interests in the Arctic, and by a whole series of practices— the reopening of bases, the building of airstrips able to accommodate fighters and bombers, and the production of military equipment specifically designed for fighting in Arctic conditions.

Stalin emphasized the importance of the Arctic, seeing it as a source of "colossal wealth," and used forced labor to extract its resources, a luxury Putin does not have. But the wealth of the Arctic is even more important to Putin that it was to Stalin. It will be his last chance to transform Russia's riches into greatness and strength. Since he has not sufficiently diversified the economy, the Arctic could well be Putin's last stand.

Some of Putin's moves have already made Russia's Arctic neighbors nervous. Russia is moving forward with a gas turbine–powered armored vehicle called Rytsar (the Knight). A sort of light Arctic tank, its motor is designed to start and operate in the extreme cold and also to travel the long distances between bases and settlements. Drones are already patrolling, especially in the eastern part of the country. Motorized rifle brigades are being formed in the Murmansk region in the western part. The FSB created an Arctic Directorate in 2004, the control of borders always part of that organization's purview. The list could go on but would thereby create an overly dramatic impression, as do some of the statements of Russian politicians and documents, like the following: "In a competition for resources it cannot be ruled out that military force could be used to resolve emerging problems."

Russia's actions in the Arctic, combined with incursions into Ukraine and Syria, have given Russia's Arctic neighbors some genuine cause for alarm, especially the Norwegians, who also share a land border with Russia. New third-generation Abrams-type battle tanks are now being stored in the huge spaces carved out of Norway's quartz and slate mountains. In 2010 Norway, the only NATO member with a permanent military base above the Arctic Circle, reopened its mountain stronghold in Bodø, which has fifty-four thousand square feet of tunnels and a five-story-high command center. At this stage, intelligence is still far more significant than the positioning of forces. "If Vienna was the crossroads of human espionage during the Cold War . . . ," says James Bamford, a columnist for *Foreign Policy*, "it's fair to say that the Arctic has become the crossroads of technical espionage today."

The Russians profess to feel threatened by the extension of NATO to their country's very borders, a result of former Eastern Bloc countries joining the organization. At the North Pole, however, Russia faces four NATO countries, all of which were members from its very inception. These were not the long-suffering countries of Eastern Europe seeking refuge inside NATO's castle, but core defenders of Western values and strategies. The Russians know how to rattle the Poles and the Baltic states, but find facing the United States, Canada, Norway, and Denmark a bit more worrisome. Still, with all its military bases and icebreakers—twenty-seven to the United States' two—Russia is the powerhouse of the north. "We're not even in the same league as Russia right now," concedes Coast Guard commandant Paul Zukunft.

That is the basic geopolitical lay of the land, but what matters even more here is the dynamic driving events. For the United States, Canada, Norway, and Denmark the Arctic is important whereas for Russia it has an edge of existential desperation. Since its land-based oil fields are browning, the promised resources of the Arctic could well mean the difference between power and collapse. If Russia loses "the battle for resources," as Deputy Prime Minister Rogozin puts it, it will also lose "sovereignty and independence." Those resources lie principally in that immense undersea extension of its territory known as the Lomonosov Ridge. The submersible that planted the titanium flag on the seafloor under the North Pole was not all about propaganda and bravado—it was also collecting soil samples as part of the scientific evidence, including the acoustic and seismic, to support Russia's claim, which was presented to the United Nations in August 2015, no quick answer anticipated.

And what if the UN rejects Russia's claim? Then, given the right desperate economic conditions, it will quickly become apparent that for Russia the Arctic is not so much a Mecca as an undersea Crimea that must be seized and annexed in defiance of all law, even at the risk of war.

9

MANIFESTING DESTINY: ASIA

We are similar in character.

—CHINESE PRESIDENT XI JINPING
ON HIMSELF AND PUTIN

Russia is pivoting east just as China "marches west." They could well collide in Central Asia.

Russia, of course, had burgeoning trade with China before the violent events in Crimea and Ukraine caused the rupture between Moscow and the West. Like other resource-rich countries, Russia saw the chance to profit by feeding the furnace of the Chinese economy, which, to take one measure of its scale, in the years 2011–13 poured more concrete than the United States did in the entire twentieth century. China had already surpassed Germany as Russia's leading trading partner in 2011. In a pronouncement both ringing and clunky, Putin declared in 2012: "In the 21st century, the vector of Russia's development is to the east."

For Russia the east has always been a vector of its manifest destiny. America's great westward sweep was matched by Russia's to the east, which even spilled over into the Western Hemisphere to include Alaska and parts of northern California. The Russians did not confront any great warlike nations like the Comanches, making their takeover of Siberia and the Far East a relatively easy conquest, not the source of both sagas and shame as the conquest of Indian territory was for America. The drive was so successful that three-quarters of Russia is in Asia.

It was Russia's eastward expansion that gave it the territorial basis for its own sense of greatness, but the east also carries associations of tragic humiliation and defeat. The only successful invasion of Russia came from the east, Genghis Khan having succeeded where Napoleon and Hitler would fail. The destruction of the Russian fleet by the Japanese navy in the Tsushima Strait during the Russo-Japanese War of 1904–5 still resonates in Russia. Billed as a "short, victorious war," a tonic for a society ailing from worker discontent and revolutionary assassination, the war had definite racist overtones. The Russian press called the Japanese "little yellow devils," while the British and some other European powers equipped Tokyo and cheered "brave little" Japan on. But the cheering stopped when the war ended with an ominous first—the first victory of an Asian nation over a white European one.

It was inevitable that Russia's eastward expansion would cause it to come up against China. Russia is the only European country that borders China. In fact, it has two separate borders with China. One is quite long, a touch over 2,500 miles in length, whereas the second, only 24 miles long and located between Kazakhstan and Mongolia, will not be visible on any map of normal size, but may well play an outsized role in the coming years because of pipelines passing through the ecologically precious lands of the Golden Mountains of Altai. In any case, unlike the United States, Russia and China are both countries with many borders, fourteen each in fact.

The first treaty China ever concluded with the West (the Treaty of Nerchinsk, 1689) was to begin establishing borders with Russia, a process that was only finally completed by Putin and Hu in 2004. But fear and grievances remain. Many Chinese believe that by force or the threat of force Russia imposed "unequal treaties" on China and unjustly seized 1.5 million square kilometers. Mao espoused that view in 1964, and five years later Soviet and Chinese troops engaged in armed border clashes. "The Politburo was terrified that the Chinese might make a large-scale intrusion into the Soviet territory that China claimed. A nightmare vision of invasion by millions of Chinese made the Soviet leaders almost frantic," wrote Arkady Shevchenko, the highest-ranking Soviet diplomat ever to defect, in his book *Breaking with Moscow.*

The fear behind the old Soviet quip—all quiet on the Finnish-Chinese border—continues to fuel Russian anxiety. Speaking off the record, a highly placed Russian government figure told me that he expects the next war to be a "resource war" and China to be the enemy. It's a pity that Russian-American relations have sunk so low, he said, when we should be forging an alliance to counter the mounting Chinese threat.

Putin has said of Russian-Chinese relations: "We do not have a single irritating element in our ties." In fact, the relationship is fraught with tension. First and foremost is what could be called Russia's demographobia. In the country's vast Far East, there are only 7 million people, while China's three northern provinces that border the Russian Far East contain more than 100 million. Many are already working in Russia, crossing the bordering as Deputy Prime Minister Dmitri Rogozin puts it, "small groups of 5 million." Putin himself has said: "I don't want to dramatize the situation, but if we do not make every real effort, even the indigenous population will soon speak mostly Japanese, Chinese and Korean."

The Russian towns and cities near the border with China are forlorn and dilapidated, whereas their Chinese counterparts gleam with steel, glass, and commercial energy. China's cheap goods, especially clothing and electronics, draw Russian customers from far and near. The few shopping centers and high-rises in the Russian towns tend to be built by Chinese companies.

But it is not only Chinese laborers who cross the border into underpopulated Russia to exploit its natural resources, and not only Russian shoppers who cross in the other direction to buy goods for themselves or for resale; there is also a flow of educated professionals moving from Russia to China, where their skills are more in demand and better paid. And, to further complicate the picture, there are cross-border romances as well, usually between Russian women, known for their beauty and warmth, and Chinese men, who, compared to Russians, have the reputation of earning more and drinking less.

Different as they are, the Russians and Chinese both share a sense of being humiliated nations. The Chinese even speak of their "century of humiliation" from the middle of the nineteenth century, when foreigners, especially the British, forced unequal treaties on them, until 1949, when Mao's victory began China's comeback. (The Map Department of the People's Press in Beijing has even published *Maps of the Humiliation of China over One Hundred Years*.)

Siberia's richness and emptiness cannot help but stimulate China's appetite for resources and lebensraum. Though all border differences were successfully negotiated in 2004, there remains a lingering sense on the Chinese side that much of the territory along the border was taken unfairly by Russia when China was weak. In some Chinese textbooks the areas on the Russian side of the border are shown in the same color as China itself. Though the borders have been fixed, that alone cannot provide Russia with much reassurance, having itself just recently violated the 1994 Budapest Memorandum guaranteeing Ukraine's sovereignty and territorial integrity.

Siberians, moreover, have never been too happy about their domination and exploitation by distant Moscow. Theirs is a mentality of self-sufficiency, rugged individualism, and distrust of the central government. In the chaos of the Russian Revolution and civil war, Siberia even briefly seceded, establishing its own republic, its flag's green and white symbolizing forest and snow. A similar logo is used by the currently existing National Alternative of Siberia—known as the Siberian Liberation Army until the group's leader was visited by the security police curious as to his choice of words, since private armies are frowned upon, to say the least. This fringe group has a near-zero chance of having any impact at the moment, though the Russian authorities are always mindful that, given the right set of conditions, small groups like the Bolsheviks and Nazis can dart from the margins to the center.

Russia and China are both content with the current arrangement and will remain so until some new dynamic brings the borders back into question. It would be a delicious historical irony if at some point China began aiding the Siberian equivalent of the breakaway groups that set up the phantasmagorical People's Republic of Donetsk.

A mixture of half-real paranoia and quite real ambition caused Putin to create an enemy out of NATO, which had obliged him by expanding its borders to outflank Russia from the Baltic to the Black Sea. Putin needed that enemy for political purposes, his rule secured by the security services, the armed forces, and the wealthy elite he has created. Funds flowed to them, which meant that they would not flow to education, nonmilitary R&D, and high-tech centers imitating Silicon Valley, where those funds could have a substantial impact on the country's economic future. Russia produces little that the world wants; its top ten exports, with the exception of some industrial machinery, include oil, gas, iron, steel, precious stones and metals, fertilizer, aluminum, wood, and cereal. Russia does of course sell weapons, planes, warships, and other military equipment, but not enough to make the top-ten list.

In the meantime, there are buyers, especially for gas and oil. Russia may be pivoting east and Europe may be desperately weaning itself off Russian energy, but their economies are still very much bound up. Though China has surpassed Germany as Russia's number one trade partner, the EU as a whole accounts for 41 percent of Russian trade, more than four times what China imports. The countries of Eastern Europe—especially Poland and the Baltic states, which feel the most threatened by Russia because of past experience, proximity, and, in the case of Estonia and Latvia, large number of ethnic Russians and Russian speakers—are also countries that depend heavily on Russia for their energy supplies. Poland gets at least half of its gas from Russia and has a supply contract with Gazprom that runs until 2022. Some of them are scrambling for inventive solutions to their problem of dependency on Russia. Lithuania is building a floating terminal to receive liquefied natural gas from the United States. Other gambits included developing domestic shale reserves, as Estonia is doing. And it's always possible to simply pay more for gas and oil from other sources.

Like Europe's liberation of itself from Russian gas and oil, Russia's search for new or enlarged markets in Asia will not be accomplished anytime soon. Alexander Ivanov, deputy head of the state-run bank VEB, put it: "Over the long term, these markets may supplant the European and American markets for us, but it won't be quick."

Indeed, the signs have been highly mixed. Russia's trade with China actually fell in 2015 by some 26 percent. The two countries had hoped to hit the $100 billion mark but came in $32 billion short. On the other hand, China's import of Russian oil for May 2016 hit a record thirty-eight million barrels.

China, of course, will never allow itself to become dependent on Russia for energy any more than Russia will settle for being a "natural resources appendage" for China. Putin is not about to turn rejection in the West to humiliation in the East. Russia is already attempting to protect itself in Asia by employing the same principle it failed to apply to its domestic economy—diversification. The Kremlin deals with both India and Pakistan, with which it lifted an embargo on arms sales in 2014. Russia sells submarines to Vietnam, also supplying it and India with nuclear power stations. Russia plays India off against China, selling it the first in a series of nuclear attack subs for $1 billion in 2012 under a ten-year contract. India declined to join in the sanctions against Russia in response to the annexation of Crimea and the incursions into eastern Ukraine. It is even possible that Russia will now be motivated to come to terms with Japan over the four southernmost Kurile Islands. The waters off those islands are rich in stocks of fish, gas, and oil, while the islands themselves contain large quantities of gold and rhenium, an exceedingly rare and costly metal used in jet engines. Seized by the USSR at the end of World War II, the islands have prevented Russia and Japan from formally concluding a peace. Wars never quite end and feelings still run high. When then president Medvedev visited one of the Kurile Islands in 2010 the Japanese prime minister, Naoto Kan, called it an "unforgiveable outrage."

Still, for all its overtures and deals, Russia may not find itself much more welcome or effective in the East than it was in the West. The United States competes there with Russia as a supplier of weapons and a guarantor of security, and there is no question that countries like Japan and South Korea will remain squarely in the American camp. "Russia's geo-strategic eyes are bigger than its stomach," says Brad Williams, a specialist in East Asia relations at the University of Hong Kong. "Simply put, Russia doesn't have the economy to support a sustained presence in Asia."

And for that very reason, implacable geopolitical logic may compel Russia to employ blunter instruments to achieve its ends in Asia.

The strategic doctrine known as "March West" was publicly articulated in an article published in *Global Times* in October 2012 by

Wang Jisi, identified by the Brookings Institution as "China's most prominent and influential foreign relations scholar and a professor at Peking University." The stated purpose of March West is to move away from possible confrontation with the United States in the maritime region off China's coast and to accelerate the "Grand Western Development," a national strategy promulgated in 2000 whose aim is to speed the development of China's western provinces, which have lagged far behind those on the eastern coast.

When it came to defining the importance of the western provinces and their relationship to China's dominant population group, the Han, no one put it better than Mao did back in 1956: "We say China is a country vast in territory, rich in resources and large in population; as a matter of fact, it is the Han nationality whose population is large and the minority nationalities whose territory is vast and whose resources are rich."

Not only do these non-Han western provinces possess land and natural wealth; they are one of the principal places through which China imports energy and exports manufactured goods. A part of the ancient Silk Road that supplied Rome with silk for togas, they are integral to President Xi's dream of building a new Silk Road as part of China's March West strategy. On a state visit to Kazakhstan in September 2013, President Xi waxed poetic on the subject: "I can almost hear the ring of the camel bells and [see] the wisps of smoke in the desert." Like Mao, Xi is physically large and imposing, given to poetic speech and a grandiose sense of self and mission that is already resulting in something of a personality cult around "Papa Xi," as he is sometimes known.

There are also affinities between Xi and Putin, the first leader he visited after assuming control of China. Men of the same generation, they face a similar task—to finally deliver their nations from a sense of humiliation and make them great powers while at the same time balancing economic dynamism with state control of information and opinion. Putin's popularity in China jumped to 92 percent after Russia's annexation of Crimea. Biographies of "Putin the Great" make the bestseller list. Major General Wang Haiyun, a former military attaché to Moscow, expressed quite clearly the Chinese image of Putin as a "bold and decisive leader of a great power, who's good at achieving victory in a dangerous situation."

Xi not only says that he and Putin are alike but has sought to further emulate the Russian leader. The modernization of China's army, the People's Liberation Army, is being closely modeled on Putin's revamp of the Russian army—leaner, meaner, more professional, gearing up to use high-tech and hybrid warfare rather than to fight great massed battles. China's island-building in the South China Sea was inspired by and modeled after Russia's actions in Crimea and east Ukraine. The two countries' militaries are now working together more closely than ever, not only in joint exercises, but in sharing "information in such a sensitive area as missile launch warning systems and ballistic missile defense, [which] indicates something beyond simple co-operation," says Vasily Kashin, an expert on China's military at the Higher School of Economics in Moscow.

Though some fear a Russia-China axis based on their shared opposition to American hegemony, the two countries are, as we shall see, ultimately more likely to collide than to coordinate.

Xi's interest in a new Silk Road is of course more prosaic than poetic. China imports huge quantities of gas and oil from Turkmenistan and Kazakhstan, which have shown themselves to be more pliant and reliable partners than Russia. But to reach China that gas and oil must flow through the western province of Xinjiang, which is restive to put it mildly.

Usually the Dalai Lama's words have a calming effect on people. But not always. One phrase that he occasionally uses can infuriate the Chinese leadership. This is not a mantra learned in the occult monasteries of Tibet but a dullish geographical term: "East Turkestan."

What does it mean? And why does it infuriate the Chinese?

East Turkestan is a huge area in northwest China amounting to about one-sixth of the country. The Chinese government absolutely insists that it be called Xinjiang or, even more officially, the Xinjiang Uighur Autonomous Region. The local people are Uighurs, Muslims who speak a Turkic language. Like the Tibetans they would prefer independence from China but would probably settle for genuine autonomy. Like the Tibetans they feel no affinity with China on any level.

When the Dalai Lama uses the phrase "East Turkestan" he is in effect saying that Xinjiang is a natural part of Turkic-speaking Islamic Central Asia, not of China, which holds it by force alone. To the Chinese this is a seditious term, a call to revolt. In 2010 China's Foreign Ministry spokesman declared that the Dalia Lama's use of such language proved "his intent of splitting the country and sabotaging ethnic unity."

Until now, Beijing has dealt with Xinjiang much as it has dealt with Tibet. It has flooded the region with Han Chinese to tip the population balance against the indigenous locals. (The current population in Xinjiang is about 45 percent Uighur and 40 percent Han.) Mandarin is the language of social advancement; the local language, culture, and religion are viewed by Han officialdom as impediments to progress. Job listings frequently stipulate native Mandarin speakers only. But perks have been offered to those who are willing to cooperate with authorities: some Uighurs were exempted from China's one-child-per-family policy, and the government has offered soft loans to small farmers.

Beijing wants a docile Xinjiang—but this seems increasingly

unlikely. China's nightmare would be collusion between the two great Western provinces of Tibet and Xinjiang. Tibetans are, however, more likely to express their discontent by means of self-immolation, whereas the Uighurs tend to opt for overt violence against Chinese officials and citizens. Though Beijing declares that these rebels are instigated and financed from abroad, their benefactors must not be very generous: an attack on a police station in Xinjiang in June 2013 that left twenty-seven dead, including nine police officers, was carried out with knives. That pattern changed briefly in 2015 with a car bomb attack in Tiananmen Square. But the Uighurs, who have an old tradition of making knives and daggers, will probably continue to favor them—knives are portable, concealable, impossible to ban. Even at close range a gun is impersonal, but there is something hideously intimate about a knife attack.

Xinjiang is important to China not only because of what is beneath the ground—the country's largest gas deposits and considerable oil—but also because of what moves across the ground. Much of China's imports and some of its exports must pass through Xinjiang. A new rail line, already called the New Silk Road, is faster than shipping through the Suez Canal. Just as important, China increasingly gets its gas and oil through pipelines that cross Xinjiang west to east. If a reasonable, just, and humane solution to the "East Turkestan" problem is not found, China can expect the Uighur rebels to graduate from knives to explosives that can cut those rail and pipe lines.

Unlike the United States, which has no offshore neighbors able to interfere with its merchant shipping or the movements of its navy, China is not blessed with a safe and open coastline. A glance at a map shows that China's coastline, though long and variegated, would not be particularly advantageous during periods of tension or conflict. China is still very dependent on oil from the Middle East that must pass through the Strait of Hormuz, which could easily be closed by the United States in the event of conflict with China. Any goods China imports (e.g., 82 percent of its crude oil) or exports by sea also have to run the gauntlet of the Strait of Malacca, also easy to choke off, not to mention passing several countries with which China has territorial conflicts: Vietnam, the Philippines, South Korea, and Japan. And then of course there is always Taiwan—that "unsinkable aircraft carrier" off China's coast, to use General Douglas MacArthur's still relevant phrase.

In the event of serious conflict at sea, the western provinces, especially Xinjiang, will attain exceptional significance as the primary conduits of energy and raw materials for China. Then China's survival will depend in large part on how well it has solved its Uighur problem. One example of how China is failing to solve that problem is Kashgar, the main city of the Uighur region. In the days of the Silk Road merchants traveling west from China would encounter a huge, forbidding desert called Taklimakan, meaning "Go In No Come Out." At that point the Silk Road split into two routes, one skirting the desert from the north, the other from the south, with both reuniting in Kashgar. Fearing the role the city could play in a Uighur resurgence, the Chinese, under the pretext of earthquake safety, are currently dismantling Kashgar's ancient labyrinth of streets and exiling their inhabitants to cheap, sterile high-rises where their culture dies.

The Uighurs are unlike the Tibetans, whose cause is better known because of the genial Dalai Lama and the support of Buddhism-embracing celebrities. The Uighurs have no such leader, no such followers. On the other hand, Tibet is for all its publicity still a world apart, whereas the Uighurs belong to the one-billion-plus Muslim world community and are subject to all that has convulsed that world in recent years. And China's policy of "Strike hard" against the "three evils" of terrorism, separatism, and extremism has been applied too indiscriminately on the Uighurs. Beards have been forbidden, government employees forced to work and eat on holy days. And it is almost a given that where the green flag is trampled the black flag will soon be raised.

Dangerous enough in itself, the "East Turkestan" problem now has its force multiplied by events developing in Central Asia.

"The Kazakhs never had any statehood," said President Putin in August 2014 in what seemed a backhanded compliment to Kazakhstan's President Nursultan Nazarbayev, whom Putin was trying to credit for creating "a state in a territory that never had a state before." These remarks caused outrage and alarm in Kazakhstan, especially in the wake of the Ukrainian incursion, which had been based in part on a similar sentiment. There are certain obvious and ominous similarities between the two countries. After the fall of the USSR both countries had voluntarily surrendered their nuclear weapons. At the time Kazakhstan had some fourteen hundred, making it the number four nuclear power in the world. However, as in the case of Ukraine, those weapons were not really operational, their codes being controlled by Moscow; but they could be repurposed for other weapon types or, falling into terrorist hands, be used for dirty bombs. Putin's declaring neither country a real state, dubious in the case of Ukraine, is less so vis-à-vis Kazakhstan, since its people were mostly pastoral nomads until the Soviet era. Both Kazakhstan and Ukraine had significant clusters of populations that were Russian-speaking and/or identified as Russians. As a progressive twenty-first-century authoritarian, Putin would never use old-fashioned Stalinist methods of swallowing nations whole, preferring only to slice off the tranche that could be justified and would prove the most useful to his strategic aims. In his attitude toward Kazakhstan Putin derives a certain moral authority from the writer Aleksandr Solzhenitsyn, on whom he bestowed the country's highest award, the State Prize of the Russian Federation, in 2007. In *Rebuilding Russia*, written in

1990, Solzhenitsyn advocated a new post-Soviet state shorn of the burdens of empire and consisting of Russia, Belarus, parts of Ukraine, including Crimea, and the north and east of Kazakhstan, which he contends were "actually part of southern Siberia."

Often described as more than four times the size of Texas (though it's hard enough to imagine the size of one Texas), Kazakhstan has copious quantities of gas, oil, and gold, and its uranium reserves rank second only to Australia's. It sells fifty-five thousand tons of uranium to China a year, supplying nearly half its needs. China's New Silk Road passes right through Kazakhstan, bringing goods to the market in the Netherlands two weeks faster than by sea. Energy flows to China through Kazakhstan. China has been assiduous in courting Kazakhstan and equally assiduous in avoiding the kind of contretemps caused by the insults, inadvertent or not, that Putin seems especially prone to.

By Central Asian standards, Kazakh president Nursultan Nazarbayev is a fairly reasonable autocrat. Early on he made a favorable impression on Margaret Thatcher, who saw him as a sort of Central Asian Gorbachev, a man you could do business with, telling Nazarbayev: "Mr. President, you seem to be moving from Communism to Thatcherism." (This incident alone gives some feel for how long Nazarbayev has been ruling Kazakhstan.) And Gorbachev himself liked Nazarbayev "very much. He had an energetic and attractive personality. He was open to new ideas." Though corrupt and authoritarian, like China and Russia, Kazakhstan is not an impossible place like its neighbor Uzbekistan, which has been called "Central Asia's heart of darkness." There, critics of the regime are routinely tortured, including being boiled alive, according to Great Britain's former ambassador to that country, Craig Murray, who documented a whole series of such appalling injustices in his book *Murder in Samarkand*.

Such misrule in Uzbekistan has led to greater resentment and resistance than in relatively unrepressive Kazakhstan. The Islamic Movement of Uzbekistan (IMU) has been a problem since the 1990s and has now pledged its allegiance to the Islamic State. Many Uzbeks are fighting with ISIS in Syria and Iraq; an Uzbek was one of the three suicide bombers in the June 2016 attack on Istanbul's airport. Terrorist groups exist within Kazakhstan and Uzbekistan and are ready to capitalize on a shift in circumstances, especially a sudden, dramatic one like the death of a leader, especially one with no named successor. Though the Uzbek president's death in September 2016 passed without immediate incident, the death of Kazakhstan's might not, and besides, as the FSB well knows, crises can be manufactured—a grievance, a slogan, some demonstrations, a few bombs, a video that goes viral.

The state-controlled media make it difficult to gauge the extent of the Islamist threat in Kazakhstan. The government prefers that terrorist incidents be presented and portrayed as the violence of criminal gangs. That leads to certain absurdities, like saying that a suicide bomber who blew himself up in the local security police headquarters was actually a crime boss who did so "with the aim of avoiding responsibility for his crimes." Uzbekistan plays it just the opposite—it treats nearly all violent acts as those of Islamist extremists, thereby allowing it to crack down on all its enemies, including oppositionists and critics, and as well to attract foreign aid, especially from the United States, in the war against terrorism.

Islamism enters all the Central Asian countries through the Internet, discs, books, and the living word of preachers. Prison, as always, is a great university. Fighters returning from Syria and Iraq enthrall the young with their tales of apocalyptic battles, video games come to life. If educated, well-to-do British and French youth can be radicalized to the point where they would go fight in Syria or commit terrorist acts at home, something of the same sort can easily occur in dictatorial Uzbekistan or authoritarian Kazakhstan.

Paradoxically, the sanctions against Russia seem to be helping ISIS. Part of it is simple math and is exemplified by the former Soviet Central Asian republic of Tajikistan. A bit smaller than Wisconsin, Tajikistan has eight million people, more than a third of whom live beneath the poverty line. For that reason, more than a million young Tajik men have traveled to Russia in search of jobs. They do the work—repairing streets, construction, shoveling snow, driving cabs—that Russians are increasingly reluctant to do. The remittances they send home account for close to 40 percent of GDP, a frighteningly high percentage.

The sanctions that have inflicted pain on the Russian economy mean there is less work for the Tajik guest workers to do. Something like 200,000 returned home in 2015: 40 percent less money was sent back than in previous years. That alone meant a 16 percent drop in GDP. Nearly a quarter million young men returned to Tajikistan to a situation that was only made worse by their arrival. Those young men will find no opportunities at home and will thus be vulnerable to the appeal of the Taliban and ISIS, which is spreading quickly throughout the former Soviet Union. And it is not only rootless, lost youth who are attracted.

In mid-May 2015 the head of Tajikistan's Special Assignment Police Force, Colonel Gulmurod Khalimov, trained in counterterrorism in the United States, simply disappeared: When he reappeared on May 27 it was in an ISIS video in which he promised to wage violent jihad against Tajikistan. He taunted his fellow countrymen as "the slaves of non-believers" and hurled them a challenge: "I am ready to die for the Caliphate—are you?"

When Kazakh president Nazarbayev decided to create Astana, his new, gleaming capital, he supposedly chose the inhospitable northern steppe for its location in order to establish a Kazakh presence in territory that was otherwise largely Russian. Russians represent something like a quarter of Kazakhstan's population, a figure that increases to half in the northern and eastern regions that border Russia, what Solzhenitsyn called actually part of Southern Siberia. The Kazakh government has instituted a program to get 95 percent of the country speaking Kazakh by 2020 while retaining Russian as both an official and an unofficial lingua franca. Kazakhstan is like Ukraine, where a great many people who consider themselves Ukrainian cannot speak the language or speak only kitchen Ukrainian at best. But one can speak only the language of the conqueror and still be fierce about independence, as the Irish, for one, have amply demonstrated.

For Putin the north and east of Kazakhstan are important because of their Russian population but even more so because that region borders Xinjiang.

In the event of turmoil and terrorism—homegrown or stimulated from without—following on the death of Kazakhstan's leader, Putin, his modernized military now well tested in Ukraine and Syria, will have at least two good geopolitical reasons for incursion.

The first is connected with the ideas of the British geographer Halford Mackinder, who is revered and reviled as the creator of modern geopolitical theory: revered because of the pioneering quality of his ideas and reviled for making them too categorical and because the Nazis used them to justify their doctrine of lebensraum. Mackinder is known to Russian historians and the history-minded Putin for his theories, but also because he was British high commissioner for Russia in late 1919 and early 1920, traveling through the south of the country during the thick of the civil war, urging London to support the Whites against the Reds, for which, on his return to London in 1920, he was knighted.

Mackinder's fame rests not on a grand opus but on "The Geographical Pivot of History," an article published in the April 1904 issue of *The Geographical Journal* in London. He did, however, publish books in which he developed his theory of Europe, Asia, and Africa as one big "world island" surrounded by a "world ocean." History was made in the world island, hence Mackinder's famous formulation:

Who rules East Europe commands the Heartland:
Who rules the Heartland commands the World-Island:
Who rules the World-Island commands the World.

In his book *The Revenge of Geography* Robert Kaplan identifies the Heartland's exact location:

"Kazakhstan *is* Mackinder's Heartland."

If Russia were in danger of becoming no more than China's gas station and lumberyard, Putin would be sorely tempted to seize control of northern and eastern Kazakhstan. That would mean controlling the thousand-mile-long border with China, specifically with Xinjiang. The following political situation, whether genuine or concocted by Russia, could turn temptation into action:

The president of Kazakhstan suddenly dies. There is still no known successor chosen nor any mechanism in place to select one. Homegrown Islamists seize the moment to unleash terror in the cities and seize the considerable amount of weapons-grade uranium that Kazakhstan is known to possess. Feeling threatened as Christians, the ethnically Russian population of northern and eastern Kazakhstan calls on Moscow for help, and Moscow is only too glad to oblige. The world is presented with a stark choice: which flag will fly over the region—the white-blue-and-red of Russia or the black banner of ISIS?

The Islamists will also have used the moment to stir up China's Uighurs, who after years of China's "Strike hard" policy are ready to strike back. China will now depend on Russia to maintain border security to keep its energy imports and manufactured exports moving; it will also depend on Russia to cease the flow of arms to the Uighurs. The balance of power will have shifted significantly in Russia's favor.

Chance, cunning, and the willingness to use force will have made Russia what it has so longed to be since the fall of the USSR—the equal of China and thus of the United States, one of a new Big Three, the Triumvirate that rules the World Island and the World Ocean, that is to say, the World.

PART SIX

THE TWILIGHT OF PARANOIA

Everything that is connected with Russia and Orthodoxy is under attack. Everything connected with the empire is under attack. Russian history, Stalin and the family are under attack.

—ALEXANDER PROKHANOV

10

HOW VLADIMIR PUTIN LEARNED TO STOP WORRYING AND LOVE THE INTERNET

Russia is a military state and its destiny is to be the terror of the world.

—TSAR NICHOLAS I

A great paradox of Putin's later reign is that as he moved away from the West after the events in Ukraine, he also began slowly, imperceptibly, to embrace the West's defining modern invention, the Internet.

By its very nature, the Internet is everything Putin dislikes. It is infinitely horizontal while he prefers the Vertical of Power. The Internet decentralizes, Putin recentralizes. The Internet eludes control and so Putin prefers television, which is easy to manipulate. Television demands that you be in a certain place at a certain time—for the large number of the VCR-less in Russia—while with the Internet you can get your news whenever and wherever you please. Television is real, large, physical, the Internet insubstantial, somehow gay.

Putin never lost his respect for television. It had been a television miniseries, *The Sword and the Shield*, that had inspired him to become a KGB agent. It had been television that had won Boris Yeltsin reelection in 1996 when a Communist resurgence was very much in the offing. And it was television that won Putin his first election and every subsequent one. It is probably not coincidental that 80 percent of the Russian population get their news from television, and 80 percent is exactly the level that Putin's popularity seems to hover at.

Putin had also felt the sting of television's power every time the satirical puppet show *Kukly* came on showing him with a rubbery nose, too red lips, watery blue eyes. In 2002 it disappeared from the air.

Even the main crisis of his presidency—the economic suffering caused by low oil prices and Western sanctions—was described as a battle between the TV and the fridge, what Russian saw on the one and *in* the other.

In Soviet times, most of the televisions were made in the Gulag by prisoners known as Zeks. Those sets often caught fire or even exploded. Whether this was due to the Zeks' indifference or to their malice will never be known. But Putin arose in post-Soviet times. The televisions were better and so were the production values. It was perfect for what Lilia Shevtsova of the Carnegie Moscow Center called "imitation democracies . . . television with fancy graphics but Kremlin-dictated scripts, elections with multiple candidates yet preordained outcomes." As Stalin's foreign minister Molotov had put it quite succinctly: "The trouble with free elections is that you never know how they're going to turn out."

Initially, it did not seem important to control the Internet—it was something only the urban intelligentsia cared about, like foreign films and foreign food. And the people involved in it as inventors and founders of companies were as alien as the Internet itself.

Pavel Durov was a perfect example. Born in 1984 of all years, Durov is habitually called the Mark Zuckerberg of Russia for having created in 2006 the social media site V Kontakte (In Contact or In Touch, both translations are good). In time VK would outdo Facebook in Russia with 46 million monthly users as compared to Facebook's 11.7 million. The year 2006 was a good time for the Internet in Russia—there was creative ferment among the young generation and benign indifference from the old. Durov said: "The best thing about Russia at that time was that the Internet sphere was completely not regulated. In some ways it was more liberal than the United States."

From the start Durov embodied the anarchic spirit of the Internet, a Merry Prankster of high-tech. Handsome, raised in Italy, always dressed all in black, he "envisioned his country as a tax-free and libertarian utopia for technologists." Durov identified himself as a libertarian, vegetarian, and pastafarian, a mock religion whose name is a blend of Rasta and pasta; it worships a supreme being called the Flying Spaghetti Monster and can involve the wearing of a colander on one's head. As Durov said, "I like to make fun of serious things."

One of Durov's more colorful pranks was to fold 5,000-ruble notes, worth about $150 at the time, into paper airplanes and sail them out his office window in the Singer Building in St. Petersburg. Needless to say, fistfights broke out on the sidewalks below. (This is reminiscent of a scene in the 1959 novel *The Magic Christian*, by Terry Southern, a screenwriter for *Dr. Strangelove*, in which a malicious billionaire, Guy Grand, opens to the public a bubbling vat filled with animal excrement and cash.)

Some of Durov's other antics did not sit so well with the international business community. A year after founding VK, Durov began allowing users "to upload audio and video files without regard to copyright. Such policies drew criticism from the United States Trade Representative and lawsuits from major record labels." Later, Durov would admit to having been "very careless."

But these were relatively small problems that were relatively easily finessed in that lax and open period of the Russian Internet. In fact, the years between the founding of VK in 2006 and 2013, when its forced sale to Putin's cronies took place, could be called the Russian Internet's "seven fat years." (Is a footnote now necessary to explain that this is a biblical reference, not one to obesity issues?)

Things began to sour in late 2011 and early 2012, when, summoned by social media, hundreds of thousands streamed into the streets of Moscow and St. Petersburg to protest the rigged parliamentary elections and Putin's return to the presidency after allowing Medvedev to pose as president while Putin retained all real power as prime minister, an arrangement that observed the letter of the Constitution while mocking its spirit.

Putin viewed those demonstrations against the background of the Arab Spring, which exploded from the same volatile mix of idealistic youth, social media, and high-tech gadgets. That quickly led to Mubarak's overthrow in February 2011 and Qaddafi's in late August. The sight of a member of his elite club of World Leaders dragged through the streets and then murdered did not sit well with Putin.

And the Americans were playing what Russia saw as their usual devious hypocritical games—abandoning some leaders, toppling others, always in the name of a democracy that never quite seemed to come or, if it did but produced the wrong results, such as an Islamist president in Egypt, that had to be repudiated at once.

In another perverse paradox, it was the ugly turn of events in 2011 that would inspire Durov with one of his most libertarian ideas. In

December 2011 an OMON (SWAT) team was banging at Durov's door demanding that he block access to opposition leader Alexei Navalny's Web site. Wishing to consult with his brother, Durov realized that he did not have any safe and secure way to do so. And thus was born the idea for Telegram, the encrypted communication app that he would create in 2013. In 2011 Durov still felt free enough to defy the Kremlin; he refused to close down Navalny's Web site and tweeted a photo of a dog in a hoodie sticking out its tongue. He could still get away with such things in 2012, probably because Putin was more occupied with putting the screws on the actual opposition leaders rather than on those who allowed them to communicate freely.

The swing year was 2013. In August, after weeks in bureaucratic limbo, Edward Snowden left Moscow's Sheremetyevo Airport and accepted asylum in Russia rather than risk any further international travel. Durov, who called Snowden "my hero," immediately offered him a job, which Snowden declined. In a gust of pro-Russian effusiveness, Durov said: "In such moments one feels proud of one's country and regret over the course taken by the United States—a country betraying the principles it was once built on."

In a perfect piece of chessboard symmetry, within a matter of months Durov the anti-Putin would be forced into exile and end up in the United States, working in secrecy and freedom in Buffalo, New York, on Telegram, his secure communication app. Putin had apparently decided that he didn't need both Durov and Snowden on his side of the chessboard, especially with Durov offering Snowden work and lionizing him. Snowden's value was not a matter of any intelligence bonanza—his value was purely symbolic, i.e., political—his presence would be a constant mocking of the United States' impotence. In the meantime Putin's cronies seized financial control of VK in a buyout that left Durov with something like $300 million to $500 million. That was money that could not be spent in prison, as Durov was reminded when a case of his driving over a policeman's foot was concocted against him, the fact that Durov didn't drive was hardly an obstacle.

Durov, now a citizen of Saint Kitts and Nevis, leads a nomadic life, traveling from hotel to hotel, country to country, with a small band of devoted techies who helped him perfect Telegram. Though it quickly gained 100 million users a month, Telegram has yet to show a profit and costs Durov something like $1 million a month. Among the hundred million users of Telegram's secure communication system were the ISIS jihadis who left 129 people dead in the November 2015 Paris attacks.

Snowden may yet prove to hold a surprise for Putin, who thus far has seen him pretty much as a godsend. Snowden provides Putin with cover for repressive actions against the Russian Internet. Granting Snowden asylum reverses the old Cold War paradigm in which persecuted Russian culture heroes like the writer Aleksandr Solzhenitsyn or the dancer Mikhail Baryshnikov were given shelter and freedom in the United States. Now in the IT twenty-first century, the most famous IT refugee is living safely in Russia, free enough even to criticize Putin from time to time—in August 2016 Snowden tweeted in response to new legislation increasing surveillance and sentences while reducing Internet freedom in Russia: "Putin has signed a repressive new law that violates not only human rights, but common sense. Dark day for #Russia."

This is a rare enough occurrence if only because common courtesy, gratitude, and the instinct for self-preservation prevent Snowden from criticizing his host overmuch. Their relationship is at best an uneasy one. Snowden's tenure in Russia is entirely based, like everything else, on the whims and interests of Vladimir Putin. Snowden is a chip that can be called in at any time—as part of a deal that, say, lifts sanctions and at least tacitly recognizes Crimea as part of the

Russian Federation, a deal that will appeal much more to a President Trump than to a President Obama.

As far back as July 2015, when Donald Trump was only one of the many vying to be the Republican presidential candidate, he called Snowden a "total traitor," adding enigmatically that Putin would immediately surrender Snowden to him: "If I'm president, Putin says 'hey, boom—you're gone'—I guarantee you that."

On the other hand, Snowden is by his very nature a wild card. He may not be cooped up in two rooms like Julian Assange in the Ecuadorian embassy in London, but when you are not free to come and go as you please, even the largest country in the world can start to feel confining. Snowden may yet once again do something bold and impulsive that snares the attention of the world.

Reluctantly, Putin was being pulled into the realm of cyberpolitics, which were proving every bit as important as geopolitics. That realm had already generated great wealth, great power, great names—Gates, Jobs, Snowden. And there was a new name on the rise—"Guccifer"— which as its creator would explain was a mix of "the style of Gucci and the light of Lucifer." That creator was a Romanian hacker in his early forties by the name of Marcel Lazar. At the time of his arrest by Romanian authorities for cybercrimes in that country he gave as his profession unemployed taxi driver, which is about as unemployed as you can get.

Using nothing fancier than an NEC desktop and a feel for how people created passwords, he cracked the accounts of, among others, Colin Powell, Candace Bushnell, and Sidney Blumenthal, confidant and adviser to Hillary Clinton. In cracking Blumenthal's account Guccifer was able to reveal that Clinton was using a private email account to conduct official State Department business, which led to an FBI investigation and haunted her throughout her presidential campaign.

Snowden had demonstrated how a state could be weakened by leaks; Guccifer had demonstrated how specific political figures could be weakened, not so much by the contents of their emails but by how they used the email system itself.

From the very start Putin had suspected that the Internet itself was a "CIA project," one whose ultimate aim was to infiltrate and weaken Russia, if only because the last thing the West wanted was a strong Russia. Putin publicly voiced those suspicions in 2014 and soon thereafter began to take actions that would wrest control of Russia's Internet away from the CIA and its various minions, witting and unwitting.

Sometime after being driven through the ghastly emptiness of Moscow's streets to his inauguration in May 2012, Putin began to slip deeper into the twilight of paranoia. This is a state of mind in which outlandish fears can be both sincerely believed and cynically exploited for political purposes.

The Moscow street demonstrations could not have been the product of injustice and outrage—someone had to be behind them, since someone always was. In this case that someone was Hillary Clinton. Putin said: "She set the tone for some actors in our country and gave them a signal. They heard the signal and with the support of the US State Department began active work."

The Arab Spring, the Moscow protests, and the damage caused by Guccifer made Putin realize that he had underestimated the power of the Internet. His parliament at once began drafting bills for laws that required foreign social media websites to locate their servers in Russia and to retain all information about users for at least six months and make it available on demand to the authorities. Another law blocks Web sites entirely even without a court ruling. Another makes any blogger with more than three thousand followers bear the same level of responsibility as mass media companies, meaning he or she can face heavy fines for positing incorrect information. Nearly any expression of critical thought can be labeled "extremist" and punished as such. Denial-of-service attacks against opposition Web sites became more frequent. An army of well-paid trolls posted pro-Putin comments on Russian and Western news outlets.

In late 2015 Putin invited Herman Klimenko, a programmer and Web entrepreneur, to serve as his official adviser on the Internet. Born in 1966, Klimenko is closer in age to Putin than are most of those active in Russia's Internet world. Balding, bearded, he has an avuncular twinkle in his eye and a wit that can cause him to refer to Russia ironically as a "banana republic," but there is no doubt about his good-soldier attitude. In fact, his first statement about his decision to accept Putin's offer was couched in military terms: "When I served in the army, there would be orders for officer appointments. Simply out of respect, you were given three days to weigh the orders. It was understood that, on the third day, the answer was always 'yes.'"

And "yes" is the word Putin is most likely to hear from Klimenko, who quickly went on record as saying: "Now the Internet is flooded with money, and criminals, and terrorists. Of course, all this needs to be regulated."

Klimenko went after Google and Apple in much the same way the EU has, demanding that they pay significantly higher taxes than they currently do. He summed the situation up rustically: "We are breeding the cow and they are milking it." Klimenko has a strong ally in parliament who is sponsoring a bill that would impose an 18 percent value added tax on the revenue generated by Google, Apple, and other such companies. In the odd-bedfellows department, Klimenko's ally in parliament is none other than Andrei Lugovoi, one of the two former KGB men accused of assassinating Alexander Litvinenko with polonium in London in 2006.

In the three years between the Guccifer revelation of Clinton's private email account and the Guccifer 2.0 hack of the Democratic National Committee, a great change took place within the citadel of Putin's mind. His initial responses to the Internet were those that were to be expected—curtail and control. At first, he failed to appreciate the full potential of hacking, being more interested in the gems of useful information that could thus be obtained and in the bragging rights that came with it—Russia's hackers are stronger than yours.

But in the case of the hacking of Sidney Blumenthal's correspondence with Hillary Clinton, there was very little useful information, and the hacker himself was a Romanian, hardly an occasion for nationalist chest-thumping (though Guccifer did use a Russian proxy server).

It was true that all the emails from Blumenthal, a former adviser to Bill Clinton and full-time employee of the Clinton Foundation, were marked "Confidential" and claimed to contain intelligence "from extremely sensitive sources." But then something rare and difficult to grasp began to happen that took Putin time to understand: It wasn't the stealthy skill of the hacker that mattered, and it wasn't the "sensitive" intelligence that was splashed all over the world's media that mattered. What mattered more than any of that was that Secretary of State Clinton was using a private server for official communications. It was the delivery system that counted, not the content. Once again the medium was the message.

Another new use for the Internet was found in connection with former KGB officer Alexander Litvinenko, who died so hideously and so publicly from polonium poisoning in London in 2006. In Putin's eyes Litvinenko had committed three unforgivable sins. He betrayed the brotherhood of the KGB, the vilest of treasons. He incriminated Putin in the supposed FSB bombing of three residential buildings in 1999, which were to set the stage for the second Chechen war and thus strengthen Putin's position as president. He accused Putin of being a pedophile.

No one can be more vicious in exchanging insults than ex-KGB.

Their accusations should be considered baseless unless supported by hard evidence. There is some evidence that the FSB was involved in the detonation of the buildings, none whatsoever for Putin being a pedophile.

In April 2015 the British police brought six charges of "making and possessing" child pornography against Vladimir Bukovsky, an even less likely candidate for the charge than Vladimir Putin himself. Yet slander is adhesive.

Bukovsky was one of the great figures of the Soviet dissident movement, not as famous as Sakharov and Solzhenitsyn—there is always a second tier—but greatly respected for what he endured, twelve years in psychiatric hospitals and prisons, and for what he achieved as an activist and writer, especially for his memoir, *To Build a Castle: My Life as a Dissenter*. Bukovsky quipped about his literary output in Soviet-era samizdat (self-publishing): "I write it myself, censor it myself, print and disseminate it myself, and then I do time in prison for it myself." He had been a dissenter since the Hungarian Uprising was crushed in 1956. "Our parents had turned out to be agents and informers, our military leaders were butchers, and even the games and fantasies of our childhood seemed to be tainted with fraud."

In 1976 he was forcibly deported from the USSR in exchange for the leader of the Chilean Communist Party. He then devoted himself mostly to neurophysiology, working mainly in Cambridge University in England.

When Litvinenko defected to the UK in 2000, he made contact with Bukovsky, calling him some twenty to thirty times a day. And it was to Bukovsky that Litvinenko would reveal how assassinations were now casually arranged over a bowl of soup in the FSB cafeteria.

After Litvinenko was himself assassinated—Bukovsky was called to testify into the inquiry conducted by former judge Sir Robert Owen. Bukovsky's conclusion was hardly a ringing condemnation:

"I am pretty sure it was done on orders from the Kremlin." Owen himself went further, naming names: "I have concluded that the FSB operation to kill Mr. Litvinenko was probably approved by Mr. Patrushev, then head of the FSB, and also by President Putin."

A month after Bukovsky testified the British police brought the multiple child pornography charges against Bukovsky based on information received from Europol. For a man of Bukovsky's proven integrity it was a particularly loathsome charge, one that would besmirch, if only by association, his last years of life.

Two things were clear to everyone but the British police: the child pornography had been planted in Bukovsky's computer and the act was an obvious allusion to Litvinenko's accusing Putin of pedophilia.

A year after the charges were brought against him, the British police forging ahead with their case, Bukovsky went on a protest hunger strike though he was in very poor health. He said of the possibility of dying: "I'm not afraid of it. How can you be afraid of something inevitable? It isn't a senseless death. It's a purposeful death. I'm an old man anyway."

In May 2016, after three weeks of a hunger strike by Bukovsky and a great international outcry, a British court postponed the criminal case against him. Bukovsky intends to file a civil case against the prosecutors, who say they need more time to determine whether his computer could have been hacked, a task difficult but doable.

One thing is clear here, one isn't. It's clear that the FSB was no more a match for Bukovsky than the KGB was. Men with that diamond-hard integrity can be killed but not broken. What isn't clear is how the example of the attack on Bukovsky might convince future Russia dissenters that the game is not worth the candle.

The FSB and its predecessors had always been adept at finding or manufacturing compromising material, *kompromat*, that could then be planted and later "discovered" when needed. Now the Internet provided a swifter, surer means—no need to break into an apartment; hacking into someone's email was all it took. Hackers had found a new purpose—not only to steal but to leave real evidence of imaginary crimes behind.

On November 9, 2016, Donald Trump, a man of boundless ambition and self-love uncorrected by character or conscience, was elected president of the United States by both the American people and the intelligence agencies of the Russian Federation. Not to be outdone by foreign competition, the FBI had also rolled up its sleeves and gotten down to work to thwart Hillary Clinton's run for president. Was this an early example of the renewed Russian-American cooperation Trump hinted at in his campaign?

Earlier in 2016 the Democratic National Committee's email account was penetrated by a group that called itself Guccifer 2.0 in homage to the original Romanian hacker of that name. There is forensic evidence to support Guccifer 2.0 being run by the FSB with some involvement by Russian military intelligence. Though it is quite certain that the Russian government used hackers in an effort to tilt the American presidential election in Donald Trump's favor, a full picture will likely never emerge unless there is a brief opening of the secret police archives after the fall of Putin's Russia as there was after the fall of the USSR.

These types of situations are always murky because four activities that are quite distinct in most countries—politics, crime, business, and the secret police—in Russia blur and merge, making them hard to tell apart. For example, cybercriminals arrested for bank fraud and extortion are offered a choice between fifteen years in prison with no access to computers or a five-year contract with the FSB as a hacker with access to unparalleled equipment and databases. One assumes they don't agonize long. And those same hackers were exploited by Russian foreign policy when Putin discovered how effective an instrument of espionage and influence the Internet can be.

In any case, the Russian hackers gathered material on everything from what the DNC itself had gathered on Donald Trump to the emails that revealed a supposedly neutral DNC covertly working against Bernie Sanders. That latter revelation of compromised integrity caused the DNC's chairperson Debbie Wasserman Schultz to resign. What mattered here was not the specific political fallout—Schultz was quickly thereafter reelected in her Florida district. Of more importance was that the DNC, and, Clinton's campaign hacked later, was revealed as compromised and hypocritical, exactly the Kremlin critique of American democracy.

Putin was hardly indifferent to the 2016 U.S. presidential election. The bad blood with Clinton went way back. Trump seemed easier to play. But more important to Putin than the winner of a particular election was the elective process itself. It needed to be revealed as unreliable, riggable if not rigged.

And for that reason the Russian hacking of the voter registration systems in Arizona and Illinois in the summer of 2016 were more significant than the DNC break-in. *The Washington Post* called the Illinois hack "the first successful compromise of a state voter registration system" and the FBI rated the threat posed by a similar attack on the Arizona system as "an eight on a scale of one to 10."

Showing the American electoral process to be vulnerable and therefore unworthy of trust weakens the United States at its very core. Putin wants a weaker United States because he sees ample evidence that the United States wants a weaker Russia. It's his golden rule—do unto others as they would do unto you, and preferably before.

But Putin himself may also be vulnerable from within. Many of Russia's freelance hackers partake of the political anarchism that seems inherent to the Internet. The main criminal/anarchist organization, known as Anonymous International or, more familiarly, as Humpty Dumpty, cracked into Prime Minister Dmitri Medvedev's twitter account and sent out the following message in his name: "I'm resigning. I am ashamed of this government's actions. Forgive me."

Other break-ins resulted in information with more substantial political content, e.g., concerning how the Kremlin prepared Crimea's secessionist referendum.

Humpty Dumpty not only engages in pranks and politics but is known to have made significant money through blackmail and extortion. Its members glide easily from crime to business to work for the secret police and the Kremlin's political aims. They have also displayed astonishing high connections in the Russian government. Sergei Mikhailov, the number two man in the FSB Information Security Center, was closely connected with Humpty Dumpty and may even have been running it. During a top-level FSB meeting in late January 2017 Mikhailov was arrested for treason and escorted from the meeting with a hood-like bag over his head.

The treason charges against Mikhailov include passing information to the United States. The U.S. intelligence agencies undoubtedly had such a high degree of confidence about accusing Russia of cyber involvement in the U.S. election not only because of forensic evidence but because they had people on the inside. That does not necessarily mean that Mikhailov was the CIA's man. There are other candidates for that role, one of them already suddenly and conveniently dead.

Mikhailov's arrest may also have been a message to the United States—the DNC break-in was a high-level rogue operation, not one approved and directed from the very top. The Kremlin wants the United States to buy this version of events so that diplomatic relations can improve. The United States may pretend to be mollified by this version, but hackers might not.

A member of Humpty Dumpty said the following in a 2015 interview:

> INT: So, the only thing you won't publish is personal data?
> HD: And we'll never publish state secrets.

INT: What if you had data like Snowden's? Would you leak that?

HD: Most likely not. Not everything needs to be released.

INT: What if the data revealed crimes by the state?

HD: Then we'd release it.

The question that was not asked during that interview was—what sorts of information might you threaten to release if members of your group were arrested?

All such caveats and dangers aside, sometime between Guccifer and Guccifer 2.0 Putin switched from viewing the Internet solely as a threat to understanding it as a weapon that can be adapted and deployed for specifically Russian aims. It could damage political enemies, smear those who would testify against you, even destabilize an opponent's political system. It was almost untraceable, utterly deniable, and wonderfully cheap. Who wouldn't love such a thing?

PART SEVEN

THE END AND AFTER

Russia is the only country in the world
whose government (its nucleus) is located
in a medieval fortress.

—EDUARD LIMONOV

11

RUSSIA WITHOUT PUTIN, PUTIN WITHOUT RUSSIA

Putin will die in the Kremlin, but when and how nobody knows.

—GARRY KASPAROV, CHESS CHAMPION

An eerie void formed when President Putin went missing for eleven days in March 2015, a void of both power and information. Not only was the leader nowhere to be seen, but his staff used cheesy, easily challengeable tricks like airing old video footage to make it appear that Putin was still diligently at work. In fact he had cancelled two quite important meetings—one with the president of Kazakhstan, the other with officials from the FSB, his power base and "alma mater."

When it became clear that the government would not be forthcoming with information, rumors streamed into the void, little prompting ever needed for that. In operatic Russian style they ran the gamut from amour to murder—Putin was attending the birth of his love child with champion gymnast Alina Kabayeva, for whom he had left his wife of many years, or else he had been discreetly poisoned in the Kremlin.

It had to be something out of the ordinary. If it was the flu, his press secretary could just announce that fact and not becloud a situation already murky with the war in Ukraine, plunging oil prices, sanctions, and the murder of opposition leader Boris Nemtsov one week before Putin's seclusion. But Russian leaders don't like their health discussed in public. It can only reduce their larger-than-life image. One Russian woman told me that Stalin's spell had broken for her when during his final illness in 1953 she began reading reports about his urine in *Pravda*. "Gods don't pass urine," she said with a crooked grin.

Contrary to some Western opinion, Putin cultivates his macho image not because he never outgrew an adolescent fascination with pecs, pistols, and espionage, but because in a Darwinian society strength is everything. In the entourage of every godfather, there's always one man who thinks he can do a better job. Stalin, in his later years, was very aware of those in his retinue checking the spring in his step, his quickness of mind.

It is also possible that the reason behind Putin's disappearance was not so primitive, but very much up-to-date. His media and image consultants may have advised him to change the Russian narrative from "Opposition leader murdered in front of Kremlin" to "Putin has disappeared." In any case, his vanishing did precisely that. Domination through absence, domination through presence, but domination at all costs.

Since the void left by Putin drew rumors at a furious pace, this was also a way for Putin to gain certain valuable information about the country's feelings for him. Of course, he knew that independent polling showed his popularity in the astronomical eighties, but he was also aware that this level was maintained because of the high price of oil, which created a boom. A decline in popularity in 2014–15 was offset by the elations of victory in Crimea and Ukraine. The problem with these polls is not that they're rigged but that many respondents will, through an instinct bred in the bone, praise the leader rather than speak ill of him, especially if it costs you nothing.

Putin may also have been testing his immediate entourage to see how some might react to what could be a crisis in the continuity of leadership. Or the whole thing might have been as banal as a bad reaction to a Botox shot that puffed him so much he couldn't show his face for a week.

Although Putin had disappeared from view a couple of times before, the March 2015 incident was the longest and therefore the most significant because it gave Russians a preview of Russia without Putin. In fact, "Russia without Putin" had already become the main slogan the opposition chanted in the streets along with "Putin is a thief." Those street demonstrations grew particularly large and vociferous in late 2011 and reached their crescendo on May 6, 2012, the day before Putin's inauguration for his third presidential term.

The mood at the anti-Putin march was both festive and sinister. People dressed as clowns seemed to be trying both to amuse and to provoke. Wearing storm trooper black, Fascists marched under their black, yellow, and white flag. The Communists held high their traditional red. But the majority of the people were part of the new middle class that had grown up and flourished under Putin. Young couples pushed strollers, followed by nerds sometimes called "office plankton" and "Internet hamsters," old intellectuals with white goatees, stylish women in chic dresses and high heels. What united them was grievance at the way Putin and Medvedev simply swapped the positions of president and prime minister in 2008, an apparent homage to the Constitution that only made their "castling" the more insulting.

Once the demonstrators passed through the metal detectors splayed across the width of the street, they moved forward like a river whose banks were formed by three rows of police and SWAT teams (OMON) standing with their arms linked. Some of the young police, who had been placed in the front line to harden them, looked like they wanted to be anywhere but there. The OMON, on the other hand, were spoiling for violence. They wore segmented black body armor that gave them a sort of outer-space Samurai look. It was *their* demonstration too. A demonstration of *their* numbers, *their* power, *their* limited tolerance.

The violence was not long in coming. Given the length of the demonstration, those at the rear never knew what happened until they went home and turned on the television, which, being state-run, of course, minimized the number of demonstrators while exaggerating the number of police injured by stones and Molotov cocktails.

Putin was so unnerved by the scale and intensity of the demonstrations, he ordered that the streets leading to the Kremlin for his inauguration the next day be kept absolutely empty. So instead of waving in triumph to adoring crowds from his limousine, he drove through a ghost town. The look on his face was one of pale, cold fury.

The demonstrators had ruined his moment, and he would never forgive them. From that day on Putin has been implacable in crackdown.

Dmitri Oreshkin, an opposition analyst who heads Mercator, a Moscow-based research group, says of the people who call for a Russia without Putin: "What do they think is going to follow him? Some liberal politician? No, things would only get worse."

One way that things could get worse is for the Russian state to disintegrate, a possibility that has haunted Putin from the late 1980s as he watched the fall of the USSR. In the chaos of a post-Putin interregnum, Chechnya and the other Muslim-dominated areas could break away to form an emirate or even to swear allegiance to ISIS. Siberia could form its own political entity, vast, strong, and finally free from Moscow. Hungry for lebensraum and arable land, China could reassert control over territory long considered taken from them in "unequal treaties." In short, this would be nothing less than the chaotic disintegration of a nuclear superpower. A more hazardous situation is difficult to imagine.

And so, to counter the formulation of "Russia without Putin," Putin's deputy chief of staff, Vyacheslav Volodin, has come up with an even more ominous version: "No Putin, no Russia."

The Russian Constitution provides that if the president resigns, is incapacitated, is impeached, or dies, his place will be taken by the prime minister. Elections have to be held within three months. There is no indication that Putin has groomed a successor. He would have considered that both premature and dangerous. It would mean both bringing someone too close to him while pushing others away and thereby turning them against him. Putin would of course have gathered or fabricated *kompromat* on all his potential successors. His main strength, however, has always been the loyalty he has demonstrated to others by keeping them in positions of power that bestow great wealth upon them. Still, among them all there is not one with whom Putin could strike the same power-for-immunity deal that Yeltsin struck with him. Putin needs his own Putin.

Whoever he is, Putin's successor will have to possess a rare amalgam of qualities—he must be able to win the respect of the masses; to keep the oligarchs, the military, and the security forces in a dynamic balance; and to manage a complex foreign policy situation. He will also have to face the country's two great unsolved problems—its dangerous dependency on gas and oil, and its failure to create a new sense of national purpose and identity.

It's possible that Mikhail Khodorkovsky, whose life has been marked by superlatives—Russia's richest man, Russia's most famous political prisoner—would return from his European exile in the event of Putin's sudden removal or demise. More than once he has indicated that he would not be averse to running the country. He gained considerable moral authority by standing up to ten years of prison, which also focused and clarified his vision for Russia. Before his imprisonment Khodorkovsky had demonstrated that he was capable of transforming himself from a looter to a leader in business as well as transforming his company, Yukos, into a modern organization, transparent, efficient, highly profitable. At the same time he also displayed the ruthless streak that he would need to stay alive in the jungle of Russian politics. Adept at transformation, he may be just the man to transform Russia.

The other obvious candidate from the opposition side is lawyer and anticorruption blogger Alexei Navalny. Born in 1976, he has enthusiastically indicated his willingness to run and is in the opinion of some prominent pundits the only electable member of the opposition. Navalny has Russian good looks, projects confidence, and has a gift for turning a phrase. He branded Putin's United Russia Party "the party of crooks and thieves," and it stuck.

He has several advantages over Khodorkovsky—he is young, he belongs to the generation that is absolutely at home on the Internet, but he also has a feel for the street. Not limited to the predictable positions of the human rights intelligentsia, he has a strong streak of anti-immigrant Russian nationalism and knows how to appeal to it in others, an increasingly valuable political skill in a global era of fast-moving rightward currents. A self-described nationalist democrat, he has, according to a *New York Times* story, "Rousing Russia with a Phrase," "appeared as a speaker alongside neo-Nazis and skinheads, and once starred in a video that compares dark-skinned Caucasus militants to cockroaches. While cockroaches can be killed with a slipper, he says that in the case of humans, 'I recommend a pistol.'" But the violent language is not reserved for non-Russians. To those who call him a network hamster, he replies: "I am a network hamster and I will slit the throats of these cattle!" At the same time he is not above posing in various high-end brand-name clothes for the Russian *GQ* while giving the magazine a hard-hitting interview. This would win him points with other "network hamsters" but would alienate the sort of Russians who would see this, like his time at Yale as a World Fellow in 2010, as proof of his treacherous otherness.

Though disapproving of Putin's methods, Navalny is already on record as saying that Crimea is now an inalienable part of Russia. Like Khodorkovsky, he too has been singled out for persecution, but, so far at least, it has been more serial harassment than the hard blow of prison. Currently, Navalny, who won 27 percent in the 2013 Moscow mayoral elections, is barred from politics by a felony conviction specifically imposed for that purpose. Under different conditions that conviction could of course be overturned. Also, unlike Khodorkovsky, he does not have the experience of running a vast and complex organization. Perhaps the two of them working together in a new party could prove a formidable force in the event of a suddenly Putin-free Russia.

The first post-Putin leader will, however, probably emerge from the inner circle of high government officials and military/security types. Dmitri Medvedev is one possibility, assuming that his years in power have made him tougher and wilier. The joke about Medvedev that began circulating as soon as he appeared on the political scene went like this: Putin and Medvedev go into a restaurant. The waiter asks Putin: "What will you have?" Putin says: "A steak." And the waiter says: "And the vegetable?" Putin says: "The vegetable will have a steak too."

Still, Medvedev ran Gazprom, a serious organization, before being chosen to replace Putin as president. Foreign leaders, especially Obama, felt comfortable with him as a twenty-first-century type, an aura Putin has never projected. Medvedev might be the right person to lead Russia out of its current political and economic impasse with the West, but most likely he would be a transitional figure, more figurehead than actual leader.

When Putin was deciding who would replace him as president

while he served as prime minister to honor the letter of the Constitution, Medvedev's main competition was Sergei Ivanov. Ivanov was, however, too much like Putin for Putin's liking. Of the same generation, a fellow Leningrader and KGB officer, Ivanov, in his capacity as Putin's chief of staff, could say that on many issues he and Putin "think more or less identically." They served together in the Leningrad KGB in the seventies, and Ivanov would later be Putin's deputy when Putin took charge of the FSB. Rumor has it that Putin envied Ivanov's height, fluency in English, and success in the KGB—Ivanov reached the rank of general as opposed to Putin's lieutenant colonel—and for those reasons chose the pliable and stubby Medvedev as his replacement. Though Ivanov insists that when it comes to being Putin's successor, "I have never regarded myself as such," others see that as a mere formal demurral. As political analyst Vladimir Pribylovsky put it: "Ivanov wants the throne."

To speculation there is no end, but one thing at least is sure—short of grave illness or death, Putin would never surrender his post as Russia's leader without a fight. And his own personal army, the 400,000-strong National Guard, which includes the OMON teams that attacked the anti-Putin marchers on the day before his inauguration, will stand him in good stead if that fight takes a literal turn. Apart from that unlikely though not impossible eventuality, the National Guard is always a part of the pressure Putin can bring to bear on any internal political situation.

What Condoleezza Rice said of him in a WikiLeaked cable—that Putin fears "law enforcement investigations"—is no doubt true. He may well believe that he has to die in the Kremlin, in prison, or in sumptuous exile, perhaps living statelessly on the $35 million yacht the oligarch Roman Abramovich gave him as a present.

A new Russian leader almost always defines himself in stark opposition to his predecessor. Anyone replacing Putin would need to show that many of Putin's actions were not only ill-considered, but criminal. Putin's successor would look deeply into his affairs and no doubt find any number of crimes ranging from rank corruption to murder most foul.

Economic crimes are easier to trace than murder though their trail is often labyrinthine, shell company within shell company until half of Siberia disappears into a tiny Caribbean island.

The Panama Papers of early 2016 did not directly implicate Putin in any questionable dealings. However, they did reveal that symphony cellist Sergei Roldugin, the friend of his youth and later godfather to his daughter, controlled some $2 billion in offshore financial assets. Putin was pleased that no direct line could be traced between him and Roldugin, but he couldn't have been happy that that particular cover was blown.

There is an almost Shakespearean profusion of corpses on the stage of Putin's presidency—the journalist Anna Politkovskaya, gunned down just after entering her apartment building; former KGB man Alexander Litvinenko, wasting away from polonium poisoning in London; opposition leader Boris Nemtsov, shot dead in sight of the Kremlin. Still, there's little chance of Putin ever being implicated in those crimes.

Putin doesn't have to ask: Who will rid me of this meddlesome person? No direct orders from Putin are necessary for this, no winks, no nearly imperceptible nods (except, one assumes, for murders committed on foreign soil). Before himself being assassinated, former KGB agent Alexander Litvinenko explained how such assassinations are conceived and carried out now under Putin as opposed to in Soviet times. Back then, the KGB was tightly controlled by the party's Central Committee. Nothing as important as a killing was possible without direct party approval and control. Now it's the opposite. There's no party, no Central Committee to which the security services must kowtow and report. It's all much more relaxed, informal, humdrum. As Litvinenko tells it, deals are made in the lunchroom: "I'm having a little soup and a guy from another section walks over and says: 'Sasha, you got any criminal connections?' 'I do,' I say. 'Listen,' he says, 'there's this guy I'm sick of, get rid of him for me.'

In Dostoevsky's novel *The Brothers Karamazov* the half-wit half brother Smerdyakov, sensing his brothers' hostility and murderous intent, carries out their secret wish and kills their father. There is a sort of Smerdyakov effect at work in Putin's Russia. Divining the leader's unspoken desires, the little Smerdyakovs of the security services have no trouble finding criminal types to do the dirty work and, if necessary, take the fall.

Putin doesn't order hits, because he doesn't have to. It can all be settled by a couple of guys over a bowl of soup.

Putin is the richest man in Russia. Putin is the richest man in Europe. Putin is the richest man in the world. There are many estimates of Putin's wealth but what they are actually based on is unclear to say the least. Apparently, Swedish economist Anders Aslund and the CIA working independently came up with the same figure, $40 billion, which has now become somewhat canonical. However, Bill Browder, who once ran the largest investment fund in Russia before he was swindled out of it and declared persona non grata, quintupled that canonical estimate to $200 billion in his 2015 book *Red Notice*. One more such quintupling leap and Putin will be the first trillionaire in history.

But all these various estimates overlook the most important thing, which is that if Mr. Putin is out of power, then he's out of pocket as well. His control of portions of Russia's largest companies would instantly evaporate with his loss of office.

If Putin was able to leave Russia, then the question would become—where would he live and on what? If his principal concern was extradition, there are any number of countries from Brazil to

Dubai where he would be safe. Many countries have fast tracks to citizenship for those who buy property, deposit money in local banks, or otherwise invest. It's possible that some deal for sanctuary could be, or has already been, worked out. The problem for Putin would not be finding a country that would accept him and not extradite him to Russia, which doesn't extradite its own citizens either. A more pressing problem would be what would support the former president in something like the style to which he has grown accustomed. Putin may well have foreign accounts containing dollars or euros, but bank accounts can be frozen and access to safe-deposit boxes denied. For that reason leaders like Putin tend to favor tangible things and thus put their trust in gold and land.

In June 2011 Putin became the only Russian president ever to visit the nation's main gold depository, located in central Moscow. A photo shows him holding up a twenty-pound ingot with one hand as his entourage looks on with smiling approval. Putin too seems to be enjoying the moment, the heft of the bar, the density of its concentrated wealth. In itself this of course proves nothing, but there are other, more significant indications of his interest in gold. Under Putin Russia became for a time the world's top buyer of gold, acquiring over 600 tons in the decade between 2004 and 2014. Despite the economic problems caused by oil prices and sanctions, or perhaps because of them, Russia became the world's number one gold purchaser in 2015 and in early 2016 was buying 500,000 ounces a month.

Russia also produces considerable gold—291 tons were mined in 2015, 208 of which were added to the nation's central bank reserves. The gold produced within Russia is shipped by FeldSvyaz, a courier service that reports directly to Putin. How difficult would it be for Putin to arrange to have a certain percentage skimmed off the top and have it shipped abroad for safekeeping? Gold is not as cumbersome as might be imagined. A million dollars in gold bars is only three times heavier than its equivalent in U.S. hundreds and is virtually untraceable.

Where might that gold be? An early 2016 *New Yorker* article, "The Bouvier Affair" by Sam Knight, about the fleecing of a Russian oligarch, offers one clue:

> The Geneva Freeport, which may be the world's most valuable storage facility, consists of seven beige warehouses and a large grain silo in La Praille, an industrial zone a short tram ride from the city's lakeside panorama of banks and expensive hotels. . . . Iris scanners, magnetic locks, and a security system known as Cerberus guard the freeport's storerooms, whose contents are said to be insured for a hundred billion dollars. . . . The freeport is eighty-six percent owned by the local government—and kinship with the opaque traditions of Swiss banking made it a storage facility for the international elite. Under the freeport's rules, objects could remain in untaxed limbo, in theory, forever. Treasures came and they did not leave. A generation ago, those goods were cars, wine, and gold.

Putin may also be funneling wealth out of the country to his children. In late 2015 there were reports that Putin's daughter Ekaterina was buying a luxury property in Biarritz, the elegant resort on the Atlantic side of the South of France where Putin was living very modestly in the summer of 1999 when Boris Berezovsky came to convince him to accept the post of prime minister. That would make a nice full circle.

Putin has also maintained close ties with European leaders like former Italian prime minister Silvio Berlusconi, who could have proved useful in assisting Putin in transferring wealth out of Russia.

But not all scenarios need end as ignominiously as those with Putin scampering away to Biarritz or some such place with bags of cash. A man extremely favored by fortune in his rise to power, he could yet prove favored again. The exploitation of the Arctic could stave off disaster for another generation.

Or a military intervention in Kazakhstan might provide the Kremlin with leverage over China, thereby completing the task of restoring Russia's greatness by restoring Russia's power.

Even if these unlikely glories are attained, they will, however, only temporarily obscure the failure at the core of Putin's reign.

Putin was given a unique opportunity by history, a period of wealth and peace that he could have used to liberate his country from its dependence on oil and on authoritarian rule. He squandered that opportunity to unleash the source of Russia's true greatness—the still untapped skills and spirit of its people. Was not his own career sufficient proof of how high an ordinary Russian could rise?

But Putin did not trust. He did not trust the world outside Russia, which in the end he could only see as the enemy at the gates. He did not trust the Russian people out of the fear that they would run rampant if given liberty. But it was a handful of well-educated men who looted the country, not ordinary Russians, who at worst filched a few boards or some cable, and proved themselves sober and canny in Russia's first real elections. And in the end on some level he did not trust himself sufficiently to manage a freer people in a world that might be opposed at times to Russia but was hardly inimical to it.

He did succeed in restoring stability and a measure of self-respect to Russia after the bitter humiliations of the 1990s, no small achievement. At the beginning of his second term, with high oil prices buoying the economy and his popularity solid and high, Putin could have done something daring and transformative. Using his immense top-down power he could have in earnest begun the transformation of Russia from a petrostate to a twenty-first-century knowledge-based economy—not because a knowledge-based economy is "nicer" and "greener," but because it is a more dependable producer of wealth over the long run and also because it involves larger numbers of people than the gas and oil industries, thereby making them stakeholders in society. In turn, that sense of belonging and connectedness could have served as the matrix for a new culture from which Russia's new vision of identity would finally emerge.

The timing was good, the timing was bad. Good from the point of view of Russia's wealth and Putin's popularity, bad from the point of view of the world situation. The Orange Revolution in Ukraine in 2004 might have been seen by Putin as only an internal question if NATO had not at the same time conferred membership on seven former Eastern Bloc countries, three of them former Soviet republics, moving the alliance right up to Russia's western border. It was then that Putin began to suffer not from a too low sense of danger but from one that would quickly become much too high.

And as people often do in times of threat and jeopardy, Putin reverted to the tried and true, in his case "the power vertical." His rule started out as authoritarianism lite but became less so with each challenge, culminating in the street demonstrations on the eve of his inauguration in May 2012. Economically, hewing to the tried and true meant sticking with gas and oil instead of transforming Russia into a knowledge-based economy that would have involved large numbers of people. Instead, the state and society ended up separate if not opposed, Russia's perennial tragic conundrum.

And because it did not involve the people enough, the House of Putin will, like the House of the Tsars and the House of the Communists, sooner or later come crashing down. When and with how much suffering is anyone's guess. All that is sure is that the Russian people, who outlasted Genghis Khan and Napoleon, Stalin and Hitler, will survive the fall of the House of Putin. Surviving is what Russians absolutely do best.

NOTES

EPIGRAPHS

xi   *"I cannot"*: Winston Churchill, "The Russian Enigma," BBC Broadcast, October 1, 1939. The Churchill Society London.

xi   *"The politics of Russia"*: Alexander Solzhenitsyn, *The Russian Question at the End of the Twentieth Century* (New York: Farrar, Straus and Giroux, 1995), p. 18.

PREFACE: PUTIN TRUMPS AMERICA

xii   *"if the Trump campaign"*: "Full transcript: FBI Director James Comey testifies on Russian interference in 2016 election," *The Washington Post*, March 20, 2017, p. 3.

xii   *"I have been authorized"*: Ibid., p. 9.

xii   "gray cloud": Glenn Thrush and Maggie Haberman, "Trump's Weary Defenders Face Fresh Worries," *The New York Times*, March 20, 2017.

xiii   *"there is smoke"*: Ibid.

xiii   *"A year ago"*: Full transcript, p. 2.

xv   *"The hotel was known"*: Full text of Christopher Steele dossier published by *Buzzfeed*, January 10, 2017, unpaginated.

xv   *"You know the closest"*: Glenn Garvin, "Donald Trump, the Unwanted Palm Beach Mansion and the Russian Fertilizer King," *The Miami Herald*, March 7, 2017.

xvi   *"provided valuable," "critical to national security"*: Eric Shawn, "Felix Sater, man at center of Ukraine plan, said he was only trying to help." Fox News Politics, February 20, 2017.

xvii   *"Russians make up"*: Glenn Kessler, "Trump's Claim that 'I Have Nothing to Do with Russia,'" *The Washington Post,* July 27, 2016.

xvii   *"were sitting in the room"*: Megan Twohey, Scott Shane, "A Back-Channel Plan for Ukraine and Russia, Courtesy of Trump Associates," *The New York Times,* February 19, 2017.

xvii   *"the Russian authorities"*: Christopher Steele dossier, *Buzzfeed.*

xviii   *"after his name surfaced"*: Andrew E. Kramer, "Paul Manafort, Former Trump Campaign Chief, Faces New Allegations in Ukraine," *The New York Times,* March 20, 2017.

xviii   *"I don't think"*: "Here's the transcript of Trump's repeated evasions on whether his campaign had contacts with Russian officials," *The Los Angeles Times,* March 26, 2017.

xviii   *"In 2006, a series of protests"*: James Miller, "Trump and Russia: All the Mogul's Men," *Daily Beast,* November 6, 2016.

xix   *"I am trying to play"*: Ibid.

xix   *"was doing a great job," "at least he was"*: Jeremy Diamond, "Timeline: Donald Trump's Praise for Vladimir Putin:, *CNN Politics,* July 29, 2016.

xix   *"Manafort proposed"*: Jeff Horowitz, Chad Day, "Manafort Had Plan to Benefit Putin Government," Associated Press, *Bloomberg News/Politics,* March 22, 2017.

xix   *"We are now of the belief"*: Ibid.

xxi   *"Ambassador Kislyak"*: John R. Schindler, "The Spy Revolt Against Trump Begins," Observer.com, February 2, 2017.

xxi   *"A senior National Security"*: Ibid.

xxii   *"The Russia Investigation"*: Glenn Thrush, Maggie Haberman, "Why Letting Go, for Trump, Is No Small or Simple Task," *The New York Times,* March 21, 2017.

xxii   *"Longtime Trump political advisor"*: Ibid.

xxiii   *"a smell of treason"*: Nicholas Kristof, "A Smell of Treason in the Air," *The New York Times,* March 23, 2017.

xxiii   *"In December, Michael Flynn"*: Full transcript, *Washington Post,* p. 6.

xxiv   *"our inability"*: Ibid., p. 2.

PART ONE: THE PRESENT AS PROLOGUE

1   *"The war between"*: Mark Galeotti, "Putin's Hydra: Inside Russia's Intelligence Services," European Council on Foreign Affairs, ecfr.eu.

CHAPTER 1: ARMS AND THE MAN

3 *"As is often the case"*: Nikolai Petrov, "How Putin Changed the Balance of Power Among Russia's Elite," *Moscow Times,* April 15, 2016.

4 *"When it comes to President"*: Mikhail Fishman, "A Bigger Bludgeon," *Moscow Times,* April 14, 2016.

5 *"There are too many"*: Pete Earley, *Comrade J* (New York: Berkeley Books, 2009), p. 299.

6 *"You could have killed him"*: Ibid., p. 301.

7 *"reckless"*: "John Kerry: We Could Have Shot Down Russian Jets 'Buzzing' US Warship," *Guardian,* April 14, 2016.

7 *"We will continue"*: Pavel Felgenhauer, "Russian Jets Fly Close to US Ship and Recon Aircraft over Baltic Sea," *Eurasia Daily Monitor,* April 21, 2016.

7 *"Narva is a part of NATO"*: "US Armor Paraded 300 Meters from Russian Border," RT News, March 23, 2015.

9 *"It's no secret"*: www.freekaliningrad.ru/tsukanov-intelligence-services-of-the-west.

9 *"creeping Germanization"*: Sergey Sukhaov, "Kaliningrad as a New Ideological Battlefield Between Russia and the West," *Eurasia Daily Monitor,* April 25, 2016.

9 *"Senior Russian intellectuals"*: Ibid.

9 *"superpower agency"*: "Putin's Personal Army," *Moscow Times,* April 7, 2016.

11 *"stressing competitors"*: Lisa Ferdinando, "Carter Outlines Security Challenges, Warns Against Sequestration," *DoD News,* March 17, 2016.

11 *"has not accepted the hand"*: Julian Barnes, "NATO's Breedlove Calls for Sharper Focus on Russia Ahead of Departure," *Wall Street Journal,* May 1, 2016.

11 *"may not be"*: Ibid.

PART TWO: BACKGROUND CHECK

13 *". . . the time is right"*: The Rolling Stones, "Street Fighting Man," *Beggars Banquet.*

CHAPTER 2: THE EDUCATION OF V. V. PUTIN

15 *"All decent people"*: Vladimir Putin, *First Person* (New York: Public Affairs, 2000), p. 81.

15 *"For the first time"*: Robert Gates, Quotation of the Day, *New York Times,* September 20, 2008.

16 *"You hold things dearer in there"*: Richard Lourie, *Russia Speaks* (New York: HarperCollins, 1991), p. 189.

17 *"When he became President"*: Ben Judah, *Fragile Empire* (New Haven, Conn.: Yale University Press, 2013), p. 20.

17 *"Once my mother"*: Putin, *First Person*, p. 6.

18 *"sun, moon and stars"*: Ibid., p. 61.

18 *"horrendous"*: Ibid., p. 10.

18 *"hordes of rats"*: Ibid.

19 *"potential, energy, and character"*: Ibid., p. 17.

19 *"He was ordinary"*: Andrew Jack, *Inside Putin's Russia* (New York: Oxford University Press, 2004), p. 52.

19 *"honest"*: Inna Lazareva, "Remembering Vladimir Putin as a boy," *New Statesman*, Jan. 15, 2015.

19 *"the streets of Leningrad"*: Daniel Triesman, "For Vladimir Putin What's at Stake in Metrojet Investigation," CNN, November 6, 2015.

19 *"The greatest criminals"*: Ben Judah, "Behind the Scenes in Putin's Court," *Newsweek*, July 23, 2014.

20 *"Books and spy movies"*: Putin, *First Person*, p. 22.

20 *"They went to see different"*: The poem "Restoration of Order" by Stanislaw Baranczak in my translation from Polish was published in *Dissent*, Winter 1984.

20 *"came on their own initiative"*: Putin, *First Person*, p. 23.

21 *"But what kind"*: Ibid.

21 *"From that moment"*: Ibid.

21 *"silent man"*: Ibid., p. 4.

21 *"only a fool"*: Judah, *Fragile Empire*, p. 10.

21 *"I didn't think"*: Putin, *First Person*, pp. 41–42.

22 *"After a breakfast"*: Lourie, *Russia Speaks*, p. 312.

22 *"Once, at Eastertime . . . Suddenly somebody's socks"*: Putin, *First Person*, p. 52.

23 *"Only the nineteenth century"*: Gary Weir and Walter Boybe, *Rising Tide* (New York: New American Library, 2003), p. 41.

24 *"This is the most"*: Jacques Margeret, *The Russian Empire and Grand Duchy of Moscow* (Pittsburgh: University of Pittsburgh Press, 1983), p. 26.

24 *"in no way distinguished"*: my translation. Appears as "wasn't too exceptional" in Putin, *First Person*, p. 48.

24 *"dangles"* and *"first stage of operational development"*: Earley, *Comrade J*, pp. 49 and 50 respectively.

24 *"We parachuted from planes"*: Yuri Shvets, *Washington Station* (New York: Simon and Schuster, 1994), p. 15.

24 *"convinced the KGB"*: Early, *Comrade J*, p. 38.

25 *"the least corrupt"*: attributed to Sakharov; Peter Baker and Susan Glasser, *Kremlin Rising* (Washington, D.C.: Potomac Books, 2007), p. 258.

25 *"he had watched in horror"*: Christopher Andrew and Vasili Mitrokhin, *The Sword and the Shield* (New York: Basic Books, 1999), p. 5.

26 *"Beginning in 1976, the KGB"*: "Soviet Cold War Tapping of the US Embassy in Moscow. A Post-Mortem," September 15, 2012. See also Sharon Maneki, "Learning from the Enemy: The Gunman Project," National Security Agency, 2012.

27 *"skills enhancement"*: www.agentura.ru/english/dossier/fsb/academy/.

28 *"the destruction of dissent"*: Andrew and Mitrokhin, *The Sword and the Shield*, p. 7.

29 *"an appropriate conversation"*: Gregory Freeze et al., ed., *The KGB Files on Andrei Sakharov* (Waltham Mass.: Andrei Sakharov Archives, Brandeis University / Yale University Press, 2005), pp. 25–26.

29 *"advisable to install"*: Ibid., p. 37.

29 *"Meeting regularly"*: Ibid., p. 58.

30 *"The Sakharov affair"*: Putin, *First Person*, p. 50.

30 *"Gradually it dawned"*: Vladimir Usoltsev, *Sosluzhivets* (Moscow: Eksmo, 2004), p. 186, my translation.

31 *"We are fleeting in this world"*: Dmitri Volkogonov, *Autopsy of an Empire* (New York: Free Press, 1998), p. 382.

33 *"They're not going to understand"*: Putin, *First Person*, p. 62.

34 *"I taught the art"*: Ibid., p. 54.

34 *"specialist in human relations"*: Ibid., p. 44.

34 *"Look at Comrade Platov"*: Ibid., p. 53.

34 *"decided to try him out"*: Ibid.

34 *"We had 'uncles'"*: Jack, *Inside Putin's Russia*, p. 58.

35 *"for the interests"*: Putin, *First Person*, p. 40.

35 *"You would be ordered"*: Earley, *Comrade J*, p. 54.

35 *"It was from the James Bond"*: Vladimir Kuzichkin, *Inside the KGB* (New York: Pantheon, 1990), p. 63.

35 *"he was somewhat withdrawn"*: Putin, *First Person*, p. 55.

36 *"I had to work"*: Ibid., p. 37.

CHAPTER 3: DRESDEN

37 *"Of course life in East Germany"*: Putin, *First Person*, p. 75.

37 *"we had the advantage"*: Markus Wolf, *Man Without a Face* (New York: Public Affairs, 1999), p. 121.

38 *"must be tons"*: Kurt Vonnegurt, *Slaughterhouse Five* (New York: Dial, 1969), p. 1.

38 *"As the Soviet Union's westernmost"*: John Koehler, *Stasi: The Untold Story of the East German Secret Police* (Boulder, Colo.: Westview Press, 1999), p. 73.

38 *"very boring"*: Wolf, *Man Without a Face*, p. 110.

38 *"blond, athletic, simpatico"*: Usoltsev, *Sosluzhivets*, p. 62.

39 *"a harshly totalitarian"*: Putin, *First Person*, p. 77.

39 *"worse than the Gestapo"*: Koehler, *Stasi*, p. 8.

39 *The entire society was infested*: Ibid., p. 9.

39 *"They not only terrorized"*: Ibid., p. 27.

40 *"a Soviet citizen"*: Kuzichkin, *Inside the KGB*, p. 82.

40 *"The work was"*: Putin, *First Person*, p. 69.

41 *"The records"*: Andrew and Mitrokhin, *The Sword and the Shield*, pp. 8–9.

41 *"if a KGB operation"*: Kuzichkin, *Inside the KGB*, pp. 86–87.

41 *"During the Cold War"*: Thom Shanker, "A Secret Warrior Leaves the Pentagon as Quietly as He Entered," *New York Times*, May 1, 2015.

42 *"Putin is a man of few words"*: Mark Franchetti, "Agent Reveals Young Putin's Spy Disaster," *Sunday Times*, London March 19, 2000.

42 *"runs on paperwork"*: Shvets, *Washington Station*, p. 27.

42 *"Our work"*: Usoltsev, *Sosluzhivets*, p. 24.

43 *"Putin's biggest success"*: Masha Gessen, *The Man Without a Face* (New York: Riverhead, 2012), p. 66.

43 *"Of course I did not"*: Earley, *Comrade J*, p. 330.

43 *"Probably"*: Putin, *First Person*, p. 67.

43 *"entirely correct"*: Ibid., p. 74.

44 *"I was a senior"*: Ibid., p. 72.

44 *"Lord Paperwork"*: Shvets, *Washington Station*, p. 25.

44 *"lived in total harmony"*: Putin, *First Person*, p. 61.

45 *"always submitted"*: This and other Lyudmila Putin quotes are in my translation from Oleg Blotsky, *Vladimir Putin: Istoriya zhizni* (Moscow: Izdatelstvo Mezhdunarodniye otnosheniya, 2002). No page numbers because the section

was from an online post. Apparently the book was published in English that same year as *Vladimir Putin: The Road to Power*.

46 *"hellish"*: Usoltsev, *Sosluzhivets*, p. 53.

46 *"Don't forget"*: Ibid., p. 185.

47 *"natural element"*: Ibid., p. 166.

47 *"if there's a holiday"*: Ibid., p. 201.

48 *"We destroyed"*: Putin, *First Person*, p. 76.

48 *"We were forced"*: Ibid., p. 78.

48 *"We cannot do anything"*: Ibid., p. 79.

48 *"That business of"*: Ibid.

PART THREE: ASCENT

49 *"The lowest card"*: Baltasar Gracián, *The Pocket Oracle and Art of Prudence*, quoted in *Lapham's Quarterly* 9, no. 3 (Summer 2016), p. 171.

CHAPTER 4: RUSSIA'S FALL, PUTIN'S RISE

51 *"Blaming Russia"*: Jakub Korejba, "Democracy? No Thanks!"; *New Eastern Europe*, January–March 2013.

51 *"were put in place"*: Andrei Soldatov and Irina Borogan, *The New Nobility* (New York: Public Affairs, 2010), p. 28.

51 *"I was happy"*: Putin, *First Person*, pp. 86–87.

52 *"there was no future"*: Ibid., p. 85.

52 *"had lost touch"*: Ibid., p. 87.

53 *"Screw it"*: Ibid., p. 88.

53 *"knew that it was wiser"*: Gessen, *The Man Without a Face*, p. 97.

54 *"Igor, I want"*: Putin, *First Person*, p. 92.

54 *"a beautiful but dangerous"* and *"As soon as the barbed wire"*: from *Quora* interview "What Are Putin's Views on Communism?" www.quora.com.

54 *"He was utterly"*: John Lloyd, "The Logic of Vladimir Putin," *New York Times*, March 19, 2000.

55 *"preserving the Soviet Union"*: Putin, *First Person*, p. 93.

55 *"Speaking from the steps"*: Obituary in the *Economist*, February 24, 2000.

56 *"Once I saw the faces"*: Putin, *First Person*, p. 93.

56 *"They were nearly all kikes"*: Richard Lourie, "Window on Russia," *Boston Phoenix*, October 18, 1991.

57 *"We are so happy"*: Ibid.

57 *"décor of laws"*: Andrei Amalrik, *Will the Soviet Union Survive Until 1984?* (New York: Perennial Library, 1970), p. 23.

57 *"most hated"*: C. J. Chivers and Erin E. Arvedlund, "Head of Russian Electricity Monopoly Survives Ambush," *New York Times*, March 3, 2005.

58 *"architect of the largest transfer"*: David Hoffman, *The Oligarchs* (New York: Public Affairs, 2002), p. 5.

58 *"I hate the Soviet system"*: TASS, Politika, June 16, 2015, tass.ru/ronika/ 2042091.

59 *"pristinely empty"*: Hoffman, *The Oligarchs*, p. 184.

59 *"Why should they"*: Ibid., p. 183.

60 *"In Sophia"*: Richard Lourie, "Pride and Prices," *Boston Phoenix*, January 3, 1992.

60 *"The schools now serve"*: Ibid.

61 *"Russia and the whole world"*: Leon Aron, *Yeltsin* (New York: St. Martin's Press, 2000), p. 317.

63 *"With a cigarette dangling"*: Gessen, *The Man Without a Face*, p. 81.

63 *"Judge his success"*: John Lloyd, "The Logic of Vladimir Putin," *New York Times*, March 19, 2000.

63 *"I found him great"*: Ibid.

64 *"not radically more serious"*: Gessen, *The Man Without a Face*, p. 124.

64 *"And what was absolutely surprising"*: Baker and Glasser, *Kremlin Rising*, p. 52.

65 *"barbaric on both sides"*: novaonline.nvcc.edu/eli/evans/his241/notes/geography /caucasus.html.

66 *"It was my salary"*: Hoffman, *The Oligarchs*, p. 117.

67 *"He uses every person"*: Chrystia Freeland, *Sale of the Century* (New York: Crown, 2000), p. 134.

67 *"He was in one place"*: Hoffman, *The Oligarchs*, p. 132.

69 *"a Faustian bargain"*: Freeland, *Sale of the Century*, p. 169.

69 *"We do not need"*: Hoffman, *The Oligarchs*, p. 308.

69 *"Isn't it clear"*: Philip Berman, review of Leon Aron, *Yeltsin*, *Philadelphia Inquirer*, April 16, 2000.

69 *"The world's most powerful"*: Hoffman, *The Oligarchs*, p. 326.

69 *"hang from a lamppost"*: Ibid., p. 328.

70 *"the cosmopolitan elite"*: Aron, *Yeltsin*, p. 596.

70 *"the turncoats"*: Ibid., p. 607.

70   *"spark and charisma"*: Ibid., p. 617.

70   *"sound bites"*: Ibid.

70–71 *"Five years ago"*: Ibid., p. 621.

71   *"I will ensure"*: Ibid., p. 622.

71   *"circles of Bolshevik hell"*: Ibid.

71   *"I was under"*: Ibid., p. 627.

71   *"Politicians like Sobchak"*: Gessen, *The Man Without a Face*, p. 134.

72   *"In the end he won"*: Aron, *Yeltsin*, p. 637.

72   *"in charge of the legal division"*: Putin, *First Person*, p. 128.

74   *"I control everybody"*: Ibid., p. 131.

75   *"the very modest . . . He wasn't sure"*: Baker and Glasser, *Kremlin Rising*, p. 53.

75   *"Do I really need"*: Freeland, *Sale of the Century*, p. 330.

76   *"forgiveness"*: "Yeltsin Resigns," *New York Times*, January 1, 2000.

76   *Any cook"*: Florence Becker, "Woman's Place," *New International* 2, no. 5 (August 1935), pp. 175–76.

CHAPTER 5: THE RUSSIA PUTIN INHERITED AND ITS SPIRITUAL ILLS

79   *"I gave Poland"*: Gorbachev press conference, July 21, 2015, AP Archive. Also "Gorbachev Denounces Putin on Rights and Corruption," *Moscow Times*, March 8, 2013.

80   *"There's a lot"*: Putin, *First Person*, p. 187.

80   *"Three people won the Cold War"*: Paul Johnson, *Heroes* (New York: Harper-Collins, 2007), p. 253.

81   *"The single most"*: Thomas Friedman, "Taking Ownership of Iraq," *New York Times*, June 25, 2006.

81   *"Russia isn't Haiti"*: Strobe Talbott, *The Russia Hand* (New York: Random House, 2003), p. 197.

81   *"You know, it's bad enough"*: Ibid., p. 76.

82   *"NATO's war"*: Ibid., p. 357.

82   *"Yugoslavization"*: Putin, *First Person*, p. 141.

82   *"is a continuation"*: Ibid., p. 139.

82   *"The entire Caucasus"*: Ibid., p. 142.

83   *"If we don't"*: Ibid., p. 140.

83   *"Under Putin's police state"*: Vladimir Ryzhkov, "Guriev Is Latest Victim of Putin's Police State," *Moscow Times*, June 4, 2013.

83 *"Russia will perish"*: Interview with Vladimir Grechukhin, "Pravda dlya nas vazhnee zakonov," *Argumenty I fakty*, no. 38, 2007.

83 *"We belong"*: Peter Chaadayev, *Philosophical Letters* (Knoxville: University of Tennessee Press, 1969), p. 38.

84 *"realm of brute fact"*: Ibid.

84 *"Russia may well fall"*: Arthur Conolly, *Journey to the North of India* 2 volumes, 1838. Also quoted in Philip Glazebrook, *Journey to Khiva.*

84 *"all sounds"*: Quoted in Avril Pyman, *The Life of Alexander Blok* (Oxford: Oxford University Press, 1979). Also quoted in *Funeral Games in Honor of Arthur Lourie* (New York: Oxford University Press, 2014), p. 12.

84 *"The Russians have"*: The hacker called "Lightwatch" quoted in Clifford Levy, "What's Russian for Hacker?" *New York Times*, October 21, 2007.

85 *"a mighty nation"*: Ibn Miskawayh quoted in Richard Lourie, *Predicting Russia's Future* (Whittle Direct Books, 1991), p. 8.

85 *"Fuck the battle"*: Peter Maas, *Underboss* (New York: HarperCollins, 1997), p. 25.

86 *"a fundamentally good man"*: Vladimir Volkoff, *Vladimir the Russian Viking* (Woodstock, N.Y.: Overlook Press, 1985), p. 223.

86 *"The Russian cannot bear"*: Richard Lourie, *Predicting Russia's Future*, p. 10. My translation.

87 *"we knew not"*: Volkoff, *Vladimir the Russian Viking*, p. 176.

87 *"directed that"*: Lourie, *Predicting Russia's Future*, p. 9.

87 *"Just as the iconostasis"*: James Billington, *The Icon and the Axe* (New York: Vintage Books, 1970), pp. 36–37.

88 *"the Bolsheviks"*: Andrei Sinyavsky, *Soviet Civilization* (New York: Arcade, 1988), p. 11.

89 *"Man will become"*: Leon Trotsky, *Literature and Revolution*, Last lines, Leon Trotsky Internet Archive.

90 *"the conviction that Russia"*: Tim McDaniel, *The Agony of the Russian Idea* (Princeton, N.J.: Princeton University Press, 1996), p. 10.

91 *"The Russians are"*: Nikolai Berdyaev, *The Russian Idea* (Hudson, N.Y.: Lindisfarne Press, 1992), pp. 20–21.

91 *"We are not suited"*: McDaniel, *The Agony of the Russian Idea*, p. 36.

92 *"Russia should not repent"*: Alexei Pankin, "Trying to Remain Moral Amid 'Dom 2'," *Moscow Times*, July 8, 2013.

93 *"accounted for far more"*: Foreword by Norman Davies in Tomasz Kizny, *Gulag* (Richmond Hill, Canada: Firefly, 2004), p. 9.

PART FOUR: CORE ISSUES

97   *"Without Ukraine"*: Mark MacKinnon, *The New Cold War* (New York: Carroll and Graf, 2007), p. 153.

97   *"The empires of the future"*: Winston Churchill, "The Gift of a Common Tongue" Harvard Commencement Ceremony, September 6, 1943, www. winstonchurchill.org.

CHAPTER 6: OIL: A WASTING ASSET

99   *"The key"*: Thane Gustafson, *Wheel of Fortune* (Cambridge, Mass.: Belknap Press, 2012), p. 27.

99   *"I vow"*: Section 1, Chapter 4, Article 92, Constitution of the Russian Federation, President of Russia Official Web Portal.

100   *"From the very"*: Putin, *First Person*, p. 186.

101   *"ORT is the most,"* *"Why are you"*: Alex Goldfarb and Marina Litvinenko, *Death of a Dissident* (New York: Free Press, 2007), p. 210.

102   *"fountain of oil"* and *"an unguent"*: Marco Polo, *The Travels of Marco Polo* (New York: Modern Library, 2001), p. 23.

102   *"revolutionary baptism"*: www.marxists.org/ . . . /stalin/ . . . /stalin/05.ht.

105   *"Stalin pointed two fingers"*: Obituary, "Stalin's Oil Minister Dies at 97," *New York Times*, April 2, 2008.

106   *"collective farming"*: Lourie, *Russia Speaks*, p. 132.

106   *"Maybe there were"*: "Nikolai Baibakov, Stalin's oil supremo, he went on to direct the Soviet economy," *Guardian*, April 16, 2008.

107   *"The timeline of the collapse"*: Egor Gaidar, "The Soviet Collapse," American Enterprise Institute, April 2007.

108   *"Yeltsin drunk"*: Talbott, *The Russia Hand*, p. 185.

108   *"Yeltzin was roaring"* Ibid., p. 135.

111   *"The gradually"*: Hoffman, *The Oligarchs*, p. 125.

111   *"A bank is like a waiter"*: Ibid., p. 126.

112   *"the biggest"*: Marshall Goldman, *Petrostate* (New York: Oxford, 2008), p. 63.

112   *"a massive scam"*: Ibid., p. 64.

112   *"Everyone knew"*: Ibid.

114   *"If the old me"*: Baker and Glasser, *Kremlin Rising*, p. 275.

116   *"a suave cop"*: Talbott, *The Russia Hand*, p. 401.

116   *"Russia will not soon become"*: Gustafson, *Wheel of Fortune*, p. 252.

116   *"Vladimir Vladimirovich"*: Ibid., p. 293.

117 *"What arrogance"*: Goldman, *Petrostate*, p. 111.

117 *"Three days"*: Ibid., p. 115.

117 *"There are worse"*: Baker and Glasser, *Kremlin Rising*, p. 288.

118 *"Some are gone"*: Gustafson, *Wheel of Fortune*, p. 296.

119 *"It was exactly"*: Boris Kagarlitsky, *Back in the USSR* (London: Seagull Books, 2009), p. 32.

120 *"Putin is probably not"*: Baker and Glasser, *Kremlin Rising*, p. 340.

121 *"excessive emphasis"*: Gustafson, *Wheel of Fortune*, p. 251.

121 *"humiliating dependence"* and *"Should a primitive"*: Dimtri Medvedev, "Go Russia!" President of Russia Official Web Portal, September 10, 2009.

121 *"ability to see"*: iipdigital. Usembassy.gov.

122 *"Nanotechnology is an activity"*: Putin quoted in "Responsible Nanotechnology," Russia and Nanotechnology, crnano.typepad.com/crnblog /2007/05/russia_and_nano.html.

122 *"super-effective weapons systems"*: Ibid.

122 *"Nanotechnology will be"*: Alexander and Zaitchik, "Russia Pours Billions in Oil Profits into Nanotech Race," Wired.com, November 1, 2007.

122 *"expansive to the point"*: Ibid.

122 *"Nanotechnology will be"*: Ibid.

123 *"As the industry expands"*: Nadia Popova, "Chubais Predicts Big Growth in Nano Jobs," *Moscow Times*, September 3, 2009.

123 *"The prospects," "technologies have brilliant"*: archive.government.ru/eng /multimedia/photo/2009/?page=95.

124 *"We were hoping"*: "Viktor Chernomyrdin, a Russian prime minister, died on November 3rd, aged 72," *Economist*, November 4, 2010. There are several translations of this brilliant formulation. None quite work.

CHAPTER 7: THE HEART OF THE MATTER: UKRAINE

127 *"In geopolitics"*: Robert Kaplan, "Old World Order," *Time*, March 20, 2014.

127 *"You have to understand"*: "Putin Hints at Splitting Up Ukraine," *Moscow Times*, April 8, 2008. I have here modified the translation of *"gosudarstvo,"* which could also be rendered as "state" or "nation-state."

127 *"It might not be"*: Ivan Nechepurenko, "Gorbachev on Russia and Ukraine," *Moscow Times*, November 21, 2014.

127 *"Our land is vast"*: quoted in Volkoff, *Vladimir the Russian Viking*, p. 39.

128 *"sacred"*: "Putin Says Crimea Sacred, Attacks US, EU over Ukraine," *Bloomberg Business*, December 3, 2014.

128 *"If anyone does not:"* Volkoff, *Vladimir the Russian Viking*, p. 234.

128 *"they must be"*: Jack Weatherford, *Genghis Khan and the Making of the Modern World* (New York: Three Rivers Press, 2004), p. 7.

130 *"The Catholic inquisitors"*: Edward Gibbon, *The History of the Decline and Fall of the Roman Empire* (New York: Fred de Fau, 1906), vol. 7, p. 4.

130 "abominable": Simon Seabag Montefiore, *Potemkin* (New York: Vintage Books, 2005), p. 362.

132 *"escaped serfs"*: Anna Reid, *Borderland* (Boulder, Colo.: Westview Press, 2000), p. 31.

133 *"the faith, language"*: Ibid., p. 29.

133 *"the language of serfs"*: Ibid., p. 30.

133 *"Oh Bohdan"*: My translation.

133 *"to Russians"*: Reid, *Borderland*, p. 64.

134 *"an odd mixture"*: Ibid., p. 79.

135 *"Shevchenko has acquired"*: Ibid., pp. 81–82.

135 *"Under the strictest"*: Ibid., p. 82.

135 *"I don't rule Russia"*: Quoted in Paul Taylor, "Frictions Created in Civil Service in Reagan Era," *Washington Post*, January 19, 1983.

135 *"not misuse"*: Reid, *Borderlands*, p. 83.

135–136 *"know nothing of God . . . family of the free"*: My translation.

137 *"gray blur"*: Remark by Menshevik Nikolai Sukhanov quoted in a review by Ian Cumming of *Stalin: Paradoxes of Power* by Stephen Kotkin, *Sydney Morning Herald*, March 2, 2015.

139 *"niggers"*: Reid, *Borderland*, p. 158.

139 *"probably the worst"*: John Thor Dahlburg, "Ukraine Votes to Quit Soviet Union," *Los Angeles Times*, December 3, 1991.

140 *"The people in Kiev"*: John Steinbeck, *A Russian Journal* (London: Penguin, 1994), pp. 53–54.

141 *"one inch east"*: "NATO's Eastward Expansion," *Der Spiegel Online International*, November 26, 2009.

141 *"the most fateful error"*: Tim Weiner and Barbra Crossette, "George F. Kennan Dies at 101," *New York Times*, March 18, 2005.

142 *"a verbal agreement"*: Like nearly all great quotes, unless by Churchill, this one may have been misattributed.

142 *"The Americans promised"*: Adrian Blomfield and Mike Smith, "Gorbachev: US Could Start New Cold War," *Telegraph* (London), May 6, 2008.

143 *"Ukraine is in many ways"*: Ivan Nechepurenko, "Gorbachev on Russia and Ukraine," *Moscow Times*, November 21, 2014.

143 *"false Leninist borders"*: Alexander Solzhenitsyn, *The Russian Question at the End of the Twentieth Century* (New York: Farrar, Straus and Giroux, 1995), p. 90.

143 *"If Ukraine were to move into NATO"*: Megan Stack, "Why Russia Is Back," *Los Angeles Times*, September 4, 2008.

143 *"threatened to encourage"*: "Putin Hints at Splitting Up Ukraine," *Moscow Times*, April, 8, 2008.

143 *"A Jewel in Two Crowns"*: *National Geographic*, April 2011.

145 *"Britain and Europe"*: Steven Erlanger, "Britain and Europe Sleepwalked into Ukraine Crisis Report Says," *New York Times*, February 20, 2015.

146 *"The E.U. operates"*: Andrew Higgins, "Upheaval Highlights E.U.'s Past Miscalculations and Future Dangers," *New York Times*, March 21, 2014.

147 *"arch-Russophobe"*: Peter Hopkirk, *The Great Game* (Oxford: Oxford University Press, 1990), p. 504.

147 *"When the Russian government"*: Peter Hopkirk, *Setting the East Ablaze* (New York: Kondasha, 1984), p. 142.

147 *"Despite the fact"*: Anna Dolgov, "Navalny Wouldn't Return Crimea," *Moscow Times*, October 16, 2014.

PART FIVE: NORTH- AND EASTWARD

149 *". . . With escalating"*: Andrew Small, "Chinese Foreign Policy Comes of Age," *New York Times*, March 26, 2015.

CHAPTER 8: RUSSIA'S MECCA: THE ARCTIC

151 *"The Arctic has always"*: "Frozen Conflict," *Economist*, December 20, 2014.

151 *"The Arctic is Russia's Mecca"*: "Norway in Arctic Dispute with Russia over Rogozin Visit," BBC News, April 20, 2015. Also appears as "The Arctic is a Russian Mecca" in Steve Lee Myers, "Arctic Council Meeting Nears in the Shadow of Tension with Russia," *New York Times*, April 24, 2015.

151 *"Tanks don't need"*: Franz-Stefan Gady, "Meet the Russian Politician Who Thinks," *Diplomat*, May 27, 2015.

152 *"Our interests"*: Adam Taylor, "Putin Thinks of the Past When Talking Ukraine—but the Arctic When He Sees Russia's Future," *Washington Post*, August 29, 2014.

152 *"main resource base"*: Bruce Panner, "Security Concerns Rising as Arctic Thaw Spurs Race for Oil," Radio Free Europe/Radio Liberty (RFE/RL), January 29, 2009.

152 *"This isn't the fifteenth"*: Roderick Kefferputz, "On Thin Ice?" CEPS Policy Brief no. 205, February 2010.

152–53 *"The Russians sent"*: Lawrence Daina and Daniel Dombey, "Canada Joins Rush to Claim the Arctic," *Financial Times*, August 9, 2007.

154 *"The Arctic has always experienced"*: Scott Borgerson, "Arctic Meltdown," *Foreign Affairs*, March/April 2008, p. 65.

154 *"the process whereby"*: CEPS Policy Brief no. 205, February 2010.

155 *"polar invertebrates"*: Ibid.

155 *"trans-Arctic Panama Canal"*: Christoph Seidler and Gerald Trauletter, "Boon to Global Shipping: Melting of Artic Ice Opening Up New Routes to Asia," *Der Spiegel Online*, September 27, 2010.

156 *"The Arctic . . . is just an ocean"*: "Exploitation of Arctic Resources Will Happen," *Der Spiegel Online*, October 26, 2012.

157 *"natural prolongation"*: "Definition of the Continental Shelf," UNCLOS 1982, Part VI, Article 76, p. 53.

158 *"the treaty's litigation"*: Keith Johnson, "GOP Scuttles Law-of-Sea Treaty," *Wall Street Journal*, July 16, 2012.

158 *"Not since we acquired"*: Secretary of Defense Leon Panetta's speech on the Law of the Sea, May 2012, Council on Foreign Relations, May 9, 2012.

158 *"designated by the Bush"*: UN Convention on the Law of the Sea, Senator Richard G. Lugar Opening Statement, September 27, 2007. www.ceanlaw .org.

158 *"As the world's"*: Ibid.

159 *"excessive claims"*: Ibid.

159 *"A crack in the ice"*: Terence Armstrong, *The Russians in the Arctic* (Fair Lawn, N.J.: Essential Books, 1958), p. 74.

159 *"This sort of thing"*: Ibid.

159 *"boldly conceived"*: Ibid., p. 78.

160 *"everything that is known"*: Ibid., p. 163.

160 *"the worst journey"*: "Worst Journey in the World," RFE/RL, March 20, 2013.

161 *"completely devoid"*: "Nuclear Waste Poses Arctic Threat," BBC News, March 1, 2013.

161 *"A Russian Academy of Sciences"*: "Arctic Oil Drilling Threatens International Radioactive Contamination from Old Soviet Nuclear Dump Sites," Bellona, www.bellona.org/articles, February 3, 2009.

161–62 *"didn't show signs"* and *"my colleagues and I,"* *"Imagine an old mouse,"* *"Experiments have already"*: Arama Ter-Ghazaryan, "Ancient Bacteria Might Help Us Live to 140," *RBTH* (*Russia Beyond the Headlines*), October 19, 2015.

162 *"a national threat"*: Michael Bohm, "Carelessness as a Russian National Trait," *Moscow Times*, August 2, 2013.

163 *"mission is suicidal"*: James Brooke, "Russia Moves into Arctic Oil Frontier with a Lax Safety Culture?" VOA (Voice of America), December 22, 2011.

163   *"inter-island"*: Ibid.

163   *"involved the kind"*: Ibid.

163   *"Some men"*: Ibid.

164   *"It is inevitable"*: Fiona Harvey and Shaun Walker, "Arctic Oil Spill Is Certain If Drilling Goes Ahead, Says Top Scientist," *Guardian*, November 19, 2003.

164   *"a completely different"*: Ibid.

164   *"We are planning"*: Christoph Seidler, "Spring Cleaning in the Arctic: Putin's Environmental Action Plan for the Far North," *Der Speigel Online*, September 24, 2010.

164   *"floating"*: Ken Stier, "In Russia, a push for Floating Power Plants," *Time*, Nov. 12, 2010.

164   *"fairly proven hardware"*: Ken Stier, "In Russia a Push for Floating Nuclear Power Plants," *Time*, November 12, 2010.

164   *"If a working"*: Alissa de Carbonnel, "Can Nuclear Power Plants Float?" Reuters, April 18, 2011.

166   *"fender bender"*: Seidler and Traufetter, "Boon to Global Shipping."

166   *"warming Arctic"*: "Tequila Sunset," *Economist*, February 9, 2013.

166   *"If there is"*: Matthew Farish, *The Contours of America's Cold War* (Minneapolis: University of Minnesota Press, 2010), p. 174.

166   *"We have no intention"*: Ivan Nechepurenko, "Oil Price Drop Puts Russia's Arctic Drive in Question," *Moscow Times*, January 15, 2015.

167   *"colossal wealth"*: Eva Stolberg review of John McCannon, *Red Arctic: Polar Exploration and the Myth of the North in the Soviet Union 1932–1939*, H-Russia networks, h-net.org.

167   *"In a competition"*: Tony Halpin, "Russia Warns of War Within a Decade over Arctic Oil and Gas Riches," *Timesonline*, *Times*, May 14, 2009.

168   *"If Vienna was"*: James Bamford, "Frozen Assets," *Foreign Policy*, May/June 2015, p. 47.

168   *"We're not even"*: Douglas Ernst, "U.S. Cedes Arctic to Russia," *Washington Times*, July 8, 2015.

168   *"battle for resources"*: "Battle for Arctic Key for Russia's Sovereignty—Rogozin," *RIA/NOVOSTI*, December 4, 2012.

CHAPTER 9: MANIFESTING DESTINY: ASIA

171   *"We are similar"*: Evan Osnos, "Born Red," *New Yorker*, April 16, 2015.

171   *"In the 21st"*: "Putin: Russia's development vector is directed eastward in the 21st century," Interfax, December 12, 2012. Translation changed slightly.

172 *"short, victorious"*: see entry on Vyacheslav Plehve in Prominent Russians in Russiapedia.

172 *"brave little"*: Denis Warner and Peggy Warner, *The Tide at Sunrise: History of the Russo-Japanese War, 1904–1905* (New York: Routledge, 2002), p. 530.

173 *"unequal treaties"*: "The Opening to China Part II," Office of the Historian, U.S. Department of State, history@state.gov.

173 *"The Politburo was terrified"*: Arkady Shevchenko, *Breaking with Moscow* (New York: Knopf, 1985), pp. 164–65.

173 *"We do not have"*: *Russian Reform Monitor* No. 1779, May 17, 2012.

173 *"small groups"*: Alex Rodriguez, "Chinese Reap Opportunity, Rancor in Russia's Far East," *Chicago Tribune*, September 27, 2006.

173 *"I don't want"*: www.president.kremlin.ru/events.

176 *"Over the long term"*: Sujata Rao and Michelle Chen, "Russian Firms Turn to Asia for Finance as Western Firms Demur," Reuters, April 30, 2014.

176 *"natural resources appendage"*: Rens Lee, "The Far East Between Russia, China, and America," FPRI (Foreign Policy Research Institute), July 2012.

177 *"unforgiveable outrage"*: J. Berkshire Miller, "Getting Serious: An End to the Russia-Japan Dispute?" *Diplomat*, April 19, 2013.

177 *"Russia's geo-strategic eyes"*: David Tweed, "Why Putin Fears China," Bloomberg Business, February 15, 2015.

178 *"China's most prominent"*: Yu Sun, "March West: China's Response to the U.S. Rebalancing," Brookings Upfront, January 31, 2013.

178 *"We say China"*: Mao Zedong, Speech of April 25, 1956, *Selected Works*, vol., 5 (Peking: Foreign Languages Press, 1977).

178 *"I can almost hear"*: Jane Perlez, "China Looks West as It Bolsters Regional Ties," *New York Times*, September 7, 2013.

179 *"bold and decisive"*: Jeremy Page, "China Turns to New Hero: Putin the Great," *Wall Street Journal*, October 2, 2014.

179 *"information"*: Charles Clover, "Russia and China Learn from Each Other as Military Ties Deepen," ft.com>world>asia-pacific, June 24, 2016.

180 *"East Turkestan"*: "China Irked by Dalai Lama's 'East Turkestan' Comment," *Tibetan Review*, July 22, 2013.

180 *"his intent of splitting"*: Ibid.

182 *"unsinkable"*: Joseph Bosco, "Taiwan and Strategic Security," *Diplomat*, May 15, 2015.

183 *"The Kazakhs never"*: Farangis Najbullah, "Putin Downplays Kazakh Independence, Sparks Angry Reaction," RFE/RL, September 3, 2014.

183 *"a state in a territory"*: Ian Traynor "Kazakhstan Is Latest Russia Neighbor to Feel Putin's Chilly Nationalist Rhetoric," *Guardian*, September 1, 2014.

184 *"actually part"*: "Alexander Solzhenitsyn on the New Russia," *Forbes* interview, August 5, 2008.

184 *"Mr. President"*: Jonathan Aiken, *Nazarbayev and the Making of Kazakhstan* (London: Continuum, 2009), p. 107.

184 *"very much"*: Ibid., p. 62.

184 *"Central Asia's heart"*: Katrina Swett and M. Zuhdi Jasser, "CIS Has a Poor Record on Religious Freedom," *Moscow Times*, August 16, 2013.

185 *"with the aim of avoiding"*: Joshua Kucera, "Kazakhstan's Islamist Threat," *Diplomat*, August 15, 2011.

186 *"the slaves of non-believers"*: Deidre Tynan, "Central Asia Is a Sitting Duck for Islamic State," *Moscow Times*, June 15, 2015.

188 *"Who rules"*: Robert Kaplan, *The Revenge of Geography* (New York: Random House, 2012), p. 74.

188 *"Kazakhstan* is": Ibid., p. 185.

PART SIX: THE TWILIGHT OF PARANOIA

191 *"Everything that is connected with Russia"*: Victor Davidoff, "Gays Are New Enemy No. 1," *Moscow Times*, June 23, 2013.

CHAPTER 10: HOW VLADIMIR PUTIN LEARNED TO STOP WORRYING AND LOVE THE INTERNET

193 *"Russia is a military state"*: Edvard Radzinsky, *Alexander II, the Last Great Tsar* (New York: Simon and Schuster, 2005), p. 53.

194 *"imitation democracies"*: Baker and Glasser, *Kremlin Rising*, p. 376.

194 *"The trouble with"*: *International Affairs* 36 (1960), p. 4.

195 *"The best thing"*: Danny Hakim, "Once Celebrated in Russia, the Programmer Pavel Durov Chooses Exile," *New York Times*, December 2, 2014.

195 *"envisioned"*: Ibid.

195 *"I like to"*: Ibid.

196 *"to upload . . . very careless"*: Ibid.

197 *"my hero"*: John Thornhill, "Lunch with the FT: Pavel Durov," *Financial Times*, July 3, 2015.

197 *"In such moments"*: Chris Boyette, "Russia's Mark Zuckerberg Offers Edward Snowden a Job," *CNN Money*, August 5, 2013.

198 *"Putin has signed"*: Andrew Roth, "Putin Signs New Anti-Terror Law in Russia. Edward Snowden Is Upset," *Washington Post*, July 7, 2016.

199 *"total traitor"*: David Sherfinski, "Donald Trump: Putin Would Return 'Total Traitor' Snowden If I'm President," *Washington Times*, July 9, 2015.

199 *"the style of"*: Andrew Higgins, "For Guccifer, Hacking Was Easy. Prison Is Hard," *New York Times*, November 10, 2014.

200 *"CIA project"*: Ewen MacAskill, "Putin Calls Internet a 'CIA Project' Renewing Fears of Web Breakup," *Guardian*, April 24, 2014.

200 *"She set the tone"*: Karl Vick, "Is Putin Taking Sides?" *Time*, August 8, 2016.

201 *"banana republic"*: Ilya Khrennikov and Stepan Kravchenko, "Putin's New Internet Czar Wants Apple and Google to Pay More Taxes," Bloomberg Technology, February 8, 2016.

201 "When I served": "Meet Vladimir Putin's new Internet advisor," *Meduza*, December 24, 2015.

201 *"Now the Internet"*: Ibid.

201 *"We are breeding"*: Khrennikov and Kravchenko, "Putin's New Internet Czar."

202 *"Confidential"*: "Hillary Clinton's 'Hacked' Benghazi Emails Sent to RT," RT, March 19, 2013.

203 *"I write"*: Ludmilla Alexeyeva, *Soviet Dissent* (Middletown, Conn.: Wesleyan University Press, 1985), p. 12.

203 *"Our parents"*: Mikhail Heller and Aleksandr Nekrich, *Utopia in Power* (New York: Summit Books, 1986), p. 544.

204 *"I am pretty sure"*: Claire Berlinski, "Update on the Bukovsky Trial," *Ricochet*, July 28, 2016.

204 *"I have concluded"*: Sir Robert Owen, *The Litvinenko Inquiry* (London, 2016), p. 244.

204 *"I'm not afraid"*: Claire Berlinski, "Did Britain Fall into Putin's Trap in Prosecuting a Russian Dissident?" *National Review*, May 11, 2016.

206 *"the first"*: Ellen Nakashima, "Russia Hackers Targeted Arizona Election System," *Washington Post*, August 29, 2016.

206 *"I'm resigning"*: "A man who's seen society's black underbelly Meduza meets 'Anonymous International'." *Meduza*, February 2, 2015.

207 *"So, the only thing"*: Ibid.

PART SEVEN: THE END AND AFTER

209 *"Russia is the only country"*: Eduard Limonov, *Drugaya Rossiya* (Moscow: Yauza, 2004), p. 66.

CHAPTER 11: RUSSIA WITHOUT PUTIN, PUTIN WITHOUT RUSSIA

211   *"Putin will die"*: Bloomberg TV Video, December 17, 2014.

212   *"Gods don't pass"*: Richard Lourie, *Russia Speaks*, pp., 279–80. I tinkered with the translation, which was mine to begin with.

214   *"What do they"*: Dmitri Oreshkin, "What Would Happen to Russia If Putin Died," *Week*, February 3, 2015.

215   *"No Putin, no Russia"*: "'No Putin, No Russia' says Kremlin Deputy Chief of Staff," *Moscow Times*, October 23, 2014.

216   *"appeared as"*: Ellen Barry, "Rousing Russia with a Phrase," *New York Times*, December 9, 2011.

216   *"I am"*: Sean Guillory, "Russian Opposition Leader Alexei Navalny," *Exiled*, December 26, 2011.

218   *"think more or less"*: Donld Jensen, "Sergei Ivanov Returns to Center Stage," *IMR*, April 2, 2013.

218   *"I have never"*: Ibid.

218   *"Ivanov wants"*: Ibid.

218   *"law enforcement"*: Luke Harding, "WikiLeaks Cables Claim Vladimir Putin Has Secret Wealth Abroad," *Guardian*, December 11, 2010.

220   *"I'm having a little soup"*: Vladimir Bukovsky, *Nasledniki Lavrentiya Beria* (Moscow: Algoritm, 2013), p. 155. My translation.

222   *"The Geneva Freeport"*: Sam Knight, "The Bouvier Affair," *New Yorker*, February 8, 2016.

BIBLIOGRAPHY

Aitken, Joanthan. *Nazarbayev and the Making of Kazakhstan*. London: Continuum, 2009.

Albats, Yevgeniya. *The State Within a State: The KGB and Its Hold on Russia—Past, Present, and Future*. New York: Farrar, Straus and Giroux, 1994.

Allison, Graham. *Nuclear Terrorism*. New York: Times Books, 2004.

Amalrik, Andrei. *Will the Soviet Union Survive Until 1984?* New York: Perennial Library, 1970.

Andrew, Christopher, and Oleg Gordievsky. *KGB: The Inside Story*. New York: HarperCollins, 1990.

Andrew, Christopher, and Vasili Mitrokhin. *The Sword and the Shield: The Mitrokhin Archive and the Secret History of the KGB*. New York: Basic Books, 1999.

Aron, Leon. *Yeltsin: A Revolutionary Life*. New York: St. Martin's Press, 2000.

Armstrong, Terence. *The Russians in the Arctic*. Fair Lawn, N.J.: Essential Books, 1958.

Baker, Peter, and Susan Glasser. *Kremlin Rising: Vladimir Putin's Russia and the End of Revolution*. Washington, D.C.: Potomac Books, 2007.

Berdyaev, Nikolai. *The Russian Idea*. Translated by R. M. French. Hudson, N.Y.: Lindisfarne Press, 1992.

Berton, Pierre. *The Arctic Grail: The Quest for the North West Passage and the North Pole, 1818–1909*. New York: Viking, 1988.

Billington, James. H. *The Icon and the Axe: An Interpretive History of Russian Culture*. New York: Vintage Books, 1970.

————. *Russia in Search of Itself*. Washington, D.C.: Woodrow Wilson Center Press, 2004.

Blank, Stephen J., ed. *Russia in the Arctic*. Carlisle, Pa.: Strategic Studies Institute, 2011.

Boym, Svetlana. *The Future of Nostalgia*. New York: Basic Books, 2001.

Browder, Bill. *Red Notice*. New York: Simon and Schuster, 2015.

Brzezinski, Matthew. *Casino Moscow: A Tale of Greed and Adventure on Capitalism's Wildest Frontier*. New York: Touchstone, 2002.

Brzezinski, Zbigniew. *Second Chance: Three Presidents and the Crisis of American Superpower*. New York: Basic Books, 2007.

Bukovsky, Vladimir. *Nasledniki Lavrentiya Beriya: Putin I Ego Komanda*. Moscow: Algoritm, 2013.

Chaadayev, Peter. *Philosophical Letters and Apology of a Madman*. Translated by Mary-Barbara Zeldin. Knoxville: University of Tennessee Press, 1969.

Cherkashin, Victor. *Spy Handler: Memoir of a KGB Officer*. New York: Basic Books, 2005.

Cockburn, Andrew, and Leslie Cockburn. *One Point Safe*. New York: Anchor Books, 1997.

Cone, Marla. *Silent Snow: The Slow Poisoning of the Arctic*. New York: Grove, 2005.

Congdon, Lee. *George Kennan, a Writing Life*. Wilmington, Del., ISI Books, 2008.

Cooley, Alexander. *Great Games, Local Rules: The New Great Power Contest in Central Asia*. New York: Oxford, 2012.

De Custine, Marquis. *Journey for Our Time*. London: Arthur Barker, 1953.

Earley, Pete. *Comrade J: The Untold Secrets of Russia's Master Spy in America After the End of the Cold War*. New York: Berkeley Books, 2009.

Eimer, David. *The Emperor Far Away: Travels at the Edge of China*. New York: Bloomsbury, 2014.

Emmerson, Charles. *The Future History of the Arctic*. New York: Public Affairs, 2010.

Freeland, Chrystia. *Sale of the Century: Russia's Wild Ride from Communism to Capitalism*. New York: Crown, 2000.

Gall, Carlotta, and Thomas de Waal. *Chechnya: Calamity in the Caucasus*. New York: New York University Press, 1998.

Gates, Robert. *Duty: Memoirs of a Secretary at War*. New York: Vintage, 2015.

Gessen, Masha. *Dead Again: The Russian Intelligentsia After Communism*. New York: Verso, 1997.

————. *The Man Without a Face: The Unlikely Rise of Vladimir Putin*. New York: Riverhead, 2012.

Goldfarb, Alex, and Marina Litvinenko. *Death of a Dissident*. New York: Free Press, 2007.

Goldman, Marshall I. *Petrostate: Putin, Power and the New Russia*. New York: Oxford, 2008.

———. *The Piratization of Russia*. New York: Routledge, 2003.

Grant, Shelagh D. *Polar Imperative: A History of Arctic Sovereignty in North America*. Vancouver, British Columbia: D & M Publishers, 2010.

Gustafson, Thane. *Wheel of Fortune: The Battle for Oil and Power in Russia*. Cambridge, Mass.: Belknap Press, 2012.

Hoffman, David E. *The Oligarchs: Wealth and Power in the New Russia*. New York: Public Affairs, 2002.

Hopkirk, Peter. *The Great Game*. Oxford: Oxford University Press, 1990.

——— *Setting the East Ablaze: Lenin's Dream of an Empire in Asia*. New York: Kodansha, 1984.

Jack, Andrew. *Inside Putin's Russia*. New York: Oxford University Press, 2004.

Johnson, Paul. *Heroes*. New York: HarperCollins, 2007.

Judah, Ben. *Fragile Empire: How Russia Fell in and out of Love with Vladimir Putin*. New Haven, Conn.: Yale University Press, 2013.

Kagarlitsky, Boris. *Back in the USSR*. London: Seagull Books, 2009.

Kalugin, Oleg. *Spymaster*. New York: Basic Books, 2009.

Kaplan, Robert D. *The Revenge of Geography*. New York: Random House, 2012.

Karamzin, Nicholas. *Memoir on Ancient and Modern Russia*. Translation and analysis by Richard Pipes. New York: Atheneum, 1981.

Kissinger, Henry. *On China*. New York: Penguin, 2011.

Kizny, Tomasz. *Gulag*. Richmond Hill, Canada: Firefly, 2004.

Klebnikov, Paul. *Godfather of the Kremlin: Boris Berezovsky and the Looting of Russia*. New York: Harcourt, 2000.

Knight, Amy. *Spies Without Cloaks: The KGB's Successors*. Princeton, N.J.: Princeton University Press, 1996.

Koehler, John. *Stasi: The Untold Story of the East German Secret Police*. Boulder, Colo.: Westview Press, 1999.

Kuzichkin, Vladimir. *Inside the KGB: My Life in Soviet Espionage*. New York: Pantheon, 1990.

Lane, George. *Daily Life in the Mongol Empire*. Indianapolis: Hackett Publishing, 2006.

Langewiesche, William. *The Atomic Bazaar: The Rise of the Nuclear Poor*. New York: Farrar, Straus and Giroux, 2007.

Laquer, Walter. *Black Hundred: The Rise of the Extreme Right in Russia*. New York: HarperCollins, 1993.

Levine, Steve. *The Oil and the Glory: The Pursuit of Empire and Fortune on the Caspian Sea*. New York: Random House, 2007.

———. *Putin's Labyrinth: Spies, Murder, and the Dark Heart of the New Russia*. New York: Random House, 2008.

Lieven, Anatol. *Chechnya, Tombstone of Russian Power*. New Haven, Conn.: Yale University Press, 1998.

Limonov, Eduard. *Drugaya Rossiya*. Moscow: Yauza, 2004.

Litvinenko, Alexander, and Yuri Feltishinsky. *Blowing Up Russia: The Secret Plot to Bring Back KGB Terror*. New York: Encounter Books, 2007.

Lourie, Richard. *Predicting Russia's Future: How 1,000 Years of History Are Shaping the 1990s*. Whittle Direct Books, 1991.

———. *Russia Speaks: An Oral History from the Revolution to the Present*. New York: Edward Burlingame Books / HarperCollins, 1991.

Maas, Peter. *Underboss: Sammy the Bull Gravano's Life in the Mafia*. New York: HarperCollins, 1997.

MacKinnon, Mark. *The New Cold War: Revolutions, Rigged Elections, and Pipeline Politics in the Former Soviet Union*. New York: Carroll & Graf, 2007.

Maillart, Ella K. *Forbidden Journey*. Introduction by Dervla Murphy. Translated by Thomas McGreevy. Great Britain: Hippocrene, 1984.

Margeret, Jacques. *The Russian Empire and Grand Duchy of Muscovy*. Translated and edited by Chester S. L. Dunning. Pittsburgh: University of Pittsburgh Press, 1983.

Marquis de Custine. *Journey for Our Time*. London: Arthur Barker, 1951.

McDaniel, Tim. *The Agony of the Russia Idea*. Princeton, N.J.: Princeton University Press, 1996.

Meier, Andrew. *Black Earth: A Journey Through Russia After the Fall*. New York: Norton, 2003.

Midgley, Dominic, and Chris Hutchins. *Abramovich: The Billionaire from Nowhere*. New York: HarperCollins 2004.

Montefiore, Simon Sebag. *Potemkin: Catherine the Great's Imperial Partner*. New York: Vintage Books, 2005.

Morgan, David. *The Mongols*. New York: Basil Blackwell, 1988.

Moynahan, Brian. *The Russian Century: A History of the Last Hundred Years*. New York: Random House, 1994.

Murphy, Paul. *The Wolves of Islam: Russia and the Faces of Chechen Terror*. Washington, D.C.: Potomac Books, 2006.

Murray, Craig. *Murder in Samarkand*. Edinburgh: Mainstream, 2006.

Poe, Marshall T. *The Russian Moment in World History*. Princeton, N.J.: Princeton University Press, 2003.

Politkovskaya, Anna. *Putin's Russia: Life in a Failing Democracy*. New York: Henry Holt, 2005.

———. *A Small Corner of Hell: Dispatches from Chechnya*. Chicago: University of Chicago Press, 2003.

Polo, Marco. *The Travels of Marco Polo*. New York: Modern Library, 2001.

Pribylovsky, Vladimir. *Chistka Vladimira Putina*. Moscow: Algoritm, 2013.

Putin, Vladimir. *First Person*. Translated by Catherine A. Fitzpatrick. New York: Public Affairs, 2000.

Reid, Anna. *Borderland: A Journey Through the History of Ukraine*. Boulder, Colo.: Westview Press, 2000.

Roxburgh, Angus. *The Strongman: Vladimir Putin and the Struggle for Russia*. London: I. B. Tauris, 2013.

Sale, Richard, and Eugene Potapov. *The Scramble for the Arctic*. London: Frances Lincoln, 2010.

Scahill, Jeremy. *Blackwater: The Rise of the World's Most Powerful Mercenary Army*. New York: MJF Books, 2007.

Schoen, Douglas, and Melik Kaylan. *The Russia-China Axis*. New York: Encounter Books, 2014.

Shvets, Yuri B. *Washington Station: My Life as a KGB Spy in America*. New York: Simon and Schuster, 1994.

Sinyavsky, Andrei. *Soviet Civilization: A Cultural History*. Translated by Joanne Turnbull. New York: Arcade, 1988.

Soldatov, Andrei, and Irina Borogan. *The New Nobility: The Restoration of Russia's Security State and the Enduring Legacy of the KGB*. New York: Public Affairs, 2010.

Solovyov, Vladimir, and Elena Klepikova. *Boris Yeltsin: A Political Biography*. New York: Putnam's, 1992.

Solzhenitsyn, Aleksandr. *The Russian Question at the End of the Twentieth Century*. New York, Farrar, Straus and Giroux, 1995.

Sorokin, Vladimir. *Day of the Oprichnik*. Translated by Jamey Gambrell. New York: Farrar, Straus and Giroux, 2006.

Talbott, Strobe. *The Russia Hand: A Memoir of Presidential Diplomacy*. New York: Random House, 2003.

Usoltsev, Vladimir. *Sosluzhivets*. Moscow: Eksmo, 2004.

Volkoff, Vladimir. *Vladimir the Russian Viking*. Woodstock, N.Y.: Overlook Press, 1985.

Volkogonov, Dimtri. *Autopsy of an Empire*. New York: Free Press, 1998.

Volodarsky, Boris. *The KGB's Poison Factory: From Lenin to Litvinenko*. Minneapolis: Frontline, 2009.

Vonnegurt, Kurt. *Slaughterhouse Five*. New York: Dial, 1969.

Wat, Aleksander. *My Century: The Odyssey of a Polish Intellectual*. Translated and edited by Richard Lourie. Berkeley: University of California Press, 1988.

Weatherford, Jack. *Genghis Khan and the Making of the Modern World*. New York: Three Rivers Press, 2004.

Weir, Gary E, and Walter J. Boybe. *Rising Tide: The Untold Story of the Russian Submarines That Fought the Cold War*. New York: New American Library, 2003.

Wolf, Markus, with Anne McElvoy. *Man Without a Face: The Autobiography of Communism's Greatest Spymaster*. New York: Public Affairs, 1999.

Yeltsin, Boris. *The Struggle for Russia*. New York: Times Books / Random House, 1994.

INDEX

Federal Security Bureau (FSB) (*continued*)
  and creation of National Guard, 10
  Internet and, 205, 207
  Kazakhstan and, 185
  political assassinations and, 203–4
  Putin's directorship of, 72, 74, 218
  and Russia without Putin, 211
FeldSvyaz, 221
Feynman, Richard, 121–22
Final Settlement, Treaty on the, 8
Financial Times, 69, 75
Finland, 157, 173
First Person (Putin), 34–35, 100
Fishman, Mikhail, 4
France, 24, 28, 75, 131, 140, 222
  Russian relations with, 146, 148
  terrorism in, 185, 198
Freeland, Chrystia, 69
Friedman, Thomas, 81
Frolov, Mikhail, 34–36
Fuchs, Klaus, 38
Fyodorov, Nikolai, 85–86

Gaidar, Egor, 59, 107–8
gas, 106
  Arctic and, 153, 155–56, 162, 165
  China and, 176, 179, 181
  comparisons between oil and, 111–12
  Crimea and, 148
  Kazakhstan and, 184
  Putin's failures and, 224
  Putin's reelection and, 121
  Russia and, 63, 102, 112, 119, 121, 144–46,
    156, 175–77, 215, 224
Gates, Bill, 117, 199
Gates, Robert M., 15
Gazprom, 112, 176, 217
genetics, 122–23
Geneva Freeport, 222
Genghis Khan, 83–84, 128–30, 172, 224
"Geographical Pivot of History, The"
    (Mackinder), 187
Geological Survey, U.S., 155
German Empire, 160
Germany, 8, 118, 131
  Arctic and, 157
  China and, 171, 176
  Kaliningrad and, 9
  reuniting of, 42, 68, 141–42
Germany, East, 8, 18, 64, 81, 141
  collapse of, 41, 47
  comparisons between Soviet Union and, 39
  economy of, 38
  Putin's posting in, 22, 36, 39, 41, 45, 47–48,
    77
  Putin's wife and, 37, 45

Germany, Nazi, 175, 187
  Arctic and, 160
  KGB and, 16
  oil and, 104–5
  tracking down criminals of, 39–40
  World War II and, 16–18, 20–21, 37–38,
    40, 85, 104–5, 138–39, 160
Germany, Weimar Republic of, 60
Germany, West, 40, 47, 118, 141
  Green Beret bases in, 41–42
Gessen, Masha, 43, 53, 71
Gibbon, Edward, 130
Gladkov, Yuri, 63
glasnost, 32, 39, 47
Global Times, 177–78
Gogol, Nikolai, 44–45
Goldman, Marshall, 112–13, 117
Google, 201
Gorbachev, Mikhail, 19, 65–66, 73, 184
  Andropov and, 25
  and collapse of Soviet Union, 79–81
  comparisons between Putin and, 75
  coup against, 55–56, 62
  criticism of, 47
  glasnost and, 32, 39
  Khodorkovsky and, 110
  oil and, 107
  presidential elections and, 68
  reuniting Germany and, 141–42
  Sakharov and, 46, 52
  Soviet economy and, 66, 106–7
  Ukraine and, 127, 143, 147
  World War II and, 138
Gosplan, 106
Gotti, John, 85
Gracián, Baltasar, 49
Gravano, Salvatore "Sammy the Bull," 85
Green Berets, 41–42
Grímsson, Ólafur Ragnar, 155
Guccifer, 199–202, 208
Guccifer 2.0, 201–2, 205, 208
Gulag, 16, 28, 54, 93, 194
Gulf of Mexico, 164
Gurevich, Vera, 19
Gusinsky, Vladimir, 69
Gustafson, Thane, 99

Han Chinese, 178, 180
Henry I, King of France, 128
Heroes (Johnson), 80
Hill, Fiona, 146
*History of the Decline and Fall of the Roman
    Empire, The* (Gibbon), 130
Hitler, Adolf, 79, 84, 172, 224
  comparisons between Stalin and, 92–93,
    104

North Atlantic Treaty Organization
(NATO) (*continued*)

and Putin's outing himself, 54
Putin's return to, 48, 51–52
and Putin's writings on snitches, 35
regular army of, 42, 48, 55, 60, 66, 80, 141
and reuniting Germany, 141–42
Russian Orthodox Church in, 130
saints of, 87
sciences and education in, 21, 121–23
scientific socialism as basis of, 67
submarine transfers of, 23–24
and television, 194
trade of, 106, 108
transition to Russian Federation from,
    57–61, 66, 72, 92, 94
and Ukraine, 135, 137, 139–40, 143
U.S. relations with, 26, 78, 141–42
and World War II, 8, 17–18, 20–21, 57, 85,
    92, 104–5, 138–39, 160
United Kingdom, 38, 80, 84, 133, 147, 172,
    184–85, 187, 199
    Arctic and, 159–60
    Berezovsky's life in, 101
    China and, 174
    exit from EU of, 148
    and pedophilia charges against Bukovsky,
        203–4
    political assassinations and, 27, 145, 201–4,
        219
    Putin's education and, 33
    Putin's statism and, 116
    Ukraine and, 140, 145
    World War II and, 37, 160
United Nations, 5, 93, 169
United Nations Convention on the Law of the
    Sea (UNCLOS), 157
United States, 24, 60, 63–64, 73
    Arctic and, 153, 155–60, 166, 168
    China and, 171, 173, 178–79, 181–82
    as Cold War victor, 80–81
    and collapse of Soviet Union, 80, 90
    comparisons between Russia and,
        83, 114, 117, 171–72
    defectors and asylum seekers in, 6, 198
    gas and, 176
    Internet and, 195–96, 199–202, 205–7
    Kazakhstan and, 185
    and Law of the Sea Treaty, 158–59
    military equipment production of, 177
    oil and, 102–3, 107
    organized crime in, 85
    politics in, 11, 46, 199–200, 202, 205–7
    Putin's education and, 33, 51
    Putin's statism and, 116
    reuniting Germany and, 141–42
    Russian aircraft buzzing military ships and
        aircraft of, 6–7, 11

Russian-Chechen wars and, 82
Russian presidential elections and, 70
Russian relations with, 15, 26, 173, 177,
    179, 206–7
Russian sanctions and, 151
sciences in, 123
slavery in, 136
Snowden and, 197
Soviet relations with, 26, 78, 141–42
terrorism and, 78–79, 185–86
Ukraine and, 139–40
World War II and, 37, 160
Usoltsev, Vladimir "Big Volodya," 30, 45–48
Uzbekistan, 184–85

VEB, 176
Vickers, Michael G., 41
Victory Day, 92
Vietnam, 177, 182
Vikings, 127–28
V Kontakte (VK), 195–97
Vladimir of Kiev, Grand Prince, 86–87, 124,
    128
Voice of America, 163
Volodin, Vyacheslav, 215
Vonnegut, Kurt, 38

Wang Haiyun, 179
Wang Jisi, 178
War and Peace (Tolstoy), 85
Warsaw Pact, 21, 41, 141
Washington Post, The, 206
Washington Station (Shvets), 24, 34
Wiesenthal, Simon, 39–40
WikiLeaks, 218
Williams, Brad, 177
Wolf, Markus, 37–38, 43–44
World Economic Forum, 69
World War I, 94, 103, 136
World War II, 8, 16–18, 20–21, 28, 40, 57,
    79, 85, 177
    Arctic and, 160
    and comparisons between Hitler and
        Stalin, 92–93
    Dresden and, 37–38
    Leningrad and, 17–18, 138–39
    oil and, 104–5
    Soviet casualties in, 18, 138
    Ukraine and, 104–5, 138–39

Xi Jinping, 171, 178–79
Xinjiang, 179–82, 187–88

Yamani, Sheikh Ahmed Zaki, 107
Yanayev, Gennady, 56
Yanukovich, Viktor, 142–44